Colonial America Almanac

Colonial America Almanac

Volume 1

PEGGY SAARI

Julie L. Carnagie, Editor

AN IMPRINT OF THE GALE GROUP
DETROIT · NEW YORK · SAN FRANCISCO
LONDON · BOSTON · WOODBRIDGE, CT

Peggy Saari

Staff

Julie L. Carangie, *U•X•L Editor*
Carol DeKane Nagel, *U•X•L Managing Editor*
Thomas L. Romig, *U•X•L Publisher*

Shalice Shah-Caldwell, *Permissions Associate (Pictures)*
Maria Franklin, *Permissions Manager*

Rita Wimberley, *Senior Buyer*
Evi Seoud, *Assistant Production Manager*
Dorothy Maki, *Manufacturing Manager*

Pamela A. E. Galbreath, *Senior Art Director*
Cynthia Baldwin, *Product Design Manager*

LM Design, *Typesetting*

Cover photographs (top to bottom): The *Mayflower* reproduced with permission of The Library of Congress; Christopher Columbus landing in the New World reproduced by permission of The Bettmann Archive; The cultivation of tobacco reproduced by permission of The Granger Collection Ltd.

Library of Congress Cataloging-in-Publication Data

Saari, Peggy

Colonial America: almanac / Peggy Saari.

p. cm.

Includes bibliographical references and index.

Summary: Examines the colonial period in America, discussing both the Native American culture before the arrival of Europeans and the exploration and settlement of different parts of the New World.

ISBN 0-7876-3763-7 (set). — ISBN 0-7876-3764-5 (v. 1). — ISBN 0-7876-3765-3 (v. 2).

1. United States—History—Colonial period, ca. 1600-1775 Juvenile literature. 2. Almanacs,   American Juvenile literature. [1. United States—History—Colonial period, ca. 1600-1775.] I. Title.

E188.S12 2000

973.2-dc21   99-39081
                                                      CIP

Printed in the United States of America

10 9 8 7 6 5 4 3 2

Contents

Volume 1

Volume 2

Advisory Board

Special thanks are due for the invaluable comments and suggestions provided by U•X•L's Colonial America Reference Library advisors:

- Katherine L. Bailey, Library Media Specialist, Seabreeze High School, Daytona Beach, Florida.

- Jonathan Betz-Zall, Children's Librarian, Sno-Isle Regional Library System, Edmonds, Washington.

- Deborah Hammer, Manager of Social Sciences Division, Queens Borough Public Library, New Hyde Park, New York.

- Fannie Louden, Fifth Grade History Teacher, B. F. Yancey Elementary School, Esmont, Virginia.

Reader's Guide

Colonial America: Almanac provides a wide range of historical information on the period in United States history between 1565 and 1760. The two-volume set describes the attempts made by European explorers and settlers to establish permanent communities on the North American continent in areas that are now part of the United States. Arranged in fifteen subject chapters, *Colonial America: Almanac* explores topics such as Native American life before the arrival of European colonists; European exploration, settlement, and colonization of the New World; the history of Africans in America during the colonial period; government and law; arts and culture; and science and medicine.

Additional features

Colonial America: Almanac includes numerous sidebars, some focusing on people associated with the colonial era, others taking a closer look at pivotal events. More than one hundred black-and-white illustrations enliven the text, while cross-references are made to people or events discussed in other chapters. Both volumes contain a timeline, a glossary, research and activity ideas, a bibliography, and a cumulative index providing access to the subjects discussed in *Colonial America: Almanac.*

Comments and suggestions

We welcome your comments on this work as well as your suggestions for topics to be featured in future editions of *Colonial America: Almanac.* Please write: Editors, *Colonial America: Almanac,* U•X•L, 27500 Drake Rd., Farmington Hills, MI 48331-3535; call toll-free: 1-800-877-4253; fax: 248-699-8097; or send e-mail via www.galegroup.com.

Introduction

Colonial America: Almanac tells the story of the period in American history when European explorers and settlers established colonies in territory that is now the United States. Presenting the story requires first answering the question: When did the colonial period begin and when did it end? According to many historians, the era started either with failed English attempts to settle on Roanoke Island (1584–87) or their successful founding of Jamestown in 1607. The conclusion is placed either before or after the French and Indian War (1754–60) or at the beginning of the revolutionary period (1775–76). These time frames, regardless of dates, put the thirteen English colonies at the center of American history. Yet the Spanish had been exploring North America since the early 1500s and had founded the first permanent European settlement at Saint Augustine, Florida, in 1565. The French were operating a thriving colony at Quebec in present-day Canada when the English arrived at Jamestown. Similarly, the Dutch established New Netherland around the time the English were colonizing New England. Although England dominated the Atlantic seaboard after taking New Netherland in 1664, Spain and France still held border regions that hemmed in the emerging English colonies.

The story of the colonial period is not confined to the European struggle for power in North America, however. By the time the Europeans stepped onto the continent, Native Americans had been developing complex civilizations since at least 30,000 B.C. Therefore, native peoples are equally significant players in the drama that began unfolding in the late 1500s. For this reason *Colonial America: Almanac* opens with a brief survey of Native American history prior to the arrival of Europeans. The narrative moves on to Spanish, French, and Dutch settlement, then finally to the founding of the "original" English colonies. Yet these groups—Native Americans, Spanish, French, Dutch, and English—did not exist in isolation from one another. They were always interacting as they competed for land, trade routes, and alliances. Colonial society became even more complex as immigrants from other European nations flooded into North America during the 1600s and 1700s.

Thus the history of the colonial period was shaped mainly by interaction among the original colonizing nations and Native Americans. The French and their native allies, in particular, had a profound impact through their continued presence on the western frontier along the Mississippi River. In fact, the English colonies' ongoing conflicts with Native Americans led to the French and Indian War. Many scholars regard the end of the war as the close of the colonial period as well, because colonists felt less militarily dependent on the British after the victory over France. It was also an important event for Native Americans, who lost their allies when the French were driven out of North America. Taking this perspective, *Colonial America: Almanac* concludes the story at the end of the war, in 1760. Although the conflict was not officially over (the Treaty of Paris was signed three years later), the hostilities had ceased and America had reached a turning point: Colonists felt newly empowered, and whatever was left of the Native American way of life began to disappear forever.

Timeline of Events in Colonial America

30,000 B.C. Native Americans arrive in North America via the Bering Sea Land Bridge.

1500 B.C. Eastern Woodland era begins in Mississippi River valley.

500 B.C.-A.D. 700 Mayans develop advanced civilizations in Mexico.

A.D. 1 Pueblo culture emerges in Southwest.

A.D. 986 The Thule Inuit encounter an expedition led by Eric the Red, who founds a settlement in Greenland.

c.1325 Aztecs build their capital, Tenochtitlán, in the Valley of Mexico.

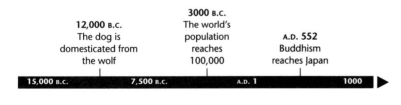

12,000 B.C.
The dog is domesticated from the wolf

3000 B.C.
The world's population reaches 100,000

A.D. 552
Buddhism reaches Japan

| 15,000 B.C. | 7,500 B.C. | A.D. 1 | 1000 |

1492	Italian sea captain Christopher Columbus, sailing for Spain, arrives in the Caribbean and founds Hispaniola, but reports that he has reached Asia.
1498	Italian navigator Sebastian Cabot, sailing for England, explores North America in search of the Northwest Passage.
1513	Seeking a mythical "fountain of youth," Juan Ponce de León of Spain lands in a part of North America he names Florida.
1519	Spanish explorer Hernando Cortes lands in Mexico; within two years, he and his expedition defeat the rich and powerful Aztec empire and claim Mexico for Spain.
1525	Giovanni da Verrazano, an Italian employed by France, reaches the North American coast; sailing north from the Carolinas, he discovers New York Harbor and the Hudson River, named at a later date for explorer Henry Hudson.
1525	Pedro de Quexco explores a huge bay on the North American coast, later known as Chesapeake Bay.
1527	Spanish explorer Panfilo de Narvaez lands on the Gulf Coast of North America with 400 explorers. The expedition is a disaster; all but a handful of members die of disease, in Indian attacks, or trying to return to Mexico by sea.
1527	The English ship *Mary Guilford* sails south along North America's Atlantic coast, from Canada to Florida.
1533	Francisco Pizarro, a Spanish explorer, conquers the great Inca empire in South America.
1534	Jacques Cartier of France lands at the mouth of the St. Lawrence River and claims the surrounding land for France.

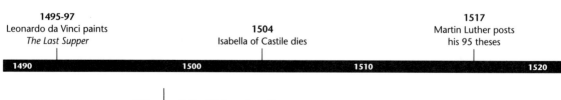

1495-97
Leonardo da Vinci paints
The Last Supper

1504
Isabella of Castile dies

1517
Martin Luther posts
his 95 theses

| 1490 | 1500 | 1510 | 1520 |

1535   Antonio de Mendoza arrives in Mexico as the first viceroy (governor) of New Spain, the name given to Spain's empire in the New World.

1539   Franciscan monk Marcos de Niza reports seeing the fabled "Seven Cities of Cíbola" while traveling in the American Southwest.

1539   Hernando de Soto, along with 600 men, sets out to explore the region that becomes the southwestern United States.

1539   Several Spanish expeditions claim the California coast for Spain, although no permanent settlements are attempted.

1540   A large expedition, commanded by Francisco Vásquez de Coronado, leaves Mexico and heads north through the Southwest. The expedition travels through the present-day states of Arizona, Kansas, New Mexico, Oklahoma, and Texas.

1540   Hernando de Alvarado travels along the Rio Grande into New Mexico.

1541   Jacques Cartier makes has last voyage to North America and explores the country around the Ottawa River.

1541   Hernando de Soto's expedition discovers the Mississippi River, near the present site of Memphis, Tennessee.

1542   A Spanish naval expedition under Juan Rodriguez Cabrillo reaches San Diego Bay, California; after Cabrillo's death, Bartolome Ferillo leads the expedition farther along the coast to San Francisco Bay.

1543   The Hernando de Soto expedition (minus its leader, who dies in 1542) returns to Mexico.

1559   Tristan de Luna y Arellano leads a Spanish expedition to Pensacola, Florida, to establish a settlement; the colony fails and the survivors leave two years later.

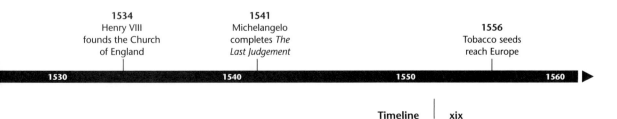

1534
Henry VIII
founds the Church
of England

1541
Michelangelo
completes *The
Last Judgement*

1556
Tobacco seeds
reach Europe

1530   1540   1550   1560

1562 Jean Ribault of France leads 150 settlers to the coast of what is now South Carolina in an attempt to found a refuge for French Protestants (Huguenots); the colony is abandoned soon after.

1564 A second French colonizing expedition commanded by Rene de Laudonniere lands in what is today Florida.

1565 Alarmed at the French presence close to Spanish Florida, a force under Pedro Menendez de Áviles attacks the colony, destroying it and killing almost all the settlers.

1565 Spain establishes Saint Augustine, its chief outpost in Florida and the oldest permanent settlement in what is now the United States.

1571 Spanish attempts to colonize northern Florida (now part of Virginia) fail when Indians overrun a Jesuit mission on the southern portion of the Chesapeake Bay.

1576 Elizabeth I of England grants Humphrey Gilbert a patent (royal authority) to colonize the New World for England and the crown.

1579 English captain Francis Drake's round-the-world expedition reaches San Francisco Bay, California; he claims the area for England, naming it New Albion. (Albion is another name for England.)

1583 Humphrey Gilbert founds a colony on the island of Newfoundland off the coast of Canada. Gilbert is lost at sea while returning to England and his patent passes to his half brother, Walter Raleigh.

1584 Captains Philip Amadas and Arthur Barlowe, sailing for Walter Raleigh, sail to the New World to pave the way for an English colony in the Chesapeake Bay region.

1585 Walter Raleigh names the land explored by his expedition "Virginia," in honor of England's unmarried queen, Elizabeth I.

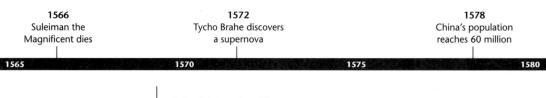

1566	1572	1578
Suleiman the Magnificent dies	Tycho Brahe discovers a supernova	China's population reaches 60 million

| 1565 | 1570 | 1575 | 1580 |

1585 More then 100 colonists under Richard Grenville establish a colony in Virginia, on Roanoke Island off the coast of modern-day North Carolina.

1586 The first Roanoke colony fails; those colonists who survive are taken back to England by Francis Drake, who arrives at Roanoke after burning the Spanish fort at Saint Augustine.

1587 Another colonizing expedition arrives at Roanoke, bringing more than 100 settlers led by John White, who sails back to England for more supplies.

1587 Virginia Dare is born to Ananias and Eleanor Dare of the Roanoke Colony; she is the first child born of English parents in North America.

1602 After exploring and naming Cape Cod and Martha's Vineyard, Bartholomew Gosnold returns from America to England with a cargo of furs and lumber, fueling the movement to colonize North America.

1602 Sebastian Vizcaino explores a bay on the coast of central California and names it Monterey after the Count of Monte Rey, viceroy of Mexico.

1603 Samuel de Champlain embarks on the first of eleven exploratory voyages along the St. Lawrence River and the northeastern Atlantic coast of North America.

1604 Samuel de Champlain and Pierre de Monts establish the first French settlement in Acadia (Nova Scotia), on an island in Passamaquoddy Bay, along the present-day United States-Canada border.

1606 The London and Plymouth companies receive charters from James I of England to establish colonies in the New World.

1607 Under the charter granted to the Virginia Company of London, an expedition led by Bartholomew Gosnold, John Smith, and Christopher Newport founds

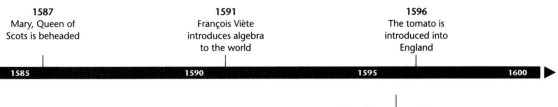

1587
Mary, Queen of Scots is beheaded

1591
François Viète introduces algebra to the world

1596
The tomato is introduced into England

1585　　　　　　　　　　1590　　　　　　　　　　1595　　　　　　　　　　1600

Jamestown, the first permanent English settlement in North America.

1608   After five years of exploring the coast and rivers of North America, Samuel de Champlain founds Quebec, the first permanent French settlement on the mainland of North America.

1609   Henry Hudson, an English navigator sailing for the Dutch East India Company, explores Chesapeake and Delaware Bays, discovers the Hudson River, and claims all the land along its banks for the Netherlands.

1610   Spanish settlers under governor Don Pedro de Peralta found Villa Real de la Santa Fe de San Francisco de Asis (now Santa Fe, New Mexico).

1612   John Rolfe establishes what will be the most important cash crop of the southern colonies by cultivating new varieties of tobacco.

1612   The Virginia Company sends sixty English settlers to the Bermuda Islands.

1613   English colonists sail north from Virginia to destroy Port Royal and other French settlements in Acadia and Maine, beginning 150 years of armed struggle between the two countries for control of eastern North America.

1614   On his second voyage to America, John Smith explores an area he names New England and maps the coast from Maine to Cape Cod.

1615   Samuel de Champlain joins the Huron Indians in attacking the Iroquois near Lake Ontario, establishing for New France both an alliance and an enemy that will continue for the rest of the century.

1615   The first Franciscan friars arrive in Quebec to begin French missionary activity in Canada.

1619   The Virginia House of Burgesses, the first elected legislature in the colonies, meets for the first time.

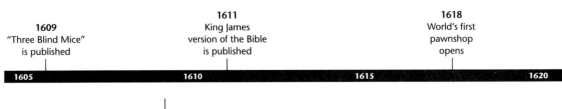

1609
"Three Blind Mice"
is published

1611
King James
version of the Bible
is published

1618
World's first
pawnshop
opens

1605   1610   1615   1620

1619 A Dutch ship arrives in Jamestown carrying the first Africans to arrive in the colony; they are put to work as indentured servants. Another ship brings women from London as wives for the settlers.

1620 Seeking religious freedom, the Pilgrims head for Virginia on the *Mayflower* but go off course, landing on Cape Cod and later founding a colony at Plymouth, Massachusetts.

1620 Peregrine White becomes the first child born among the New England colonists.

1621 The Plymouth settlers establish a peace treaty with Massasoit, chief of the local Wampanoag Indians, who help the Pilgrims survive the winter.

1621 James I of England grants the Acadian lands already claimed by France to William Alexander for the purpose of founding the colony of Nova Scotia (New Scotland).

1622 One-fourth of the Jamestown colonists, 357 people, die in an attack by the Powhatan Indians, which begins two years of war.

1623 The Council for New England, which succeeded the Plymouth Company, establishes fishing and trading settlements in Portsmouth and Dover, New Hampshire.

1623 Thomas Warner establishes a settlement on St. Kitts (St. Christopher), the first successful English colony in the West Indies.

1624 On behalf of the Dutch West India Company, Dutch colonists establish fur-trading settlements at Fort Orange (Albany, New York) and New Amsterdam (Manhattan Island).

1624 James I revokes the Virginia Company's charter and takes control of the settlement, making it a royal colony.

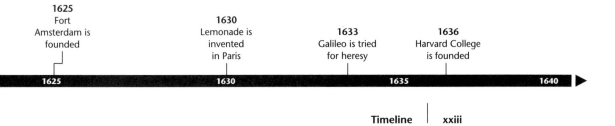

1625
Fort Amsterdam is founded

1630
Lemonade is invented in Paris

1633
Galileo is tried for heresy

1636
Harvard College is founded

1625   1630   1635   1640

1626 By the end of the summer, the Dutch construct over thirty wooden frame houses on the southern tip of Manhattan.

1627 A Swedish company receives a charter for that nation's first colony in the New World, although the colony (New Sweden, on the Delaware River) will not be founded for another decade.

1628 John Endecott, leading a group of about sixty Puritans fleeing religious persecution in England, founds Salem, Massachusetts, for the New England Company.

1629 The Massachusetts Bay Company receives a royal charter granting the company rights to establish settlements between the Charles and Merrimack Rivers in New England.

1630 John Winthrop and 900 Puritans found a self-governing settlement at Boston in the name of the Massachusetts Bay Company.

1631 The Council for New England, with Englishman Fernando Gorges as president, establishes a single plantation settlement at Saco Bay, Maine.

1632 The English return Quebec and Acadia to French control by a treaty under which each nation recognizes the other's established North American colonies.

1634 Under a charter granted to Cecilius Calvert, the second Lord Baltimore founds Maryland as a refuge for English Catholics who are seeking religious tolerance and civil rights.

1635 Seeking greater freedom than the Massachusetts Bay Colony offered, Thomas Hooker and sixty followers found Hartford, the first permanent settlement in Connecticut.

1635 English Puritans build the settlement of Fort Saybrook at the mouth of the Connecticut River, beginning competition with the Dutch for control of the river valley.

1646	1648	1650
England's civil war ends	Europe's Thirty Years' War ends	England's first coffeehouse opens

| 1645 | 1647 | 1649 | 1651 |

1635 French colonists under Pierre Belaine, sieur d'Esnambuc, establish a settlement on Martinique and seize the island of Guadaloupe, the first permanent French colony in the West Indies.

1636 Banished from Massachusetts for his religious and political views, Roger Williams founds Providence Plantation (later the colony of Rhode Island) on land he purchases from the Narragansett Indians.

1637 Colonial forces in Connecticut and Massachusetts, allied with the Mohegan and Narragansett Indians, destroy Pequot Indian villages, kill 500 to 600 Pequots, and scatter or enslave the surviving members of the tribe to avenge the murders of several colonists.

1638 Banished from Massachusetts for challenging the Puritan clergy, Anne Hutchinson moves to Pocasset (later known as Portsmouth), the second settlement in Rhode Island.

1638 Swedish colonists led by Peter Minuit establish Fort Christina (Wilmington, Delaware), the oldest permanent settlement in the Delaware River Valley.

1639 The Hartford and New Haven colonies establish a democratic, representative system of self-government under the Fundamental Orders of Connecticut.

1639 The charter for Maine grants the territory already claimed by the French as part of Acadia to aristocratic English proprietor Fernando Gorges.

1641 The colonial government of Massachusetts takes control of the region known as New Hampshire.

1642 Paul de Chomedey, sieur de Maisonneuve, founds the settlement of Montreal, expanding New France's fur trade south and west.

1643 Four New England settlements (Plymouth, Massachusetts Bay, Connecticut, and New Haven) form the

1653
Thomas Bartholin
describes lymphatic
system

1655
Sweden invades
Poland

1657
First fountain pens
manufactured

| 1653 | 1655 | 1657 | 1659 |

United Colonies of New England, joining in defense against both Indians and the Dutch.

1644   Roger Williams returns from England after obtaining a royal patent for the colony of Rhode Island.

1647   Four Rhode Island settlements (Providence, Portsmouth, Newport, and Warwick) join in a loose confederacy, drafting a code of civil law that expressly separates church and state.

1652   The Massachusetts Bay Colony takes over the territory of Maine and declares itself independent of the English Parliament.

1653   The Dutch West India Company allows New Amsterdam, with more than 800 residents, to incorporate as a self-governing city.

1654   Ships carrying Dutch settlers from Brazil, where they had been expelled, bring the first Jews to New Amsterdam.

1654   In their continuing effort to monopolize the northern fishing and fur trade, English colonists capture Acadia from the French.

1655   Led by Peter Stuyvesant, the Dutch capture Fort Christina and take control of all of the Delaware Valley.

1664   The English capture New Amsterdam, which they rename New York, and England's King Charles II grants to his brother, the Duke of York, all land from Maine to Delaware not already settled by English colonists.

1665   The colony of New Jersey, presented by the Duke of York to his friends George Carteret and John Berkeley, is founded.

1668   Jesuit priest Jacques Marquette founds a mission at Sault Ste. Marie in present-day Michigan.

1669   French fur trader Louis Jolliet begins his exploration of the Great Lakes region.

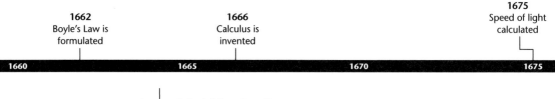

1662
Boyle's Law is
formulated

1666
Calculus is
invented

1675
Speed of light
calculated

| 1660 | 1665 | 1670 | 1675 |

1673   Dutch forces recapture New York and the colonies along the Delaware River from the English, only to be forced to give them back again a year later.

1673   Louis Jolliet and Jacques Marquette, hoping to find a river route to the Pacific, explore the Mississippi River as far south as the Arkansas River.

1675   King Philip's War, between English colonists and Native American tribes in Massachusetts, Rhode Island, and Connecticut, causes damage or destruction in sixty-four colonial towns and destroys Indian villages and food supplies.

1682   After almost two years of traveling the Mississippi River, René-Robert Cavalier de la Salle reaches the river's mouth and claims for France all the land along its banks, a territory he names Louisiana.

1682   William Penn founds Philadelphia and the Pennsylvania colony as a refuge for Quakers and other persecuted religious minorities.

1698   Eusebio Francisco Kino leads a three-year expedition that charts a land course from Mexico to California, disproving the previous belief that California was an island.

1699   Brothers Pierre and Jean Baptiste Le Moyne establish Old Biloxi (present-day Ocean Springs, Mississippi), the first of several French settlements along the coast of the Gulf of Mexico.

1700   French settlers begin to construct forts, settlements, fur-trading posts, and Jesuit missions in the Illinois Territory.

1702   Queen Anne's War, the second war between England and France for control of North America, begins. Most of the fighting over the next twelve years will take place in the outlying settlements on the New England-Canada frontier.

1681
France annexes
Strasbourg

1687
The University of
Bologna is founded

1692
Aesop's Fables
is published

1680   1685   1690   1695

1710 British and New England troops capture Port Royal, which they rename Annapolis Royal, and the region now known as Nova Scotia, from the French.

1711 Almost 200 North Carolina settlers are massacred by the local Tuscarora Indians, initiating the year-long Tuscarora War, which results in the deaths of hundreds of Tuscaroras and the migration of the survivors to New York, where they join the Iroquois Confederation.

1716 Virginia governor Alexander Spotswood leads an expedition into the westernmost Virginia territory, crossing the Blue Ridge Mountains into the Shenandoah River Valley.

1718 On behalf of the French Company of the West, Jean Baptiste Le Moyne founds a city (New Orleans) at the mouth of the Mississippi that becomes the capital of the Louisiana territory four years later.

1718 Spanish settlers found the military post and mission of San Antonio, the first of several missions established in an attempt to counter French settlements along the western Gulf coast.

1720 France's treasury is bankrupted after the Mississippi Company is revealed to be a sham in a financially disastrous settlement plan known as the Mississippi Bubble.

1722 The Six Nations of the Iroquois Confederation (Mohawk, Oneida, Onondaga, Cayuga, Seneca, and Tuscarora), under a treaty with Virginia colonists, agree not to cross the Potomac River or move west of the Blue Ridge Mountains.

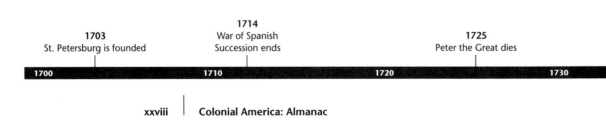

1703
St. Petersburg is founded

1714
War of Spanish
Succession ends

1725
Peter the Great dies

| 1700 | 1710 | 1720 | 1730 |

1729   French soldiers in the Louisiana territory massacre Natchez Indians. A ten-year war begins between the French and Indians.

1733   James Edward Oglethorpe founds the city of Savannah and the colony of Georgia, the last of the original thirteen English colonies, as a haven for the poor.

1747   Settlers from Virginia and Pennsylvania move onto land granted to the Ohio Company, prompting French settlers to construct a line of forts across western Pennsylvania.

1749   Georgia permits large landholdings and slavery, leading to economic prosperity for plantation owners. Following five years of war between French and British colonies (King George's War) in which little territory changes hands, the British found Halifax to strengthen their hold on Nova Scotia.

1750   German craftspeople in Pennsylvania develop the Conestoga wagon, soon to become the standard vehicle on the frontier.

1752   A year before their original charter is due to expire, the trustees of Georgia give all administrative power to the British government.

1754   Competing British, French, and Native claims to territory from the Appalachians west to the Mississippi River lead to the nine years of fighting known as the French and Indian War.

1755   Britain banishes defeated French colonists from Acadia, some of whom travel to Louisiana, where they become known as Acadians (Cajuns).

1760   The English capture Montreal from the French, essentially ending the French and Indian War.

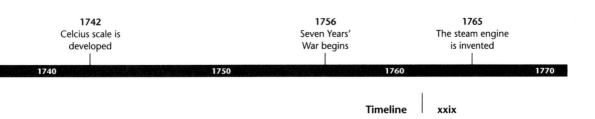

1742
Celcius scale is
developed

1756
Seven Years'
War begins

1765
The steam engine
is invented

1740   1750   1760   1770

Words to Know

A

American Revolution: A conflict lasting from 1775 to 1783 in which American colonists gained independence from British rule.

Anabaptists: Those who oppose the baptism of infants; also know as Baptists.

Anglican Church: The official religion of England; also know as the Church of England.

Antinomianism: The belief that God has predetermined who would be saved from sin.

Apprentice: A person who learns by practical experience under skilled workers.

Archaeologists: Scientists who study ancient cultures.

Aristocrat: A member of the nobility, or ruling class.

B

Banished: The forced removal of someone from a colony.

Baptism: The initiation into Christianity through anointment with water.

Borough: An area under the jurisdiction of a local government.

C

Calvinists: Followers of French Protestant reformer John Calvin.

Capital: Money used for business purposes.

Capital offenses: Crimes requiring the death penalty.

Catechism: Religious instruction that involves questions and answers.

Charters: Land grants and governing contracts.

Common law: The body of law determined by custom and precedent.

Commons: A grassy area in the middle of the village.

Communion: The ritual in which bread and wine represent the body and blood of Jesus of Nazareth, the founder of Christianity.

Congregations: Separate groups of church members.

Conquistadors: Conquerors.

Constitution: A document that establishes an independent government.

Covenants: Solemn and binding agreements.

D

Deeds: Legal contracts.

Democracy: Government by the people exercised directly or by elected representatives.

Deported: Forcibly sent.

Dissenters: Those who oppose the church.

Doctrine: Policy and teachings.

Duties: Taxes.

Dysentery: A disease characterized by severe diarrhea.

E

Emigrated: To leave one country or region and settle in another.

Encomienda: A land grant.

English Civil War: A conflict lasting from 1642 to 1648 that pitted Parliament and the Puritans against Charles I and the Church of England.

Evangelicals: Those who emphasize salvation by faith, the authority of the scripture, and the importance of preaching.

F

Fords: Part of a body of water that may be crossed by wading.

Franciscan friars: Priests belonging to the order of Saint Francis of Assisi.

Freedom dues: Items given to a servant at the end of service.

Freedom of the press: The right of newspapers to print truthful information.

Freemen: Men with the full rights of citizens; women had no rights.

Free will: The idea that all people can make voluntary choices or decisions independently from God.

G

Gallows: A structure used for hanging people for execution.

Gentry: The upper or ruling class.

Glorious Revolution: The name given to the ascension of Protestant monarchs William III and Mary II.

H

Head right: A grant from the colony to a settler who paid his own way to North America.

Heresy: A violation of church teachings.

Huguenots: Members of a Protestant religious group.

Hydrography: The science of charting bodies of water.

I

Immigration: To come into a foreign country to live.

Indentured servants: Laborers who worked for a specific number of years.

Indigo: A plant used to make blue dye.

J

Jesuits: Members of the Society of Jesus, a Roman Catholic religious order.

M

Malaria: A disease transmitted by mosquitoes.

Magistrates: Judges.

Mass: The Catholic Eucharist, or holy communion service.

Matrilineal: Relating to a family headed by a woman

May Day: A celebration held in England on May 1 honoring the tradition of spring fertility rights in Egypt and India.

Maypole: A flower-wreathed pole that is the center of dancing and games during a May Day celebration.

Mercantilism: A system that advocates government intervention in the economy to increase the power of the state.

Mestizos: People having mixed Native American and white parentage.

Midwife: A person who assists women in childbirth.

Militia: Citizens' army.

Missionaries: People sent to do religious or charitable work in a foreign country.

Monopoly: An exclusive ownership through legal privilege, command of supply, or action.

Mulattos: People of mixed white and black ancestry.

N

New World: European term for North and South America.

Notaries: Officials who process legal documents.

P

Pacifists: People who do not believe in bearing arms.

Paganism: Having little or no religion.

Palisade: A fence of stakes for defense.

Parishes: Areas of church jurisdiction.

Parliament: England's lawmaking body.

Patent: A contract granting specific rights.

Patrilineal: Relating to a family headed by a man.

Patroons: Proprietors of large estates.

Pelts: Animal skins.

Penal colony: A settlement for convicted criminals.

Penance: The confession and punishment of sins.

Persecuted: Being punished or discriminated against because of religious beliefs.

Pig iron: Crude iron that has been made in a blast furnace.

Pirates: Bandits who robbed ships at sea.

Pope: The head of the Roman Catholic Church.

Pounds: The name of British currency.

Presbyterianism: A democratic system of church organization in which ministers and elders formed the governing body in a district.

Priest: An ordained clergyman of the Roman Catholic Church.

Privateer: A pirate licensed by the government.

Privy Council: The king's council.

Proprietary grant: A contract giving an individual or group the right to organize and govern a colony.

Proprietors: Individuals granted ownership of a colony and full authority to establish a government and distribute land.

Protestantism: A branch of Christianity formed in opposition to Catholicism; its consists of many denominations, or separate organized churches.

Provinces: Local regions.

Puritans: A Protestant group that advocates strict moral conduct and reform of the Church of England.

Q

Quakers: Members of the Society of Friends.

Quitrents: Fixed taxes on land.

Quorum: A minimum number of members required to approve legislation.

R

Revival meetings: Religious events based on spontaneous spiritual awakening.

Rickets: A disease that affects the young during the period of skeletal growth.

Roman Catholicism: A branch of Christianity based in Rome, Italy, and headed by a pope who has supreme authority in all church affairs.

Royal colony: Colony under direct rule of the king.

Royal council: A committee appointed by the governor, with the approval of the king, that helped administer the colony.

Royal governor: The highest colonial official, appointed by the king.

S

Salvation: The forgiveness of sins.

Scurvy: A disease caused by a lack of vitamin C.

Seditious libel: Making a false statement that exposes another person to public contempt.

Shilling: An early American coin.

Slaves: Permanent servants regarded as property.

Smallpox: A deadly skin disease caused by a virus.

Stocks: A wooden frame with holes for the hands, feet, and head used to punish people.

Surveying: A branch of mathematics that involves taking measurements of the Earth's surface.

Syndic: Representative.

T

Tariffs: Trade fees.

Tenant farmers: People who pay rent for farmland with cash or with a share of the crops they produce.

Theocratic state: Government ruled by the church.

Treason: Betrayal of one's country.

Tribute: Payment.

Trust: A property interest held by one person for the benefit of another.

Typhus: A disease transmitted by lice.

V

Vestryment: Members elected to make decisions regarding the church.

Veto power: The authority to prohibit.

Viceroy: Representative of the king.

W

Wampum: Woven belts of shells often used as currency by the Native Americans.

Whiskey treaties: Agreements signed while Native Americans were under the influence of alcohol.

Research and Activity Ideas

The following list of research and activity ideas is intended to offer suggestions for complementing social studies and history curricula, to trigger additional ideas for enhancing learning, and to suggest cross-disciplinary projects for library and classroom use.

Activity 1: Teen life in colonial America

Assignment: Imagine that you and two of your friends are living in colonial America and you possess the power of time-travel. The three of you have been invited by a present-day social studies class to tell about colonial American life from a teenager's perspective. You accept the invitation, promising to make your presentation both informative and entertaining.

Preparation: First you must select your roles. For instance, you could be Puritan teenagers living in a small town or on neighboring farms. You might be African slaves working together on a southern plantation. Or you could be Native Americans living in a village near one of the colonies. Next, using *Colonial America: Almanac* as a starting point, gather information about the daily life of the teenagers you have chosen to portray. Consult the library and Internet Web sites for additional material, including illustrations and other graphics. As you conduct your research, focus on food, clothing, shelter, community and family life, recreation, religion, education, and other relevant topics. You can facilitate this stage of the project by making specific assignments. For instance, each team member can gather information on two or three areas such as community and family life or food, shelter, and clothing.

Presentation: After you have gathered information, prepare a twenty-minute team presentation. Keep in mind that your goal is to tell about life in colonial America, but you also want to engage your audience. Use various strategies to bring your colonial teenagers to life: Wear colonial-style clothing, prepare a colonial recipe and share the food with the class, or distribute handouts that feature interesting facts. Explore other possibilities to draw upon the knowledge and talents of each team member.

Activity 2: A trip to the colonies

Assignment: Your teacher has asked you to start a travel service that specializes in planning family vacations to historic sites in the United States. To launch your venture, you must prepare a promotional brochure that features a one-week "trip through colonial America." The teacher has chosen you for this assignment because you know about colonial-period sites that are uncommon tourist attractions.

Preparation: You must first decide on a destination for the trip, so you need to gather more information. As an expert on the colonial era, you know there are several possible itineraries for a trip to colonial America—New England, the middle colonies, the southern colonies, the Southeast, and the Southwest. Using *Colonial America: Almanac* as a starting point, check the library and Internet Web sites for more information. In addition to obtaining facts, you want to find photos and illustrations of colonial sites.

You will probably discover that well-known places such as Plymouth Rock or Williamsburg, Virginia, will have to be included on your itinerary. But you can also guide travelers to less familiar sites. Examples are John Bartram's gardens outside Philadelphia, Pennsylvania; the oldest French building in the United States, at Cahokia, Illinois; and the statue of Jacques Marquette in Rotunda Hall in Washington, D.C. Once you have decided on a destination, select several sites that can be visited within a seven-day period, including as many lesser-known locations as possible.

Presentation: Now that you have completed the information-gathering phase, you are ready to create the brochure. One approach is to write a three-page paper in which you describe the itinerary of the trip to colonial America. Include the following information: (1) historical background on the region, (2) a detailed description of each site, and (3) an explanation of its significance. Then provide a trip map along with photos and illustrations of the sites. If you feel especially creative, you can use a computer to produce an actual brochure, then distribute copies to your classmates.

Activity 3: A "live" historical event

Assignment: For a school assembly program, your class has been asked to dramatize an important event in colonial American history. You are expected to base your dramatization on historical facts, although you are free to use your own dialogue and interpretation when necessary. Your goal is both to inform and entertain your audience. You must also involve each member of the class in the project.

Preparation: The first task is to choose an historical event. Possibilities include the Pilgrims' first winter at Plymouth, Bacon's Rebellion, or the Salem witch trials. To make a decision you might put the question to a class vote. Once you have chosen the event, you need to gather information for a script and other aspects of the dramatization. One approach is to form teams that will do research on a particular aspect of the event. For instance, if you are dramatizing a Salem witch trial, one team can find information about the accusations brought against so-called witches. Other teams could locate transcripts of accused witches' trial testimony, do research on how the judges made their decisions, and find out how the Salem community reacted to the trials.

Using *Colonial America: Almanac* as a starting point, the teams must find information at the library and on Internet Web sites. Look for historians' accounts of the event, which can provide a narrative frame for your dramatization. Also look for documents from the period, which can be used as the basis of speaking parts. For instance, William Bradford wrote about the Pilgrims' landing and first winter at Plymouth. Nathaniel Bacon issued a manifesto during his rebellion, and there are eyewitness accounts of the Salem witch trials.

Presentation: When all the teams have gathered their information, assign roles and responsibilities, such as script writers, a director, a narrator, major and minor speakers, "extras" for crowd scenes—perhaps even a publicity team, costume and prop crews, and lighting and sound crews, depending on the complexity of your production. Be sure everyone in the class is involved, and concentrate on making the dramatization both informative and entertaining.

Native North Americans

U ntil the latter half of the twentieth century, accounts of American history usually began with the arrival of Christopher Columbus (1451–1506) in 1492. Before Columbus went ashore on a small island in the Bahamas (a group of islands south of present-day Florida in the Caribbean Sea), however, native peoples had lived in North America for thousands of years. Nevertheless, for centuries historians chose to concentrate only on the story of Europeans in the "New World" (a European term for North and South America). Native Americans thus remained in the background of the narrative, portrayed either as passive observers or as wild savages.

One reason for the incomplete portrait of Native American culture was that documents from the colonial period presented only the European point of view. For instance, European explorers and settlers wrote detailed observations of Native American people and customs, kept records of treaties, and transcribed the speeches of great chiefs. Some wrote about conflicts with Native Americans, others expressed admiration for the Native American way of life, and many documented atrocities the colonists and Native Americans committed against one

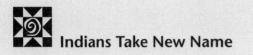

Indians Take New Name

The way the native peoples of North America came to be known as "Indians" is a familiar tale: Italian explorer Christopher Columbus, who led the first successful Spanish expedition to North America, mistakenly assumed he had reached the East Indies. When he stepped ashore on an island in the Bahamas, members of the Taino tribe came out to greet him. He called them Indians, and the misnomer (mistaken name) endured for more than four hundred years. In the 1920s, "Native American" became an alternative name, and by the 1980s it had been adopted as standard usage.

another. Yet there was no way to produce a true picture of native peoples—especially the origin and development of their ancient societies—because Native Americans themselves did not maintain written records. Instead, they relied on oral traditions that were passed down from generation to generation within close-knit tribes or clans. After nearly five hundred years of European conquest, however, those communities had virtually disappeared.

Native American story recovered

In the 1970s historians made efforts to reconstruct the history of the Native Americans through a method known as ethnohistory. The approach combines traditional American history with archaeology (the study of objects left behind by previous societies), anthropology (the classification and analysis of humans and their societies), and ethnology (a branch of anthropology devoted to studying the origin and functioning of human cultures). Extensive information about ancient Native American life has been discovered by archaeologists, who excavate (dig up) the ruins of old societies. They have found homes and other buildings, as well as tools, arts and crafts, and even food consumed by ancient Native Americans. They dated these discoveries through scientific methods. By studying things people used in their daily lives, archaeologists were able to make informed judgments about the way Native Americans lived in the remote past.

Additional knowledge has come from anthropologists and ethnologists, a large number of whom are Native American. These scholars have studied cultural traditions that explain the origins and history of native peoples, such as the stories a tribe tells about itself. The stories have yielded extensive information about the way early Native Americans perceived the world and how they remembered their own history. One example is an Iroquois creation myth. (The Iroquois lived in present-day New York state.) According to the myth, the world began when Sky Woman was cast out of heaven by her jealous husband. As she plummeted toward a vast lake, ducks and other birds slowed her fall. Then a turtle came out of the water and

A Native American pictograph. *Reproduced by permission of UPI/Corbis-Bettmann.*

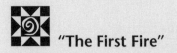

"The First Fire"

Stories like "The First Fire," a Cherokee myth, help anthropologists learn how early Native Americans explained the processes of nature.

The story opens: "In the beginning there was no fire, and the world was cold, until the Thunders (Ani´-Hyûñ´tikwalâ´ski), who lived up in Galûñ´lati [a level between heaven and earth], sent their lightning and put fire into the bottom of a hollow sycamore tree which grew on an island. The animals knew it was there, because they could see the smoke coming out at the top, but they could not get to it on account of the water, so they held a council to decide what to do. This was a long time ago."

The story continues as the Raven, the Screech-owl (Wa'huhu'), the Hooting Owl (U´guku´), and the Horned Owl (Tskili) fail to get fire from the tree. The Raven's feathers are scorched by the fire and turn black, and the owls acquire white rings around their eyes from trying to rub out the smoke. Since the birds cannot reach the fire through the air, the Uksu´hĭ snake volunteers to approach the tree through the water. He is overcome by heat and smoke, however, and his body is scorched black. The great black snake Gûle´gi, "The Climber," meets the same fate. The world is still cold, so the animals hold another council. Kanane´ski Amai´yehi (the Water Spider) offers to make an attempt. Although the animals concede that she can go over or under the water, they wonder how she will bring back the fire. The Water Spider answers by spinning thread from her body and weaving it into a tusti bowl that she fastens onto her back. The story concludes: "Then she crossed over to the island and through the grass to where the fire was still burning. She put one little coal of fire into her bowl, and came back with it, and ever since we have had fire, and the Water Spider still keeps her *tusti bowl."*

Source: Elliott, Emory, and others, eds. American Literature: A Prentice Hall Anthology. *Englewood Cliffs, N.J.: Prentice Hall, 1991, pp. 18–19.*

she landed on his shell. After animals piled soil onto the turtle's back, Sky Woman turned it into the continent of North America. She soon had a daughter, who in turn had twin sons—one good and one evil. The Good Twin brought humans to life, but the Evil Twin tried to destroy them. The brothers had a fight and the Good Twin won. He then taught humans about farming, self-government, and communicating with the spirit world.

Not only does the Sky Woman myth describe the Iroquois' worldview, but it also suggests that women were important in Iroquois society. Scholars have collected thousands of similar stories that provide invaluable details about native cultures throughout North America. They have also gathered information from other methods used by native peoples to record their history. For example, many groups created pictographs (simple pictorial representations of historical events) on animal hides and on tepees (cone-shaped tents made of animal skins) and other dwellings. They also etched pictographs into the rocks of cliffs and caves. Some groups used wampum belts (broad, woven bead belts) to record treaties and other events.

Early Native Americans

Archaeologists speculate that Native Americans may have come to North America as early as 30,000 B.C. However, this theory has not yet been proved and the date is currently placed closer to 11,000 B.C. On the basis of various types of evidence, scholars have identified at least three major eras in early Native American history: the Paleo-Indian Period (11,000–8000 B.C.), the Archaic Age (5000–2500 B.C.), and the Formative Period (1500 B.C.–A.D. 1500). Since there is no way to set exact time frames, the beginning and ending dates of these eras often vary.

Early peoples cross Bering Sea Land Bridge

Archaeologists have determined that early native peoples, called Paleo-Indians, began to migrate (move from one place to another) to North America during the fourth and last Ice Age, which ended in 10,000 B.C. During the Paleo-Indian Period, glaciers (massive sheets of ice) covered much of the earth. In North America the glaciers spread as far south as present-day Kentucky. As the glaciers melted, the levels of the oceans rose, causing dramatic changes in climates around the world. Deserts appeared where lush plants had once grown, and warm weather brought new plants to life in areas that had once been too bitterly cold for plants to grow. Over hundreds of years, small groups of hunters crossed the Bering Sea Land Bridge (also called Beringia) from Asia to Alaska. (Perhaps 1,000 miles wide in some spots, the bridge was formed when land that is now under the waters of the Bering Strait was exposed after the last Ice Age.) According to this theory, over many centuries these people and their descendants slowly moved south, settling in present-day Canada, the United States, Central and South America, and the Caribbean Islands.

Paleo-Indian Period

The Paleo-Indians were nomads who had no permanent home and moved in groups from place to place in search of food and water. They collected berries and nuts, caught fish and wild birds, and hunted animals such as mammoths (large Ice Age elephants), camels, and bison (buffalo). When food became scarce in one area, the groups

Natives Contradict Archaeologists

Archaeologists speculate that around 11,000 B.C., early native peoples crossed the Bering Sea Land Bridge from Asia to Alaska. Yet very few Native American teachings support this theory. Most tribal stories say that native peoples originated within their own homelands. For instance, a Caddo group that once inhabited modern-day Texas and Louisiana believed their people once lived under the earth. They then emerged through the mouth of a cave near the site where the Mississippi River meets the Red River in Louisiana. In the Southwest, Cochiti Pueblo teachings hold that all native peoples originated in the north at a place they called "White House." Although this story may support the Bering Sea Land Bridge theory, scientific speculation and Native American teaching represent different ways of thinking. Oral traditions about the origins of various Native American tribes are part of deeply held religious beliefs.

moved to new territory, perhaps only a few miles away. The tribe generally chose its leaders for bravery in hunting and war. Most Paleo-Indians lived in caves or tents and other temporary shelters that could be moved easily. They made their clothing from animal hides. Although they used simple canoes or logs to cross rivers, they hunted and traveled on foot. Horses had disappeared from the continent not long after the first humans arrived.

Paleo-Indians skillfully crafted stone tools such as spear points, axes, scrapers, and knives, which they used for hunting bison and cutting apart meat. Although Paleo-Indians did not have bows and arrows or advanced types of spears, some groups used highly effective hunting methods. They often drove bison herds into an arroyo (deep gully), then surrounded and killed the animals. Sometimes hunters simply drove whole herds of bison off cliffs, but this was wasteful. Tribes could neither eat all the meat from the bisons they killed using this method nor preserve it for future use.

Archaic Age

Around 9000 B.C., temperatures began to grow warmer in North America. Glaciers melted, forming rivers and vastly changing the environment to something like its present state. Over many generations, people adapted to the shifts in their local environment. These adaptations marked the end of the Paleo-Indian Period and the beginning of the Archaic Age. During this time native peoples were still hunter-gatherers, but they had to kill smaller animals for food. Large mammals had begun to disappear, possibly as a result of climate change or a natural catastrophe.

Rise of agriculture

With the end of the Archaic Age around 2500 B.C. came the rise of agriculture (farming), which began in the Tehuacan Valley in present-day central Mexico. All Native American groups did not change immediately from hunting and gathering to agriculture. Instead, the trend came about slowly through changes in climate conditions and weather patterns. At first crops such as beans, squash, and maize (corn) were grown from wild plants, but eventually farmers learned to produce higher yields through cross-pollination (the transfer of pollen from one the male part of a flower to the female part of a flower). The development of agriculture had a tremendous effect on many Native American groups. Hunter-gatherers had tended to live in small bands that moved frequently and therefore did not form settled cultural patterns. But when a tribe planted a crop, it stayed in one place to reap the harvest. As farming methods and tools were perfected, permanent communities with some form of government often followed.

Formative Period

The Formative Period, also known as the post-Archaic Age, began around 1500 B.C. It continued until Native Americans' first extensive contact with Europeans nearly three thousand years later. Despite regional differences, native groups during this time had many similarities. Agriculture, ceremonial buildings, trade, and village

Oldest Art Works

The oldest works of art found in North America date back to 3000 B.C. They were made from or etched onto stone, bone, and antler. After 3000 B.C., Native Americans created ceramic art pieces. Artworks that Native Americans produced prior to this time did not survive because the objects were made of wood, hide, or fiber, which rarely endure for long periods of time.

communities became common among most Native American societies. Weaving, ceramics, metallurgy (the making of tools and other objects from metal), and jewelry making were also introduced in the early Formative Period. Throughout North America, settled cultures gradually began to establish unique economic, linguistic (language), political, and religious practices.

Advanced civilizations evolve

During this time highly advanced civilizations evolved among the Olmecs, Maya, Toltecs, Aztecs, and Incas in Central America and the Andes Mountains in Peru. The two greatest cultures were the Maya and the Aztecs. The Maya (500 B.C.–A.D. 700) built large, vaulted stone structures that are still standing in such villages as Chichén Itzá in the Mexican state of

Mayan temple pyramids demonstrate the advanced skills and creativity that the Mayan people possessed. *Reproduced by permission of Andrea Henderson.*

Yucatán. They also domesticated (tamed) dogs, made beautiful cotton fabrics, and crafted gold and silver jewelry. They developed hieroglyphic writing (a system using pictorial characters), which they carved into stone or painted on paper. Other Mayan achievements were advances in mathematics and a detailed calendar based on close observations of the solar system.

Near the end of the twelfth century, the Aztecs moved from northern Mexico into the Valley of Mexico (in the central part of the country). When they built their capital, Tenochtitlán (c. 1325), on an artificial island in the middle of a lake, they were still a poor nomadic tribe. Gradually the Aztecs absorbed the cultures of Texcoco and Tlacopán, nearby city-states that they conquered in the 1400s. Soon they created an empire of 6,000,000 people around Tenochtitlán, which eventually had a population of 100,000. By the time the Spanish arrived in 1519, the Aztec capital was connected to the mainland by a series of stone causeways (highways raised above water). The city featured squares, paved streets, stone temples, and other impressive buildings.

Early mound builders flourish

While sophisticated societies thrived in Mexico during the Formative Period, agriculture remained the basis of life for native peoples in areas north of the Rio Grande (the river that forms part of the border between present-day Mexico and Texas). A significant development was the mound-building culture that emerged in eastern North America during the Woodland Era (which roughly coincides with the Formative Period). Civilizations flourished in the river valleys of present-day Alabama, Arkansas, Kentucky, Mississippi, Missouri, Ohio, southern Illinois, southern Indiana, and Tennessee. People formed cultures based partly on farming and partly on hunting and gathering. They were organized into republics (societies in which the leader is elected or appointed by the citizens) dominated by a large city surrounded by smaller ones. Each city consisted of a plaza, one or more pyramid-like temple mounds, chiefs' houses, and other dwellings.

As early as 1400 B.C., people living along the Mississippi River were constructing large burial mounds and forming planned communities. Important people in the tribe were buried in the mounds, which often had temples built on top of them. Archaeologists consider these communities the first chiefdoms (villages governed by one principal leader) north of Mexico.

Hopewell community forms trade network Among the most prominent mound-building groups were the Adena and the Hopewell. In 500 B.C. the Adena culture was developing in the Ohio River valley. The Adena built burial mounds and lived in small villages of circular, semipermanent dwellings. The Adena were followed four hundred years later by the Hopewell societies, interrelated groups centered in present-day Ohio and Illinois. The Hopewell built massive earthen mounds for burying their dead and probably for other religious purposes as well. The Hopewell were among the first groups of Native Americans to determine an individual's status in society according to family standing rather than personal merit.

Hopewell societies participated in trade networks that extended from the Great Lakes to the Gulf of Mexico. Some of the items traded were conch (a type of marine mollusk) shells, shark's teeth, lead, copper, and various kinds of stone. Archaeologists speculate that art-

 Cahokia

During the height of Mississippi mound-building culture, the city of Cahokia was constructed on the site of present-day St. Louis, Missouri. Cahokia occupied an enclosed area of several square miles and had a population of thirty thousand people. The settlement contained more than one hundred mounds, including one that was built in four levels and stood 100 feet high.

works sometimes traveled thousands of miles through many hands to end up in burials of native leaders of numerous cultures. Over the centuries small family-based groups came together to trade goods and find mates. By A.D. 1700, however, the mound builders had disappeared. Scholars have been unable to determine why they became extinct. One of several theories is that the invention of the bow and arrow resulted in the elimination of entire tribes during war.

Pueblo culture thrives

Around A.D. 1, small permanent villages appeared in the Southwest (present-day Texas, Arizona, New Mexico, Utah, and Colorado), ending a nomadic hunting and gathering way of life. In the Sonoran Desert of south-central Arizona, the Hohokam turned to agriculture and developed massive irrigation systems to water their fields.

Bow and Arrow

By A.D. 700 the use of the bow and arrow was widespread throughout the North American continent. This was a major advance in hunting and warfare among Native American groups. More "efficient" bow-and-arrow warfare is cited as one of the possible reasons that mound builders eventually disappeared.

Around A.D. 200, in southern New Mexico, eastern Arizona, and parts of Mexico, the Mogollon people developed small villages of earth-covered houses. Later they built multistoried pueblos—small towns made up of stone or adobe (earthen brick) buildings that often housed many families. The Mogollon people also developed systems for farming in a dry climate.

Within two hundred years the Anasazi group had emerged in the Four Corners region of Arizona, New Mexico, Utah, and Colorado. They eventually designed large multistoried apartment buildings to house their communities, some with more than twelve hundred rooms. Skilled potters as well as farmers, the Anasazi were known for the black-on-white geometric designs of their pottery. By A.D. 1040, pueblos were flourishing in Chaco Canyon in northern New Mexico. Among the largest were Pueblo Bonito and Chetro Ketl. The pueblos of Chaco Canyon were connected by an extensive road system that stretched for many miles across the desert.

Aztlán perfects agriculture

Agricultural communities continued to develop over the next several hundred years. In A.D. 900 the area that is now the southwestern United States and northern Mexico was called Aztlán by the Aztecs. To conserve scarce rainfall in the arid (dry) climate, farmers in Aztlán developed advanced agricultural techniques. They designed a variety of irrigation systems such as canals and dams and devised various planting methods. Aztlán communities consisted of multistoried pueblos and large ceremonial centers. The ceremonial centers resembled *kivas,* the round underground chambers found among present-day Hopi communities in Arizona and Pueblo villages in eastern New Mexico.

Inuit inhabit Canadian Arctic

As agricultural societies were developing in eastern and southwestern North America, a village-centered hunting culture had gradually emerged in the extreme northern regions of the continent. When hunters moved south at the end of the Archaic Period, the area they left behind—the Canadian Arctic—was inhabited by Inuit (Eskimo) peoples. The Inuit maintained their hunting cultures. Inuktitut, the Inuit language, was spoken

This multistoried pueblo built by Native Americans living in New Mexico probably housed many families at one time. Scholars believe that it signals a shift from a nomadic way of life to a more settled, permanent one. *Reproduced by permission of National Archives and Records Administration. Photograph by Ansel Adams.*

across the entire Canadian Arctic, which included present-day Alaska and Greenland. Population density was low and social groups were usually small. Leadership was generally informal, with no official chiefs. The opinion of the most experienced and respected elder usually carried the greatest weight in group decisions. All groups relied on hunting both land and sea animals as well as fishing. Caribou (large deer similar to reindeer) and seals were the primary food sources, although some groups hunted walrus

and whales. Because plant life was scarce, gathering played a minor role in the Arctic economy.

Caribou were also important for their hides. The Inuit took the hides in the fall, when they were in the best condition, and used them to make winter clothing—two layers of coats, pants, stockings, and boots. Summer clothing consisted of a single layer and was often made of sealskin. The Inuit lived in large villages in log houses built of driftwood and partly covered by earth. During the winter most groups moved far out onto the frozen sea to hunt seal through holes made in the ice. There they lived in dome-shaped snow houses called igloos. The Inuit also domesticated dogs for working and invented the dogsled, which is still in use among Arctic peoples today.

First Native American-European encounter

The Thule Inuit in Greenland were the first Native Americans to come in contact with Europeans. In about A.D. 986, Inuit hunters encountered the Norse (inhabitants of present-day Scandinavia; also called Vikings) expedition led by Erik the Red, who founded a settlement in Greenland. Inuit, Beothuk, and Micmac peoples are said to have met him and members of his party along the eastern coast of North America. In 1002 Erik's son, Leif Eriksson, made one of the first documented European contacts with Native Americans. According to the "Saga of Erik the Red" (contained in a collection of Norse sagas titled *Hauksbok*), Leif Eriksson spent the winter of 1002 in a place called "Vinland." Historians disagree about the exact location of Vinland, though many speculate it could have been Nova Scotia (a peninsula on the coast of eastern Canada) or northern New England (the northeast part of modern-day United States).

Vikings describe Native Americans

According to the "Saga of Erik the Red," the Norsemen who encountered Native Americans were named Karlsefni and Snorri, leaders of a party that set up camp on an estuary (inlet) called Hop in Landlock Bay. One morning they were astonished to see strangers (now known to be Native Americans) come ashore from nine "skin-boats" (canoes covered with animal hides). The saga states that the Native Americans (whom the Norsemen called "Skraelings") were "small ill favoured [unattractive] men, and had ugly hair on their heads. They had big eyes and were broad in the cheeks." The Native Americans stayed for a while and then went away.

The following spring the Native Americans returned. They engaged in friendly trading with the Norsemen—they wanted to exchange hides for red cloth—until they were scared away by one of Karlsefni's bulls. Three weeks later a "great multitude" came back and attacked the Norsemen. According to the "Saga of Erik the Red," Karlsefni and Snorri "could see the Skraelings hoisting up on poles a big ball-shaped object . . . which they sent flying inland over Karlsefni's troop, and it made a hideous noise when it came down." Two Norsemen and four Native Americans were killed in the battle. Karlsefni's party decided that, "though the quality of the land was admirable, there would always be fear and strife dogging them there on account of those who already inhabited it. So they

The Norse in Greenland

The Norse explorer Erik the Red, who founded and settled Greenland in A.D. 986, was the first European to encounter Native Americans. After being banished (forced to leave) from Iceland because he had killed two men in a feud, he established a community in Greenland according to Viking traditions. He was distressed when his son, Leif Eriksson, brought Christianity to the colony from Norway. In 1002 Leif Eriksson made one of the first documented European contacts with Native Americans. The Norse prospered in Greenland for several hundred years, but a changing climatic pattern gradually made the country too cold for European farming practices. Harsh conditions eventually led to the extinction of the Norsemen in Greenland by the early sixteenth century.

The Norse explorer Erik the Red and his crew were the first Europeans to encounter Native Americans while establishing a settlement in Greenland. *Reproduced by permission of Corbis-Bettmann.*

made ready to leave, setting their hearts on their own country. . . ."

Europeans come to stay

Over the next five centuries, Native Americans along the east coast of North America had occasional contact with Europeans. Although Europeans continued to hunt and fish south of Greenland, they did not establish permanent settlements. The situation changed drastically, however, when the Columbus expedition arrived in 1492 (see Chapter 2). From that time onward, Europeans came to stay. According to some scholars, the native population of North America north of the Rio Grande was between 7,000,000 and 10,000,000 in 1492. Others place the figure lower, around 2,000,000 to 3,000,000. Native peoples grouped themselves into approximately 600 tribes and spoke numerous languages, perhaps more than 1,000 different dialects (some estimates reach as high as 2,000). They differed in physical appearance—some were dark-skinned, while others had light complexions; they were tall and short, plump and slender. In fact, historians have noted that Native North Americans were as diverse as Europeans. Although native groups had distinct social and cultural characteristics, they were all centered on the family, clan, and village. Historians point out that in this respect, they were again like most Europeans. Yet life for Native North Americans was tied to the cycles of nature. And, unlike Christian Europeans, their religions revolved around the belief that nature was alive and pulsating with spiritual power.

Native Americans initially encountered European explorers and colonists in three distinct regions north of the Rio Grande—the Southwest, the Southeast, and the Northeast.

In 1565 the Spanish founded the first permanent European settlement—Saint Augustine, Florida—in North America. Although the Spanish had also settled in New Mexico, Native Americans drove them back to Mexico in the late sixteenth century. The Spanish therefore did not play a major role in colonization north of the Rio Grande. Yet they remained a significant presence in the lives of Native Americans from their slave-trading base in the Caribbean (see Chapter 2). Native peoples had the most sustained and long-lasting contacts with the French, English, and Dutch, who began arriving on the continent soon after the Spanish.

Native American world destroyed

The arrival of Europeans in North America produced dramatic changes in the ancient native cultures that had evolved since 11,000 B.C. Native American interaction with explorers, settlers, and colonists began immediately—initially with beneficial results for both Native Americans and Europeans. Most native peoples welcomed the strangers who began swarming onto the shores of the Atlantic Ocean in the early seventeenth century. They taught inexperienced colonists how to farm and live off the land. They established trade networks with Europeans, who had huge markets for their goods. In return, the Native Americans received useful European-made products. Within a few decades, however, tensions began to rise between Native Americans and Europeans and among Native American groups themselves. Europeans became greedy for more land to accommodate the increasing number of settlers, and they competed for exclusive control of trade. Moreover, the Europeans were intent on "saving" the souls of pagan Native Americans by converting them to Christianity. The introduction of European weapons and warfare took a tremendous toll, producing Native American-European alliances that ripped the fabric of Native American life. In less than a century after Columbus had been greeted by "Indians," the Native American way of life had been virtually destroyed.

"How the Spaniards Came to Shung-opovi"

In 1540 Francisco Vásquez de Coronado (c. 1510–1544) led a Spanish expedition into present-day New Mexico. The area was inhabited by the Hopi, a native group that included numerous tribes. At first the Hopi welcomed the Europeans, but tensions arose when the Spanish tried to convert them to Christianity. The Spanish enslaved the Hopi, forcing them to build a Roman Catholic mission. The Hopi finally revolted in the late 1600s and drove the Spanish out of New Mexico. The following excerpt, from a long Hopi tale, describes the coming of the Spanish:

> It may have taken quite a long time for these villages to be established. Anyway, every place was pretty well settled down when the Spanish came. . . . When the Spaniards came, the Hopi thought that they were the ones they were looking for—their white brother, the Bahana, their savior.

> The Spaniards visited Shung-opovi several times before the missions were established. The people of Mishongnovi welcomed them so the priest who was with the white men built the first Hopi mission at Mishongnovi. The people of Shung-opovi were at first afraid of the priest but later they decided he was really the Bahana, the savior, and let him build a mission at Shung-opovi.

> Well, about this time the Strap Clan were ruling at Shung-opovi and they were the ones that gave permission to establish the mission. The Spaniards, whom they called Castillia, told the people that they had much more power than all their chiefs and a whole lot more power than the witches. The people were very much afraid of them, particularly if they had much more power than their witches. They were so scared that they could do nothing but allow themselves to be made slaves. Whatever they wanted done must be done. Any man in power that was in this position the Hopi called To-ta-achi, which means a grouchy person that will not do anything himself, like a child. They couldn't refuse, or they would be slashed to death or punished in some way. There were two To-ta-achi.

> The missionary did not like the ceremonies. He did not like the Kachinas [elaborately costumed and masked male tribe members who represent spirits] and he destroyed the altars and the customs. He called it idol worship and burned up all the ceremonial things in the plaza.

The tale goes on to describe how the Hopi were forced to build the mission and how they finally destroyed it.

Source: Gunn, Giles, ed. Early American Writing. New York: Penguin Books, 1994, pp. 12–13.

The Southwest

The earliest European explorers of the present-day United States were Spanish conquistadors (con-querors). After invading Mexico in the early sixteenth century, they pushed north across the Rio Grande in search of gold and other precious metals (see Chapter 2). They created Nuevo México (New Mexico) and founded missions (religious centers with schools and churches) to convert native peoples to Christianity. Around the same time, the Spanish moved into present-day California, building a network of missions. Spanish settlement of the far West, however, played no role in the history of the colonial period.

The Pueblo peoples of the Southwest initially accepted the Spanish presence in New Mexico without resistance. They even adopted European innovations in cooking, architecture, and town planning. Yet the Spaniards profoundly disturbed the local ecology (pattern of relations between living things and their environment). They brought cattle and sheep that grazed on the land, consuming large amounts of prairie grasses. Spanish baking ovens greatly increased the need for firewood, depleting local supplies. To expand the existing network of irrigation canals, the Spanish enslaved the native peoples as laborers. When the Acoma Pueblo finally refused to submit to the intruders, hundreds of Native Americans were killed or enslaved. The Spanish policy of "blood and fire" produced a legacy of resentment. Never finding gold or silver, the Spanish struggled economically and maintained an uneasy peace with their neighbors. In the late 1600s, Native American warriors expelled the Spanish, driving them back into Mexico and keeping them out for a decade (see Chapter 2).

The Southeast

Native Americans in the Southeast encountered Europeans—Spanish, English, and French—in two major regions. The first stretched along the Atlantic coast from present-day Virginia down to Florida, and the other extended along the Mississippi River in present-day Mississippi to the Gulf of Mexico. During the late 1500s, the English made several unsuccessful attempts to establish colonies in Virginia. Finally, in 1607, the Powhatan confederacy (an alliance of Powhatans and other native peoples of the Chesapeake region) was instrumental in saving the Jamestown settlement (see Chapter 4). The confederacy covered nearly all of eastern Virginia, and until 1609 Powhatan relations with the English were peaceful. When English leaders attempted to dictate unfavorable terms of trade and colonization, however, the Powhatans retaliated by withholding corn from the colony. War immediately broke out, and by 1611 the English had forced all native peoples out of the Jamestown area. Native American uprisings in 1622 and 1644 did not slow the number of English settlers. Immigration (people moving from one country to another) remained high, and the English moved westward into Native American country.

Creeks ally with British

In the mid-1500s, Native Americans living along the mid-Atlantic coast encountered Spanish slave traders, who were seeking slaves—Native American as well as

African—to work on prosperous sugar plantations in the Caribbean Islands. A century later, in 1669, English investors founded the colony of Carolina in order to cash in on the African slave trade, which had become a booming business for the Spanish (see Chapters 2 and 6). The Carolina proprietors gained a monopoly on trade with a nearby native group, whom they called the Westos. (The Westos were the surviving members of the Eries, who had earlier been driven from the Great Lakes region during tribal conflicts.) When colonists attempted to enslave the Westos, they retaliated with violent raids on English settlements. Aided by Shawnee, the colonists eventually destroyed the Westos. The English then expanded trade with the Creeks. This group of Muskogee-speaking (Muscogulge) peoples were called Creeks by the English because they lived along the tributaries of the Oconee and Ocmulgee Rivers (in present-day Georgia). The Creeks were highly diverse, encompassing many distinct peoples united loosely by language and broad cultural and political patterns.

By the turn of the eighteenth century, the Creeks were military allies of the English. Creek forces destroyed several Spanish missions in Florida (see Chapter 2). They took more than one thousand Apalachee and other native people to Charleston (a port city in present-day South Carolina) and sold them as slaves to Caribbean sugar planters. Afterward the Creeks achieved a balance of power in the region by playing Europeans against one another and trading with the British, French, and Spanish alike. The British had the best trade goods at the lowest prices, however, and their economic strength and military advantages gave them the greatest staying power in North America. The links between the Creeks and the British endured. The introduction of firearms also caused conflict between the Creeks and neighboring Cherokee.

Especially bloody was the Yamasee War (1715–16), which nearly destroyed the British (see Chapter 4) and unleashed Creek-Cherokee hostilities that lasted for several generations. Five years later, in a treaty at Coweta (in Georgia), the Cherokee acknowledged their weakened position by giving up territory in North Carolina and Georgia. The Creeks continued to move west, struggling to keep their land and adapt to the presence of European colonists.

Seminoles coexist with Spanish

Among the Creeks were the Seminoles, a group that originally lived in the Oconee River area. Their name is a form of *cimmaron,* the Spanish word for wanderer or runaway. The Seminoles began to take up temporary residence in Florida as early as the 1500s. In the aftermath of the Yamasee War, they stayed in Florida, eventually establishing permanent settlements near present-day Tallahassee and Gainesville. The Seminoles also built a village called Cuscowilla outside Saint Augustine. Since Cuscowilla was strategically located

James Oglethorpe, founder of the Georgia colony, meeting with the Native Americans. The colony became a new trading partner for the native peoples in the area.
Reproduced by permission of The Library of Congress.

Georgia colony changes native life

The founding of the colony of Georgia, south of Carolina, had a profound effect on native peoples along the Atlantic coast. In 1732 a society of Christian missionaries and philanthropists (people who give money for charitable works) based in London, England, established the settlement of Georgia for debtors who had been released from English prisons. Georgia represented a new trading partner for Native Americans, who now had access to superior British goods. English immigration to the region also created population pressure on the Creeks at the same time they began to fall into debt to the traders. The result was repeated cessation (giving up) of Native American land to the British. Finally, Georgia became a pathway for escaping African slaves who sought safety and freedom among the Seminoles in Florida. They eventually formed a distinct subgroup of black Seminoles (see Chapter 6).

Choctaw, Chickasaw, and the French

Meanwhile, along the Mississippi River, the Choctaw and Chickasaw had established trading relations with the French. The Choctaw were a large group that inhabited central and southern Mississippi near the mouth of the river and along the coast of the Gulf of Mexico. They were known for their advanced agricultural methods. Since French settlers were more interested in the fur trade than in taking

inland, the Seminoles thus prevented the Spanish from expanding beyond the coast. The Seminoles were generally friendly to their European neighbors. Nevertheless, they remained remote from Spanish settlements, preferring to hunt and fish in nearby lakes and woods. By the eighteenth century, when many other tribal bands were withering away, the Seminoles had developed a separate identity from the Creeks.

Delaware Meet Europeans

Initial contacts with Europeans were quite unsettling for Native Americans. The following are excerpts from a Delaware account of sighting the *Half Moon*, the ship carrying English explorer Henry Hudson (d. 1611) and his crew. They had anchored off the coast of present-day Manhattan. The story was written down in the eighteenth century by John Heckewelder (1743–1823), an English missionary who interviewed descendants of the Delaware:

A long time ago, when there was no such thing known to the Indians as people with white skin, some Indians who had been out fishing, and where the sea widens, espied [saw] at a great distance something remarkably large swimming, or floating on the water, and such as they had never seen before. They immediately returning to the shore, appraised their countrymen of what they had seen, and pressed them to go out with them and discover what it might be. . . . [Some concluded] it either to be an uncommon large fish, or other animal, while others were of the opinion it must be some very large house. . . . [Finally] they sent runners and watermen off to carry the news to their scattered chiefs. . . . [The chiefs] arriving in numbers, and themselves viewing the strange appearance . . . concluded it to be
a large canoe or house, in which the great Mannitto (great or Supreme Being) himself was, and that he was probably coming to visit them. By this time the chiefs of the different tribes were assembled on York island, and were counseling (or deliberating) on the manner they should receive their Mannitto on his arrival. Every step had been taken to be well provided with plenty of meat for a sacrifice; the women were required to prepare the best victuals [food]; idols or images were examined and put in order; and a grand dance was supposed not only to be an agreeable entertainment for the Mannitto, but it might, with the addition of sacrifice, contribute toward appeasing him, in case he was angry with them. . . . Between hope and fear, and in confusion a dance commenced. While in this situation fresh runners arrive declaring it a house of various colours, crowded with living creatures . . .; but other runners soon after arriving, declare it a large house of various colours, full of people of a different colour than they [the Indians] are of; that they are also dressed in a different manner from them, and one in particular appeared altogether red, which must be the Mannitto himself. . . . Many are for running off into the woods, but are pressed to stay, in order not to give offense to their visitors.

Source: Calloway, Colin G., ed. The World Turned Upside Down: Indian Voices from Early America. Boston, Mass.: St. Martin's Press, 1994, pp. 35–38.

land, they treated the Choctaw as equals. The two groups became friendly, sharing knowledge of hunting and farming and even encouraging intermarriage. Although this alliance often involved the Choctaw in war with the Chickasaw and the pro-British Creeks, the Choctaw generally benefitted from their relations with the French.

Museum Tells Pequot Story

In 1998 the Mashantucket Pequots opened the Mashantucket Pequot Museum and Research Center on their reservation in Connecticut. The largest Native American museum in the nation, the architecturally stunning complex features exhibits that combine science and storytelling to bring alive the history of the Pequots. Among them is a re-creation of a Pequot village as it existed before the arrival of the Europeans. There are also demonstrations of Pequot customs and a diorama of a caribou hunt. A central focus of the museum is the story of the Pequots' near-extinction at the hands of the Puritans.

The Chickasaw lived in north-western Mississippi, along the banks of the river. They spoke a Muskogee language that was distinct from the dialect used by the Creeks. Small in numbers compared with their neighbors, the Chickasaw maintained their culture partly by developing a reputation for fierceness. They formed a century-long alliance with the British, who had traveled overland to Chickasaw territory from Carolina in the late 1600s. To facilitate trade, a group of Chickasaw settled in Carolina early in the eighteenth century. Beginning in the 1720s, the Chickasaw were frequently at war with the Choctaw and their French allies. In the

1750s the Chickasaw achieved a final victory over their rivals, remaining undefeated until the American Revolution (1775–83; a conflict in which American colonists gained independence from British rule).

The Northeast

In the Northeast dwelled numerous Native American groups that played an important role in European settlement and determined the course of American history. Among them were the Pequots, who inhabited territory in the present-day Connecticut River valley. During the 1620s English colonists called Puritans (a Christian group that advocated strict moral conduct) formed the Massachusetts Bay Colony on the north Atlantic coast. Between 1634 and 1638 the population of the settlement rose from around four thousand to more than eleven thousand as a result of increasing migration from England. When new arrivals began to crowd the coastal region, Puritan leaders looked for more land to the west, an area controlled by the Pequots, the Niantic, and other native groups. These groups were frequently at war with the Narraganset, who were friendly to the English.

In 1635 the Puritans established three colonies on Pequot land near the mouth of the Connecticut River. Consequently tensions increased between the English and the Pequots. Despite an earlier treaty, English authorities sought to drive Native Americans out of the Connecticut valley. The resulting con-

A depiction of the first encounter between Native Americans and Puritans in the New World. This first meeting would lead to the end of the traditional way of life for all Native American people. *Reproduced by permission of Corbis-Bettmann.*

flict, known as the Pequot War (1637), culminated in the Puritan massacre of five hundred Pequots. The surviving members of the tribe were either killed or fled to other areas of the country. In the Treaty of Hartford the Puritans declared the Pequot Nation dissolved (see Chapter 4).

Iroquois gain power

During the early 1600s Native American groups that lived farther to the north, along the Saint Lawrence River valley in present-day southeastern Canada, established trading relationships with the French (see Chapter 3). Gradually other Native American nations entered into trade with the French. Among them were the Hurons and the Algonquians, who lived between Lake Simcoe and Georgian Bay. Against this alliance of French and native groups in Canada were the Iroquois nations of Mohawk, Oneida, Onondaga, Cayuga, and Seneca, who inhabited present-day western New York. Around 1570 these groups had united as the Five Nations under Hiawatha and Deganawidah (see box

The Iroquois Confederacy

The Iroquois Confederacy (or Iroquois League) was an alliance of native peoples living in present-day western New York state. Around 1570 the Five Nations—the Seneca, Cayuga, Onondaga, Oneida, and Mohawk—were united by the Onondaga wise man Daganowedah (Deganawidah) and his disciple Hayowenthah (Hiawatha). The league was formed to bring an end to years of warfare and cannibalism (eating of humans by humans) among the nations. The following excerpt from an Iroquois legend describes how the union came about:

> [Daganowedah] made arrangement with the Mohawk Chief to act as his spokesman when they should be in council [at Onondaga]. [The spokesman] was also to take the lead in the file, and to perform all the duties necessary to the completion of the Alliance, but he was to act as Daganowedah should direct. [Daganowedah's] reason for choosing a spokesman, was that he had not been heard when the [Onondaga] council first opened, and that probably they might listen to a wise man of the Mohawks. To this arrangement the Mohawk agreed. He agreed also to divest Tadodahoh of his snakes [Tadodahoh was a giant who had snakes tangled in his hair and extending from his ears, nose, lips, eyebrows, fingers, and toes. The warrior who could remove the snakes would strip Tadodahoh of his power], and to make him as other men, except that he should clothe him in civil power as the Head of the Confederacy that should be formed. They then proceeded with a delegation of the Mohawks to the council grounds at Onondaga. When they had arrived they addressed Tadodahoh the great military despot [ruler]. The Mohawk divested him of his snakes, and for this reason he was styled [named] Hayowenthah, or one who takes away or divests.

Source: Gunn, Giles, ed. Early American Writing. New York: Penguin, 1994, p. 19.

on p. 22). The Iroquois gained a European ally in 1609, when Dutch colonists arrived in New York, seeking to copy the economic success of the French (see Chapter 4). The Iroquois and the Dutch signed a treaty called a Covenant Chain. In exchange for exclusive fur-trading rights, the Dutch supplied the Iroquois with metal weaponry—hatchets, knives, and arrow points—that they needed to combat their native and French enemies. Dutch traders ultimately penetrated the Delaware River valley into present-day Pennsylvania and Delaware.

In 1620 the British finally entered the northeastern trading market by establishing an Atlantic port at the Plymouth Colony in present-day Massachusetts (see Chapter 4). The Wampanoag, the Native American group that inhabited the area, had initially resisted English settlement. When they finally accepted the colony,

British traders began to compete for native products. With the French positioned in Canada, the Dutch in New York, and the British in New England, the Iroquois now held the strategically important central territory the Europeans depended on for their trade routes. All sides therefore needed the Iroquois for trading partners and were willing to make concessions in exchange for their business. By maintaining unity and continually playing one group of colonists against the other two, the Five Nations maximized their power and held on to their territory.

Iroquois-British Covenant Chain

In 1677 the Iroquois took a regional leadership position by establishing a Covenant Chain with Britain (see Chapter 4). Through this series of treaties the British declared the Iroquois to be the leaders of all native peoples in most of present-day New York and Pennsylvania. By thus empowering the Native American nations, English colonists made life easier for themselves. While non-Iroquois tribes retained some sovereignty (political independence), they were willing to become clients of the Iroquois and the British in order to obtain arms and trade goods at low prices. Further, by elevating the Iroquois, the Covenant Chain created a mechanism for resolving differences among native nations. For instance, it would in the future prevent such catastrophes as Metacom's War (1675–76), also called King Philip's War, which is considered the costliest war in American history (see Chapter 4). Dur-

ing this conflict the Wampanoag chief Metacom led a campaign against British colonists who had been gradually intruding on ancestral Native American land on Narragansett Bay (in present-day Rhode Island). Metacom asked for Mohawk support, but the Mohawk refused to help the Wampanoag and the colonists gained the upper hand.

In the eighteenth century the Covenant Chain enabled the Iroquois to avoid war by agreeing to give the British the lands of the Delaware and the Shawnee over the objections of those groups. Despite the covenant, however, the Iroquois consistently tried to show the British that their loyalty could not be taken for granted. Although they sided with the British against the Dutch and later against the French in wartime (see Chapter 4), the Iroquois attempted to remain independent during peacetime.

Trade brings conflict

By the third decade of the seventeenth century, the region bounded roughly by the Hudson River, the Saint Lawrence River, and the Atlantic Ocean had become the most complex zone of interaction between natives and Europeans. The traders' influence grew considerably after wampum, originally a sacred object used in Native American religious rituals, was converted into currency. The use of wampum accelerated the pace of trade and heightened competition among native peoples, producing commercial rivalries that sometimes were settled through warfare. This situation intensified for the Iroquois when they overhunted their own territory in New York and needed skins to continue trading with the Dutch at Fort Orange (on the site of present-day Albany, New York).

Farther to the west, competition for hunting territory led to raids and counterraids. North of the Great Lakes, the Ottawas defeated the Winnebago, forcing them to the western shore of Lake Michigan at present-day Green Bay, Wisconsin. Later a people known as the Neutrals drove out the Sauk, Fox, and Potawatomi, who also relocated to the Green Bay area, where the defeated Winnebago—recovering from an epidemic (widespread outbreak of disease)—had little choice but to accept them. The native refugees at Green Bay formed a strong anti-Iroquois, pro-French alliance. In the 1640s the Iroquois attacked the remaining Hurons, defeating them and driving the remnants of the nation and their allies toward Green Bay. Some of the Shawnee and Erie allies of the Hurons instead fled to the south, where they would face still more conflicts with Europeans.

French need native allies

By the early eighteenth century, British trade goods had become extremely attractive to the native peoples of the Northeast, and the French turned to military force to keep their native allies in line. They built Fort Pontchartrain at Detroit (a city in present-day Michigan) in an attempt to enforce their monopoly of the fur trade

in the northern Great Lakes region and keep the English at bay. Yet French attempts to block access to British trade made the Hurons, Petun, and other allies resentful and strengthened opposition to the French among the Iroquois. The Five Nations took part in two unsuccessful British attempts to invade Canada (see Chapter 4). In 1706 conflict pitted the Hurons, Petun, and Miami against the Ottawas, who had relocated from upper Lake Superior to the Detroit River.

The Miami, meanwhile, returned to their former homes on the Maumee River in present-day Indiana. In 1712 the Fox people fled toward Detroit after being attacked by Ojibwa and Sioux. More than 1,000 Fox arrived at Detroit to claim their traditional hunting grounds. Other tribes near Detroit resented the newcomers, and the historic links between the Fox and the Iroquois fed French fear. The French supported their allies in a combined attack on the Fox in 1712, triggering a sequence of Fox wars that compromised French relations with native peoples for the rest of the century (see Chapter 3).

Iroquois form Six Nations

During the 1720s the Tuscarora were driven from North Carolina after losing a war with the British. They journeyed north into the territory of the Iroquois, who adopted the Tuscarora and henceforth became known as the Six Nations. Two other groups—the Shawnee and Susquehannock—also moved up into Iroquois territory. Strengthened by the new arrivals, the Iroquois attempted to make peace with both the French and the British. These new people made the Iroquois a feared military power. Furthermore, the newcomers brought anticolonist sentiments that reinforced the views of Iroquois who opposed cooperation with European missionaries and settlers. Finally, the number of newcomers coincided with a smallpox (a deadly skin disease caused by a virus) epidemic, which the Iroquois leadership blamed on Europeans (see Chapter 3). Overall, "traditionalist" Iroquois favored isolation and withdrawal, becoming dominant over those who wanted to maintain connections with traders and missionaries. In the next generation the Iroquois turned to the south, making war against the Cherokee (old enemies of the Tuscarora) and living in harmony with the Hurons, Petun, and other peoples of the Great Lakes.

Europeans bring devastation

Culture, climate, location, and timing determined the nature of a native group's contact with Europeans—but usually the results were disastrous. As a consequence, great stresses were placed on the economic, social, political, and religious systems of Native Americans. Scholars estimate that within a century of Columbus's arrival, the Native American population had been reduced by nearly 50 percent. Several factors contributed to

this dramatic decline. European weapons and warfare were fatal to native peoples, many of whom were nearly exterminated. Native Americans routinely died as a result of mistreatment, especially slavery. Population loss also occurred when Native American farming and hunting methods were disrupted. Europeans brought horses, cattle, sheep, pigs, and chickens; they introduced crops such as sugarcane, wheat, and rice, along with new species of weeds and grasses. They even brought rats and cockroaches. As a result, many Native American groups could not sustain their own traditions and eventually died out. Yet native peoples were most devastated by disease: in virtually every encounter with Europeans, Native Americans succumbed rapidly to diseases caused by microbes (tiny organisms) the Europeans unwittingly carried into North America.

Europeans bring disease

Before the arrival of Europeans, Native Americans had experienced syphilis (a disease of the genital organs), hepatitis (inflammation of the liver), encephalitis (inflammation of the brain), poliomyelitis (paralysis of limbs), and dental infections. The Europeans, however, brought worse illnesses. Among them were highly contagious viral diseases (caused by a virus, an infectious agent) that produce eruptions on the skin, such as smallpox, measles, and chicken pox. Native Americans also suffered from frequent outbreaks of influenza,

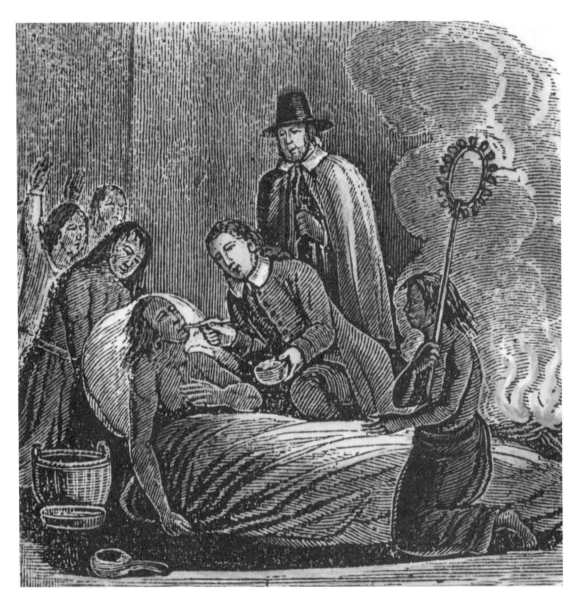

A depiction of two colonists nursing a sick Native American. The arrival of the Europeans brought several diseases that resulted in the deaths of thousands of Native Americans. *Reproduced by permission of The Granger Collection.*

another viral affliction. In addition, they contracted bacterial diseases such as diphtheria (inflammation of the heart and nervous system), whooping cough (a severe respiratory condition), and scarlet fever (respiratory inflammation accompanied by a red rash). Also deadly were typhus (a disease carried by body lice), dysentery and cholera (intestinal diseases), and yellow fever (a viral disease carried by mosquitoes). Whereas the Europeans had developed immunity (acquired resistance) to most of these diseases, Native Americans had no built-in resistance. As a result, when they recovered from one epidemic, they were more likely to catch the next. People could not tend crops or hunt for food, and the sick had to take care of themselves. Entire communities were thus wiped out. European explorers saw evidence of the devastation as they came upon uninhabited villages littered with bones from bodies that had not been buried.

Trade destroys traditions

Life for native peoples throughout North America was also severely undermined by European trade. From 1492 until the Revolutionary War, trade was the central theme of interaction between Native Americans and Europeans. This relationship shifted over time, transforming native life by drawing North America into a web of global economic connections. The fur trade set the pattern for relationships between Native Americans and Europeans, as both sides competed and negotiated for the best price. Typically, when populations of fur-bearing animals died out in one area, Europeans wanted to trade directly with Native Americans whose furs were still plentiful. At the same time, native peoples with depleted fur stocks became middlemen who made deals between other tribes and European traders. During the eighteenth century this pattern

was repeated in the Southeast, with deerskins replacing furs.

In a relatively brief time, European trade items became an essential part of native culture. For instance, guns replaced the bow and arrow, wool cloth substituted for buckskin, and glass beads took the place of natural adornments. Durable cast-iron pots soon replaced fragile pottery. When the pots were worn out, warriors used the metal to make knives, arrowheads, and other tools. By the early eighteenth century, native groups from the Northeast to the Gulf of Mexico were dependent upon European goods—everything from fishhooks to gunpowder—that they had no way to make for themselves. Lacking a market for their own handmade products, many Native American craftsmen died without passing on their skills. Within a few generations many arts and crafts were all but lost in many native groups.

Native Americans lose land

Land became a crucial item of exchange during trade negotiations between Native Americans and Europeans. Immediately, misunderstandings led to disputes about land. The main reason was that the two groups had different ideas about ownership. In general, native peoples did not consider land to be something they could own, buy, or sell. They revered the earth as a sacred gift that is inseparable from the people who live on it. Initially, at least, Native Americans were willing to share their land with Europeans. Yet the colonists mistook the native peoples'

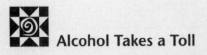

Alcohol Takes a Toll

Alcohol was by far the most destructive aspect of European trade for native peoples. Before 1500 Native Americans had had virtually no exposure to alcoholic beverages. Consequently, they were as vulnerable to alcoholism as they were to diseases. By the late seventeenth century, brandy and rum had become important trade items. Since many Native Americans found liquor highly addictive, they would do anything to obtain it. The demand for alcohol caused distortions in the native economy, as hunters would trade skins for alcohol and then go into debt for goods that had become necessities. In the Southeast, for instance, English traders accumulated huge debts when they supplied Native Americans with European-made items and received no payment in return. (Today we would say the Native Americans were buying on credit.) By the early 1770s, London merchants withheld shipments of goods to the traders until they received 2,000,000 acres of Native American land as payment.

willingness to share as an agreement to sell. When colonists followed the European practice of drawing up legal contracts, Native Americans responded according to their own traditions and assumed they were signing peace treaties. In order to claim land, Europeans began relying on so-called whiskey treaties (agreements signed while Native Americans were under the influence of alcohol). Soon the Europeans were acquiring vast stretches of territory throughout North America.

First reservation established

The fate of Native Americans was finally sealed when European colonists conceived of the idea of taking the good land in a particular area for their own use. They then set aside undesirable lands (called reservations) for use by native peoples. In New England a combination of military defeats and diseases weakened the power of Native Americans to oppose this arrangement. In 1638 the Puritan leaders of the colony of New Haven forced the sixty surviving members of the Quinnipiac tribe to surrender land around the mouth of the Quinnipiac River and harbor. The Native Americans were allowed to keep about 1,200 acres east of the river's mouth.

The Quinnipiacs agreed to have little or no contact with the English. They were also required to obtain the consent of Puritan colonists before allowing any other Native Americans on their reservation. The English appointed a supervisor to oversee the Quinnipiacs' affairs. Although the Native Americans could only hunt outside the reservation on a restricted basis, the English had full rights to cut timber on Quinnipiac land. The Quinnipiacs had to pay for any English livestock they killed, but they were not compensated for damage English cattle did to their crops. In addition to being forced to renounce their own religion and accept Christianity, the Native Americans could not purchase alcohol or firearms.

Reservations fail . . .

Additional reservations were established in New England. After Metacom's War ended in 1676, the surviving Wampanoag, Narraganset, and Mohegan were reduced to about fifteen hundred people and confined to the reservation towns of Natick, Punkapoag, Hassamesitt, and Wamesit. Colonial officials expected native leaders to run these towns like New England settlements, with annual town meetings and elected officers. But the plan failed because town life was incompatible with the native hunting economy. Living under European law was impractical for native peoples. In Native American culture, everyone used land and other property, whereas Europeans strictly enforced laws protecting private property. Moreover, native practice allowed criminal offenders to pay some form of mutually acceptable compensation to the victim or his or her family. European law was far more complicated and rigid. Native Americans living on reservations were also frequently cheated out of their land. Within a few generations, towns that had been set aside for natives came under the control of Europeans, eventually losing their native character.

. . . but set policy for the future

After Bacon's Rebellion of 1676 (see Chapter 5), the Powhatans and other native groups in Virginia were also sent to reservations. In the rebellion, Nathaniel Bacon led a band of farmers who protested that Virginia governor William Berkeley was allowing Native Americans to raid white settlers' farms along the frontier. Berkeley eventually responded by confining Native Americans to designated areas. They suffered a fate similar to that of the native peoples of New England. Elsewhere, Native Americans were relocated to lands on the western frontier rather than to reservation islands surrounded by Europeans. As a model for relations between native peoples and white settlers, reservations failed miserably. It is not difficult to understand why the concept of a colony of Christian Native Americans within a colony of Europeans did not succeed. Native peoples living on large reservations were numerous enough to resist the colonists, but they could not agree among themselves. Smaller groups were located on borderland, and they were defeated by poverty, alcoholism, and oppression. The idea of reservations, however, became a basic part of Native American policy set by the new United States government in the late eighteenth century.

Spanish Exploration and Settlement

2

E xploration and settlement of the New World (the European term for North and South America) began in the late fifteenth century as a direct result of events in Europe, the Middle East, and Africa. One of the most significant influences was the Crusades (1095–1291), a failed Christian movement to recapture the Holy Land (a region in the Middle East comprising parts of modern Israel, Jordan, and Egypt; today known as Palestine) from the Muslims (followers of the Islamic religion). During four hundred years of interaction with Middle Eastern cultures, Europeans discovered the learning of the Muslims, which enabled them to make significant advances in exploration. For instance, they drafted more accurate maps of the known world, built swifter ships, and charted sea routes by observing the position of the Sun. Another important development was the introduction of luxury goods, such as silks and spices, that came from China and the East Indies (India and adjacent lands and islands in the Far East), which created a thriving market in Europe.

Motivated by visions of huge profits, adventurers were willing to take risks in searching for trade routes to previously unknown lands. At that time, the only way for Europeans to reach the Far East was to sail south along the west coast of Africa and then east into the Indian Ocean. The most direct route was through the Mediterranean Sea, but the eastern end of that waterway was controlled by Turkey, a Muslim foe of the Europeans. Portugal was the first country to send explorers eastward. Financed by merchants, they traveled down the African coast in search of gold and ivory. The Portuguese also became involved in the small but lucrative business of buying African slaves from Muslim traders. Soon Spain began competing with Portugal to find the best trade routes. The Spanish had also assumed the role of defender of Roman Catholicism throughout the world, and they seized the opportunity to conquer new lands and convert "pagans" to Christianity. (Roman Catholicism is a branch of Christianity that is based in Rome, Italy, and headed by a pope who has supreme authority in all church affairs.) Thus the stage was set for the discovery of the New World by Christopher Columbus (1451–1506), an Italian navigator who sailed for Spain.

After Columbus opened the way into the New World, the Spanish moved into Peru and Mexico, where they conquered wealthy native civilizations. Then in the 1530s they began exploring the southeastern and southwestern regions of North America in hopes of finding more treasure. Spanish settlement in North America was limited to these areas, which are often called the borderlands, by the French (see Chapter 3) and the English (see Chapters 4 and 5). Consequently, Spain did not settle in any of the original thirteen colonies that became the United States. Nevertheless, the Spanish presence in the borderlands—especially on the Atlantic coast and near the Gulf of Mexico—significantly shaped the history of the colonial period.

Columbus finds the "East Indies"

In the early 1480s, Columbus began to seek a sponsor for a voyage of exploration to prove his theory that he could reach China and the East Indies by sailing west across the Atlantic Ocean. If he succeeded, he would also confirm a long-held European belief that the world was round. (Contrary to popular belief, Columbus was not the first European to speculate that the world was round. Rather, he was the first to have an opportunity to prove it.) For several years Columbus failed to sell his idea to the king of Portugal, primarily because Portuguese explorer Bartholomeu Dias (c. 1450–1500) had found a sea passage from Europe to India, which was considered the best route at the time. Undaunted, Columbus decided to try his luck in Spain. He first met with Queen Isabella I in 1486. Finally, in April 1492, Isabella and her husband, King Ferdinand V, agreed to finance Columbus's expedition.

On August 3, 1492, Columbus set sail from Cádiz, Spain, with three ships—the *Santa Maria* (with Columbus as captain), the *Niña*, and the *Pinta*. At first the expedition made rapid progress. By October 10, however, the crew had

An artist's rendering of Christopher Columbus claiming land in the New World for Spain. He had mistakenly thought that he had arrived in the East Indies, but he actually discovered the Bahama Islands. *Reproduced by permission of The Bettmann Archive.*

turned mutinous (rebellious) because they had not come in sight of land. Luckily for Columbus, two days later they reached a small island in the present-day Bahamas (a group of islands south of Florida). Columbus mistakenly assumed he had reached the East Indies. After going ashore, he spent several weeks meeting the native peoples, the Taino, and exploring the islands. On December 25, 1492, he founded the first European settlement in the Americas on an island he named Hispaniola. Called La Navidad ("the birth"; in commemoration of being founded on Christmas Day, or the birthday of Jesus), it stood on the site of present-day Limonade-Bord-de-Mer, Haiti. Columbus returned to Spain in early 1493, leaving twenty-two men at La Navidad.

Becomes harsh ruler

Columbus had no difficulty persuading Ferdinand and Isabella to sponsor a second voyage. When the expedition reached La Navidad in November 1493, however, they found the settlement in ruins. Either the Native Americans had turned against

Christopher Columbus

Christopher Columbus was born in 1451 in Genoa, Italy, where his family had been textile merchants for three generations. As a young man Columbus served as a sailor on merchant ships and warships in the Mediterranean Sea. In 1476 he went to Lisbon, Portugal, to study mathematics and astronomy, subjects that were vital for navigation. During this time he made several voyages, including one to Iceland. Two years later he married and settled on the island of Madeira, where his son Diego was born. In 1488 he had another son, Fernando, with his Spanish mistress, Beatriz Enriquez. Since the early 1480s Columbus had been trying to find a sponsor for an expedition to prove that he could reach Asia by sailing west across the Atlantic Ocean. Finally the Spanish monarchs Ferdinand V and Isabella I agreed to support the venture. Columbus made his first voyage in 1492, when he "discovered" the New World, which he mistakenly assumed was the East Indies. Yet his triumph was short-lived. While he was governor of Hispaniola, he was accused of

Christopher Columbus.
Reproduced by permission of Corbis-Bettman.

mistreating Native Americans and he failed to fulfill his promises of huge supplies of gold for Spain. Although Ferdinand and Isabella funded three other expeditions, they eventually lost confidence in him. Columbus spent his final years as a wealthy but disappointed man in Valladolid, Spain, where he died in 1506.

the Europeans or the Spaniards had fought among themselves—no one had survived to tell what had happened. Columbus decided to move 75 miles east, where he started building a settlement called Isabela. He immediately sent a party of men in search of gold while he explored the nearby islands.

When Columbus returned to Isabela in late September 1494, he learned that his men had found very little gold. He also faced mounting tensions between the Native Americans and the Spaniards. Having been mistreated by the colonists, the Native Americans were organizing an army to drive the

Spanish Abuses of Native Americans

Bartolomé de Las Casas (1474–1566), a Spanish missionary, witnessed many horrible abuses of Native Americans on Hispaniola. In a report to Ferdinand and Isabella around 1514, he revealed that Spaniards "made bets as to who would slit a man in two, or cut off his head at one blow. . . . They tore the babes from their mother's breast by their feet, and dashed their heads against the rocks. . . . They spitted [impaled like meat over a fire] the bodies of other babes, together with their mothers and all who were before them, on their swords." Las Casas also described the psychological impact of the mistreatment: "In this time, the greatest outrages and slaughterings of people were perpetrated, whole villages being depopulated. . . . The Indians saw that without any offence on their part they were despoiled [robbed] of their kingdoms, their lands and liberties and of their lives, their wives, and homes. As they saw themselves each day perishing by the cruel and inhuman treatment of the Spaniards, crushed to the earth by the horses, cut in pieces by swords, eaten and torn by dogs, many buried alive and suffering all kinds of exquisite [extreme] tortures, some of the Princes . . . decided to abandon themselves to their unhappy fate with no further struggles, placing themselves in the hands of their enemies that they might do with them as they liked. There were still those people who fled to the mountains."

Source: Sale, Kirkpatrick. The Conquest of Paradise: Christopher Columbus and the Columbian Legacy. *New York: Knopf, 1990, p. 157.*

Europeans off the island. In retaliation the Spanish took drastic measures, which led to the near-extermination of the native inhabitants of Hispaniola. During the next three years Columbus ruled harshly, imposing heavy taxes on the Native Americans and forcing them into slavery. While he was exploring the islands around Isabela in 1496, a curious incident took place: Columbus assembled his men and made them take an oath that they had been sailing along the mainland of Asia, not the coast of an island. Apparently he was still convinced—or was trying to convince himself—that he had found the "Indies." If he suspected he had made a geographical error, he did not want the news to come from his men.

Sees South America

Soon reports about the terrible conditions on Hispaniola were reaching Spain. Ferdinand and Isabella were already displeased because they were receiving little gold from the New World and very few Native Americans

New World Named for Vespucci

Italian navigator Amerigo Vespucci (1454–1512) led two voyages to the New World for Spain. On the first (1499–1500) he discovered the mouth of the Amazon River, but his second trip was more historic. In 1501 and 1502, when he explored South America, he realized that the two continents in the New World were not part of Asia. In 1507 German mapmaker Martin Waldseemüller published a map showing that North America and South America were separate from Asia. He named the land "America" in honor of Vespucci.

becoming the first European to see the continent of South America.

When Columbus returned to Spain in 1496, he had left his brother Bartholomeu in charge at Isabela. Bartholomeu had subsequently moved the settlement to the south side of the island, to a place called Santo Domingo. Upon reaching Santo Domingo in August 1498, Columbus was beset by problems. The Spaniards could find only small quantities of gold, and they no longer had enough native workers. Friction had also continued between the surviving Native Americans and the colonists. Death and sickness were rampant, supplies were scarce, and living conditions were poor. Soon the Spanish colonists were openly challenging Columbus's authority.

had converted to Catholicism. No longer confident of Columbus's ability to govern the colony, the monarchs recalled him to Spain in 1496. Columbus tried to persuade Ferdinand and Isabella to send him on a third voyage to Hispaniola. During that time he wore the coarse dress of a Franciscan friar (member of the Roman Catholic monastic order of Saint Francis). His strange attire has never been completely understood. Some historians speculate that he may have adopted it to express regret for wrongdoing, to show humility, or to use as a disguise. In 1498 he succeeded in persuading the king and queen to send him back. On this third voyage Columbus sailed along the coast of Venezuela, thus

Sent back to Spain in chains

Finally Ferdinand and Isabella sent Francisco de Bobadilla to replace Columbus as governor of Santa Domingo. When de Bobadilla arrived in 1500, he found the colony in chaos. The bodies of seven rebel Spaniards were hanging in the town square, and Columbus's brother Diego was planning to hang five more. Columbus himself was trying to put down a rebellion on another part of the island, and Bartholomeu was making similar efforts elsewhere. After arresting all three men, Bobadilla ordered that they be put in chains and sent back to Spain for trial. Although Columbus subsequently lost all of his titles except admiral, during his years in Hispaniola he had become a wealthy man. In 1502 he set out on a fourth voyage to the Caribbean, but the trip ended in humiliation: he had to be rescued after spending a year stranded on the island of Jamaica. Ferdinand refused to send Columbus on another expedition, so the explorer spent the last three years of his life in splendid retirement at Valladolid, Spain.

Conquistadors invade Mexico and Peru

Although Columbus's career ended in personal disappointment, the explorer opened the way for European conquest of North and South America. During the early 1500s Spanish settlement spread to other Caribbean Islands—present-day Puerto Rico, Jamaica, and Cuba—that Columbus had visited. While Columbus's wild promises of huge deposits of gold and other riches failed to materialize, the Spanish still made comfortable profits from tobacco, sugar, and ranching in the Caribbean. Soon they moved onto the mainland of South America and set up trading posts in Venezuela and Colombia. Then in 1519 Hernán Cortés (1485–1547) led an expedition into Mexico in Central America, conquering the Aztec empire ruled by Emperor Montezuma II (1466–1520). In Mexico the Spaniards found advanced civilizations that had perfected sophisticated architectural and agricultural techniques. They also discovered an abundance of gold and silver, which enticed other Spanish conquistadors

 They Came from the East

The following poem was written by the Maya in 1541, after the Spanish conquered the native peoples of Central America.

They came from the east when they arrived.

Then Christianity also began.

The fulfillment of its prophecy is ascribed [attributed] to the east . . .

Then with the true God, the true Dios,

came the beginning of our misery.

It was the beginning of tribute [a form of taxation],

the beginning of church dues,

the beginning of strife with purse-snatching,

the beginning of strife with blow-guns [European weapons];

the beginning of strife of trampling people,

the beginning of robbery with violence,

the beginning of forced debts,

the beginning of debts enforced by false testimony,

the beginning of individual strife,

a beginning of vexation [worry].

Reprinted in: Elliott, Emory, and others, eds. American Literature: A Prentice Hall Anthology. Englewood Cliffs, N.J.: Prentice Hall, 1991, p. 25.

(conquerors) to mount expeditions to the continent. Francisco Pizarro (c. 1475–1541) invaded the Incas of Peru (a country in South America) in 1531, and in 1541 Spaniards conquered the Maya in Central America.

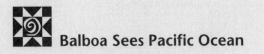
Balboa Sees Pacific Ocean

In 1510 Spanish explorer Vasco Núñez de Balboa founded a settlement called Darien on the isthmus (a narrow strip of land connecting two larger land masses) of Panama. Three years later he led a small party across the mountains in the center of the peninsula. Legend has it that on the morning of September 25, 1513, Balboa and his dog climbed a peak and looked out over a vast ocean. Balboa thus became the first European to see the Pacific Ocean from its eastern shore.

Spanish move into Southeast

While conquistadors were conquering rich empires in Peru and Mexico, the Spanish were also pursuing tales of riches farther north. Beginning in the late 1530s, they simultaneously explored two principal regions: the Southeast (modern-day Florida, Alabama, and South Carolina) and the Southwest (modern-day New Mexico, Arizona, Kansas, and Texas). The Spanish initially moved into Florida and several years later were accidentally made aware of possible treasures in the Southwest.

The first European explorer to venture into present-day Florida was Juan Ponce de León (1460–1521), who had founded a colony in Puerto Rico in 1508. In March 1513 he led an expedition in search of the "Fountain of Youth," which he had learned about from Native Americans. According to their myths, anyone who drank from the fountain would be restored to youth. The following month Ponce de León arrived on the west coast of a peninsula, which he mistakenly thought was an island, and claimed it for Spain. Since his discovery occurred during the Easter season, he called the new land La Florida for the Easter feast *Pascua Florida.* Ponce de León spent some time exploring the coast down to present-day Key West (an island at the western tip of Florida) before returning to Puerto Rico. In 1514 he was granted a commission (authority) to colonize "the isle of Florida." Seven years later he took two vessels, two hundred men, fifty horses and other animals, and farm implements to La Florida. The expedition landed on the west coast near present-day Charlotte Harbor or Tampa Bay. They were immediately attacked by Native Americans, who wounded Ponce de León with an arrow. The Spaniards escaped to Cuba, where Ponce de León died soon afterward.

Stranded party explores Southwest

By 1521 Spanish explorers had traveled along the coasts of the Atlantic Ocean and the Gulf of Mexico, and Spanish slave traders had gone as far north as the Santee River in present-day South Carolina. Seven years later Pánfilo de Narváez (c.

1480–1528) set out with four hundred men to conquer and settle La Florida. The Spanish ships landed on the west coast in April 1528. Disregarding his captain's advice, Narváez abandoned the ships and marched into the interior in search of gold. The expedition was attacked by Native Americans near the site of present-day Tallahassee. The Spaniards made their way to a bay on the Gulf of Mexico and constructed five boats, in which they hoped to travel along the coastline to a Spanish outpost in Mexico. They set sail in September. Commanding two of the vessels were Álvar Núñez Cabeza de Vaca (c. 1490–1560) and Andrés Dorantes de Carranca. Sailing with Dorantes was his African-Moroccan slave, Estevanico (c. 1500–1539).

In November the small fleet was hit by violent storms. The only survivors were the parties led by Dorantes and Cabeza de Vaca, who wrecked off the coast of Texas, possibly on Galveston Island. They spent the winter on the island, and by spring 1529 only fifteen men of the original eighty were still alive. Thirteen of them, including Estevanico and Alonzo de Castillo, another survivor, left Galveston to try to reach Mexico by walking overland. Cabeza de Vaca was too sick to travel and was left behind, presumably to die. The party led by Dorantes headed west and south. Several men died along the way. The rest, including Dorantes and Estevanico, were captured by Native Americans at San Antonio Bay on the Texas coast. They were harshly treated by their captors, and by the autumn of 1530 only Dorantes, Estevanico, and

Alonzo de Castillo were still alive. Dorantes managed to escape, traveling inland to a village of the Mariame tribe, where he was held captive. In spring 1532 Estevanico and Castillo also escaped and joined Dorantes at the Mariame village.

During the winter of the following year, the men were surprised to encounter Cabeza de Vaca. He had not only survived but had also been working as a trader among various Native American tribes. The four Europeans were not allowed to stay together, so before parting they planned to meet in September 1534 at the annual Native American festival that celebrated the harvest of prickly pears. From there they would escape back to Mexico. Their plan went according to schedule, and they managed to flee from a site near the present-day city of San Antonio, Texas. They encountered a camp of the Avavares people, where they were warmly greeted as medicine men (spiritual healers) with special powers, probably because of their foreign appearance.

Tales of golden cities

Estevanico, Cabeza de Vaca, Dorantes, and Castillo performed healing rituals for the Native Americans. Estevanico was especially noted for his ability to learn other languages and to use sign language. When the four men left the Avavares in spring 1535, they found that their reputation as healers had preceded them and they were welcomed wherever they went. As they traveled farther west, they saw evi-

A drawing of Álvar Núñez Cabeza de Vaca while on his quest for the "Seven Cities of Cíbola." *Reproduced by permission of Corbis-Bettmann.*

dence of many different cultures. Visiting the Pueblo groups in the area that is now New Mexico, they saw metal bells and medicine gourds the Pueblo had made. Estevanico kept one of the gourds (a vegetable similar to a pumpkin or squash) to use in his healing rituals. When they reached the Rio Grande (a river that runs between Texas and Mexico) at the end of 1535, Castillo and Estevanico headed upstream, where they came upon the permanent towns (pueblos) of the Jumano tribe. When Cabeza de Vaca and Dorantes joined Castillo and Estevanico, they found Estevanico surrounded by Native Americans, who treated him like a god.

As they traveled toward Mexico, the men heard tales of fabulously rich cities in the interior called the "Seven Cities of Cíbola." From the Rio Grande they traveled to what is now the Mexican state of Chihuahua. As they moved south, they began to see more and more evidence of contact with Europeans, and they even met a party of Spaniards in March 1536. They reached Tenochtitlán (present-day Mexico City) the following July, more than eight years after they had landed on the coast of La Florida. Viceroy (governor) Antonio de Mendoza welcomed the three Spaniards and Estevanico in Mexico with generous hospitality. Eventually Dorantes sold or gave Estevanico to Mendoza. Intrigued by the tales Cabeza de Vaca told of wealthy cities to the north, the viceroy commissioned two expeditions. He sent the first to La Florida under the command of conquistador Hernando de Soto (c. 1500–1542), who left Spain in 1538. (Mendoza received all funding, explorers, and supplies for major expeditions from Spain.) The second was a small party led by a Franciscan missionary, Marcos de Niza (1495–1558), that set out from Mexico in 1539. Both arrived at their destinations around the same time, initiating the settlement of regions that would be dominated by the Spanish until the late seventeenth century.

Hernando de Soto

Hernando de Soto was born around 1500 in Estremadura, a Spanish province near the border of Portugal. Embarking on a life of adventure as a young man, he joined an expedition to Nicaragua led by Spanish explorer Francisco Fernández de Córdoba in 1524. De Soto participated in founding the city of Granada. Sometime after their arrival in Nicaragua, de Soto sided with Córdoba's adversary, Pedro Arias, in a dispute that resulted in Córdoba's death. De Soto then settled in Nicaragua and began to prosper, partly through his involvement in the slave trade. Once again lured by adventure, he joined Francisco Pizarro in an expedition to Peru, where they conquered the Inca Empire. De Soto stayed in Peru until 1536, when he returned to Spain. In 1537 the king of Spain appointed him governor of Cuba, granting him the right to conquer and colonize the territory north of Cuba on the mainland of North America. In

Hernando de Soto. *Reproduced by permission of The Bettmann Archive.*

1539 de Soto was the first European to explore Florida, and his party became the first Europeans to see the Mississippi River. He died on the voyage from Florida to the Gulf of Mexico in 1542.

De Soto lured to La Florida

De Soto had only recently returned to Spain after participating in the conquest of Peru when he heard of Cabeza de Vaca's stories about the "Seven Cities of Cíbola." Although Cabeza de Vaca had failed to find any treasure, de Soto felt that he might discover riches elsewhere in the unex-plored territory around the Gulf of Mexico. He sailed from Spain in April 1538, with six hundred men and two hundred horses. After stopping in Cuba for supplies, his party landed on the western coast of Florida, at the site of modern-day Tampa Bay, in May 1539. They then traveled overland along the coast.

Five months later the Spaniards reached the town of Apalachen near the present-day city of Tallahassee. Ignoring a hostile reception from Native Americans, the explorers spent the winter in the area. When spring came, de Soto and his party left in search of a place called Cofitachequi, which they heard was ruled by a powerful and wealthy queen. In April 1540 they reached Cofitachequi, which was located 75 miles north of the Savannah River in territory that is now eastern Georgia. The Spaniards discovered that the city was indeed ruled by a queen, but they were disappointed to learn that her treasure consisted of a few freshwater pearls (small gems that are formed in the shells of oysters).

Again fails to find gold

De Soto's party left Cofitachequi two weeks later, moving north to the land of Chiaha, which was also rumored to be rich in gold. In early June, after crossing the Appalachian Mountains, the Spaniards reached Chiaha. Once again they had been led astray: Chiaha turned out to be simply an island (now called Burns Island) in the middle of the Tennessee River, and it offered no wealth. From there de Soto led his men south. Along the way they met two great Native American chiefs, Cosa and Tuscaloosa. Cosa lived on the Coosa River north of the site of present-day Childersburg, Alabama. Tuscaloosa lived in a village on the shores of the Alabama River.

At Mabila (possibly near present-day Choctaw Bluff, Alabama) de Soto received word that his ships had sailed into the Gulf of Mexico to meet him. As the Spaniards continued to move south toward the Gulf, they engaged in a fierce battle with a group of Native Americans. During the conflict they were pushed to the north and west and forced to set up a winter camp about 125 miles east of the Mississippi River. The following spring they were attacked by members of the Chickasaw tribe, who killed twelve of de Soto's men.

First Europeans to see Mississippi River

Leaving winter camp in late April 1541, the Spaniards reached a site south of Memphis, Tennessee, on the Mississippi River in early May. They were the first Europeans to sight the great river, which explorers had been hearing about for decades from Native Americans. By June, de Soto and his men were again searching for treasure. This time de Soto had heard rumors of gold and silver in the Ozark Mountains, so he built some barges and crossed the river. The party spent several months traveling through the region that is now the state of Arkansas, but they found no riches. After spending a difficult winter near modern-day Camden, they found themselves in a desperate situation by spring. Several men had died, and they had lost most of their horses. De Soto decided to turn back and sail down the Mississippi to the Gulf of Mexico.

Upon reaching the river, the Spaniards raided a Native American village so they would have a place to build boats for the trip down to the Gulf.

Hernando de Soto raiding a Native American village after reaching the Mississippi River.
Reproduced by permission of The Bettmann Archive.

During the night of May 21, 1542, however, de Soto fell ill with a fever and died. His men reportedly tossed his body in the river so it would not be discovered by Native Americans. Led by Luis de Moscoso, the survivors completed seven barges. In July they went down the Brazos River (in present-day Texas) to the mouth of the Mississippi. After sailing along the Gulf to the settlement of Pánuco in northwestern Mexico, they embarked for Spain. It was now September 10, 1543—more than five years since de Soto's expedition had set out for La Florida. Of the 600 men in the original party, only 311 had survived. Moreover, their leader had died without ever finding treasure. Nevertheless, de Soto is remembered today as the leader of the first Europeans to sight the Mississippi River.

Menéndez drives out French

The Spanish returned to La Florida sixteen years later when explorer Tristán de Luna y Arellano led an expedition to the site of modern-day Pensacola, on the Gulf of Mexico. They started a colony, but it failed and

▣ The Founding of Saint Augustine

Francisco López de Mendoza Grajales, a member of the Spanish force led by Pedro Menéndez de Avilés, gave the following account of the founding of Saint Augustine, Florida. The first permanent European settlement in the present-day United States, Saint Augustine is the oldest city in the United States.

On Monday, August 27, while near the entrance to the Bahama Channel, god showed to us a miracle from heaven. About nine o'clock in the evening a comet appeared, which showed itself directly above us, a little eastward, giving so much light that it might have been taken for the sun. It went towards the west,—that is, towards Florida,—and its brightness lasted long enough to repeat two Credos [Catholic oaths]. According to the sailors, this was a good omen [sign].

Wednesday morning, September 5, at sunrise, so great a storm arose that we feared we should be shipwrecked. The same evening, about sunset, we perceived a sail afar off, which we supposed was one of our galleys [ships], and which was a great subject of rejoicing; but, as the ship approached, we discovered it was the *French flagship Trinity we had fired at the night before. At first we thought she was going to attack us; but she did not dare to do it, and anchored between us and the shore, about a league [a unit of measure] from us. That night the pilots of our other ships came on board, to consult with the Admiral. The next morning, being fully persuaded that the storm had made a wreck of our galley, or that, at least, she had been driven a hundred leagues out to sea, we decided that so soon as daylight came we would weigh anchor and withdraw to a river which was below the French colony, and there disembark, and construct a fort, which we would defend until assistance came to us.*

Our fort is at a distance of about fifteen leagues from that of the enemy. The energy and talents of these two brave captains, joined to the efforts of their brave soldiers, who had no tools with which to work the earth, accomplished the construction of this fortress of defence; and, when the general disembarked, he was quite surprised with what had been done.

Reprinted in: Colbert, David, ed. Eyewitness to America. New York: Pantheon Books, 1997, pp. 9–10.

the survivors finally left in 1561. Four years later the Spanish became alarmed at the presence of the French north of La Florida. French Huguenots (members of a Protestant religious group) had founded Fort Caroline, a settlement on modern-day Parris Island off the southern coast of South Carolina (see Chapter 3). In 1565 Spanish military leader Pedro Menéndez de Avilés arrived in the area with a small party and built a fort called Saint Augustine on a site less than seventy-five miles south of Fort Caroline. It was the first permanent European settlement in what would become the United States.

A view of Saint Augustine. The fort, which still stands, marks the first permanent settlement in the United States. *Reproduced by permission of The Library of Congress/Corbis.*

Menéndez then led ships up the Atlantic to attack Fort Caroline. They were chased away by a French fleet under the command of Jean Ribault, who then tried to stage a counterattack on Saint Augustine. Ribault's move left Fort Caroline undefended, so Menéndez led his troops overland and slaughtered most of the French colonists. During this time Ribault's ships wrecked on an island south of Saint Augustine, where he and his men were captured by Menéndez. Nearly all of the Frenchmen, including Ribault, were killed.

Spanish remain in Southeast

The Spanish had scored a decisive victory against the French. Yet the following winter they endured disease and starvation at Saint Augustine, which was little more than a ditch. In 1566 the Spanish began building a town, laid out in a grid with narrow streets and small blocks, and constructed narrow houses. As Saint Augustine grew, it was constantly vulnerable to attack by the French and English. For instance, in 1669 the English pirate John Davis killed sixty settlers. The Spanish constructed eight or nine wooden forts, and in 1672 they started work on the great stone presidio (fort) Castillo de San Marcos, which still stands.

By 1700 Saint Augustine had a population of around one thousand, but the town was totally dependent upon support from Spain to keep it going. In 1702 South Carolina Governor James Moore attacked Saint Augustine with a combined force of English, Creek, and Yamasee troops, destroying everything outside the walls of the fort. Nevertheless the Spanish held the town. In 1740 they also fought off an attack led by James Oglethorpe, founder of the colony of Georgia, who was trying to claim Florida for Great Britain. As part of the 1763 Treaty of Paris that ended the French and Indian War, Florida was finally granted to Britain. A year earlier, however, France had secretly given "the Isle of Orleans" and the area west of the Mississippi River to Spain in the Treaty of Fontainebleau (see Chapter 3). Therefore the Spanish maintained a presence in the Southeast and would play an important role in American history during the nineteenth century.

"All the reputation and honor himself"

While de Soto was exploring Florida, Spanish friar Marcos de Niza was leading his small party to the Southwest in search of the "Seven Cities of Cíbola." De Niza had appointed Estevanico to be a guide on the expedition. They began their journey on March 7, 1539. Two weeks later de Niza decided to set up camp while Estevanico went ahead to scout the trail. After four days Native American messengers returned to de Niza to report that Estevanico was within thirty days' march of Cíbola and he wanted de Niza to join him. De Niza immediately started north, but Estevanico did not wait for him. As the friar entered each new village, he found a message from Estevanico saying he had continued on. De Niza chased after him for weeks but was unable to catch up.

In the meantime Estevanico had been traveling through the vast desert region of the Mexican state of Sonora and the area that is now southern Arizona. He was the first Westerner to enter the area of Arizona and New Mexico. In May he reached the Zuni pueblo of Hawikuh, which was supposedly the first of the Seven Cities of Cíbola. Estevanico was captured and killed by the Zuni, who thought he was a spy. Later Pedro de Casteñeda, a member of the expedition led by Francisco Vásquez de Coronado (1510–1554) in 1540, gave an explanation for Estevanico's actions. According to Casteñeda, Estevanico left de Niza behind because he "thought he could get all the reputation and honor himself, and that if he should discover those settlements with such famous high houses, alone, he would be considered bold and courageous."

"Of How They Killed the Negro Estevan at Cíbola, and Marcos de Niza Returned in Flight"

Pedro de Casteñeda, a member of the Francisco Vásquez de Coronado expedition, recorded a Zuni eyewitness account of the killing of Estevanico in *The Narrative of the Expedition of Coronado* (published 1896):

> After Estevan [Estevanico] had left the friars, he thought he could get all the reputation and honor himself, and that if he should discover those settlements with such famous high houses, alone, he would be considered bold and courageous. . . . Estevan reached Cíbola loaded with the large quantity of turquoise . . . and some beautiful women. . . . These had followed him from all the settlements he had passed, believing that under his protection they could traverse the whole world without any danger. But as the people in this country [the Zuni] were more intelligent than those who followed Estevan, they lodged him in a little hut

they had outside their village, and the older men and the governors heard his story and took steps to find out the reason he had come to that country. For three days they made inquiries about him and held a council. The account which the negro gave them of two white men who were following him, sent by a great lord, who knew about the things in the sky, and how these were coming to instruct them in divine matters, made them think that he must be a spy or a guide from some nations who wished to come and conquer them, because it seemed to them unreasonable to say that the people were white in the country from which he came and that he was sent by them, he being black. Besides these other reasons, they thought it was hard of him to ask them for turquoises and women, and so they decided to kill him.

Reprinted in: Gunn, Giles, ed. *Early American Writing*. New York: Penguin, 1994, pp. 48–49.

Coronado continues search for gold

De Niza returned to New Galicia, a province on the west coast of Mexico, alone after Estevanico was killed at Hawikuh. De Niza said he had seen the very rich and very large city of Cíbola from a distance. It is believed that he was referring to Hawikuh, which in actuality is a small pueblo. Since his own journal was contradictory, de Niza embellished the tale, impressing the governor of New Galicia, Francisco Vásquez de Coronado.

Coronado traveled with de Niza to Mexico City and submitted the report to Mendoza. The viceroy had long been interested in exploring the territory north of Mexico, so he decided to equip an expedition at royal expense and appointed Coronado to head the venture. Coronado assembled a force of about three hundred soldiers, six Franciscan friars, one thousand Native Americans, one thousand horses, and six hundred pack animals at the western coastal town of Compostela. Mendoza traveled to Compostela to review the expedition in person as it started out on February 25, 1540. The viceroy then sent two ships up the Gulf of California under the command of Hernando de Alarcón to support the expedition from the sea. But the fleet soon lost contact with Coronado.

Grand Canyon sighted

Coronado traveled with his army to Culiacán. On April 22, he left with an advance force of about one hundred Spaniards, a number of Native Americans, and four friars. They proceeded up the Yaquí River valley (in present-day New Mexico), where they founded the town of San Geronimo. Leaving one of his officers, Melchor Díaz, in charge, Coronado took a group of soldiers toward the Gila River (in New Mexico and Arizona). Díaz went up the Colorado near present-day Yuma, Arizona, and crossed into territory that is now California, becoming the first European to explore this region. Meanwhile, Coronado and his men had crossed the Gila River and entered the Colorado Plateau. They reached Hawikuh in early July. The Spanish had no difficulty in capturing the town, but once inside they realized it did not come close to matching de Niza's glowing description. As a result, Coronado sent the friar back to Mexico in disgrace. One observer reported, "[S]uch were the curses that some hurled at Fray Marcos that I pray God may protect him from them."

At that point Coronado sent expedition members Pedro de Tovar and Fray Juan Padilla northwest to a province called Tusayan. They found the ancient villages of the Hopi (a Native American tribe) in what is now northern Arizona. Then they heard about a great river—the Colorado—to the west. The following month Garcia López de Cárdenas, another explorer under Coronado's command, led a group in search of the river. Finally, they reached the edge of a great canyon and became the first Europeans to see the Grand Canyon, one of the world's natural wonders.

Duped yet again

In late August 1540 Coronado sent out another party to the east under the command of Pedro de Alvarado (c. 1485–1541). They reached the pueblo of Acoma, perched high on a rock, where the inhabitants gave the Spaniards food. Alvarado then went to Tiguex in the Rio Grande valley (near present-day Bemalillo). When he reported back that Tiguex had plenty of supplies, Coronado decided to make his headquarters there. During the winter of 1540–41, the demands of the Spaniards for supplies and friction over women led to the "Tiguex War." After seizing one pueblo, the Spanish burned two hundred of their captives alive. During various other engagements, several Spaniards were also killed and Coronado was wounded many times.

Alvarado then traveled east to Cicuye (on the Pecos River), where he captured a Native American (perhaps a Pawnee), whom the Spanish named "the Turk." The Turk told stories of the land of Quivira, which was ruled by a

Francisco Vásquez de Coronado

Francisco Vásquez de Coronado was born in 1510 in Salamanca, Spain, into a family of minor nobility. He sailed to Mexico in 1535 as a member of the party of Antonio de Mendoza, the first viceroy of New Spain, as Mexico was then called by the Spanish. Coronado married Beatriz de Estrada, the wealthy heiress of the former treasurer of New Spain. He took part in putting down an uprising in the Spanish royal mines and in October 1538 was named governor of New Galicia. In 1538 he headed an expedition to locate the fabled "Seven Cities of Cíbola" and claim their treasures for Spain. On two different occasions, however, Coronado was misled by two different men. During his three-year search for riches, he explored parts of the Rio Grande River valley and Kansas, and he became the first European to reach Palo Duro Canyon in Texas. He was later accused of brutal

Francisco Vásquez de Coronado.
Reproduced by permission of Corbis-Bettmann.

treatment of Native Americans in his army but was exonerated (found innocent) of the charges. Coronado died in Mexico City in 1554.

powerful king and contained abundant quantities of gold. In April 1541 Coronado left Tiguex to find Quivira and headed east into the Great Plains, where they saw enormous herds of buffalo. When they finally observed the meager material possessions of the nomadic Plains tribes, the Spanish realized they had been tricked once again. A frustrated Coronado sent his main force back to the Rio Grande with large sup-

plies of buffalo meat. He then took command of a small detachment that headed north and east for forty-two days, probably reaching central Kansas near the present-day town of Lyons. A member of the party reported that "Neither gold nor silver nor any trace of either was found." When the Turk confessed that he had lied in order to draw the Spaniards farther into the interior so they would be ambushed, some of the soldiers strangled him to death. (It is said that Coronado opposed his execution.)

Coronado charged with brutality

Now completely defeated, Coronado returned to Tiguex in October 1541. Shortly thereafter he was seriously injured in a riding accident and lingered near death for some time. By early 1542, however, the Spaniards were ready to return to Mexico. They left Tiguex in April and arrived in Mexico City in late autumn. Mendoza was angry that the expedition had not resulted in the discovery of treasure, but he gradually concluded that Coronado had done his best. Mendoza reappointed Coronado governor of New Galicia in 1544. Soon, however, a royal judge began a formal investigation of accusations that Coronado was guilty of brutality toward the Native Americans. He was relieved of his duties as governor but was cleared of all charges two years later. He then became an official in the municipal (city) government of Mexico City, where he served until his death in 1554.

Spanish colonize Southwest

The first major colonizing effort in New Mexico was headed by Juan de Oñate (d. 1614), who had grown up in a wealthy family in New Spain. In 1598 Oñate set out with 400 soldiers, colonists, missionaries, and Native Americans for the Rio Grande valley. Upon reaching their destination they started a settlement. They soon had conflicts with the Pueblo, however, when Oñate demanded food and other goods. The Pueblo revolted, and in 1610 Oñate was replaced as governor by Pedro de Peralta. The Spaniards then moved to Santa Fe, establishing the third-oldest permanent European settlement in the United States after Saint Augustine and Jamestown (see Chapter 4). By the 1630s there were 250 Spaniards, 750 Native Americans, and about 24 Franciscan friars who served 75 Catholic missions.

The Pueblo initially accepted the Spanish presence, even adopting European innovations in cooking, architecture, and town planning. They also offered the Franciscans the same respect they gave their own spiritual leaders because they considered the white friars to be assistants of their gods.

Pueblo turn against Spanish

The Spaniards soon found that land in the Southwest offered few mineral resources, and the only way to get rich was to use the Pueblo as forced labor for tasks that included herding, farmwork, blacksmithing (shaping iron), silver crafting, and domestic chores. Spanish-Native American relations were thus based on exploitation (using another person for selfish purposes). Over time, the Pueblo came to resent the Spaniards, who profoundly disturbed the ecology (pattern of relations between living things and their environment) in New Mexico. For instance, they brought cattle and sheep that consumed large amounts of prairie grasses. Spanish baking ovens greatly increased the need for firewood, depleting local supplies. To expand the existing network of irrigation (watering system) canals, the Spanish had to rely even more heavily on forced labor. When the Acoma Pueblo finally refused to submit to the intruders, the Spanish killed or enslaved hundreds of Native Americans.

In 1680, after eighty-two years of Spanish occupation, the Pueblo revolutionary leader Popé (c. 1625–1690) led a revolt against the Spanish. Popé urged the Pueblo to return to their traditional religion and way of life in defiance of Spanish law. He organized a massive force of followers at Santa Fe and led a siege in which 434 Spanish missionaries and colonists were killed. The 1,946 surviving colonists fled south to El Paso del Norte (now Ciudad Juárez across the Rio Grande from Laredo, Texas). As the new leader of the Pueblo, Popé set about removing all traces of Spanish influence. He outlawed the Spanish language, destroyed Catholic churches, and cleansed the people who had been baptized by missionaries. Within a decade, however, Popé's power was weakened by Apache raids, internal Pueblo dissension, and his own harsh rule.

 Franciscans Convert Pueblo

By the 1630s the Spanish had made progress in colonizing the Southwest. They were also fulfilling their Old World destiny of spreading Christianity among the "pagans" and "heathens" of the New World. While military leaders created New Mexico, Franciscan friars founded missions for the conversion of the Pueblo peoples. One of the Franciscans, Fray Alonso de Benavides, reported on the success of their venture:

> . . . All the Indians are now converted, baptized, and very well ministered to, with thirty-three convents and churches in the principal pueblos and more than one hundred and fifty churches throughout the other pueblos; here, where scarcely thirty years earlier all was idolatry [worship of idols as gods] and worship of the devil, without any vestige [trace] of civilization, today they all worship our true God and Lord. The whole land is dotted with churches, convents, and crosses along the roads. The people are so well taught that they now live like perfect Christians. They are skilled in all the refinements of life, especially in the singing of organ chants, with which they enhance the solemnity of the divine service.

Reprinted in: Kupperman, Karen Ordahl, ed. Major Problems in American Colonial History. Lexington, Mass.: D. C. Heath, 1993, p. 43.

Spain needs California

During the late 1600s the Spanish turned their attention to present-day California. Although Spain had already claimed land in the region, it had not yet been explored. By that time, mapping and settling the territory had become crucial. The Spanish conquest of the Philippines in

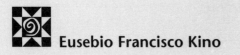
Eusebio Francisco Kino

Eusebio Francisco Kino was a pioneering Jesuit missionary. Born around 1645 in Tirol, Austria (now Italy), he was also an explorer, mathematician, mapmaker, astronomer, and businessman. In 1665 Kino joined the Jesuits, and he later participated in an expedition to establish Spanish settlements in Mexico. Beginning in 1687, he spent almost twenty-five years in Primería Alta, the area that is now northern Mexico and southern Arizona. He built missions and explored the southwestern region of North America. His explorations led to the Jesuits' return to the present-day Baja Peninsula in 1697. Kino was also responsible for establishing ranching as a viable economic enterprise in Primería Alta. He died in 1711, during a visit to dedicate a chapel at the mission of Santa Magdalena.

the 1650s had opened trade between Mexico and Manila across the Pacific Ocean. But the present route from Mexico to the Philippines skirted California because ships had to avoid dangerous currents. Moreover, English and Dutch pirates lay in wait, hoping to plunder heavily laden Spanish ships. Spain therefore needed a harbor on the coast so the voyage would be safer and more direct. The Spanish government also wanted to take advantage of the abundant pearl fishing in California waters.

Kino explores Southwest

In 1683 the Spanish government sent two Jesuit missionaries to California. One of them was an Austrian, Eusebio Kino (c. 1645–1711), who became an important explorer of the Southwest. The party was given the assignment of exploring the area, befriending the Native Americans, and establishing missions. When a drought forced the cancellation of the enterprise in 1685, Kino was sent to Primería Alta (now northern Sonoma, Mexico, and southern Arizona). After reaching Primería in March 1687, he lived and traveled among the Yuma and Pima tribes. At this time there were no European settlers remaining in the Southwest because the Pueblo had driven them out. Kino explored the area, built missions, and attended to his religious duties. Moving from his previous mission at the town of Cucurpe, he founded the mission of Nuestra Señora de los Dolores. Kino remained at Dolores from 1687 until 1711, from that location establishing missions in the Santa Cruz, San Miguel, Magdalena, San Pedro, Sonóita, and Altar River valleys. Some of these missions eventually grew into modern-day towns and cities. For instance, in April 1700 he founded San Xavier del Bac, which is now Tucson, Arizona.

Confirms Baja is a peninsula

Kino did more than build missions. He also led explorations that pushed as far north as the Gila and Colorado Rivers. His discoveries ultimately encouraged the Jesuits to settle on the Baja Peninsula of California in 1697. Up until this time the area was believed to be an island, but Kino confirmed that it was actually a peninsula and could therefore be reached by land. Kino traveled thousands of miles on horseback, sometimes with Europeans and other times with Native Americans. In 1695 he rode to Mexico City, taking fifty-three days to make the 1,500-mile journey.

Introduces ranching to Southwest

Kino was also a skilled businessman. He is credited with introducing ranching as a viable economic enterprise in Primería Alta. The older missions had supplied him with a few animals, but he went on to establish cattle ranches in at least six river valleys in northern Mexico. The missions bred cattle, horses, mules, and sheep. The animals not only fed Native Americans but also enabled the missions to be self-sufficient. This was an important factor because it meant that the missions could survive regardless of what was happening politically and economically elsewhere in the Spanish domains. In addition, it allowed Kino to develop new missions without relying on outside help. For example, when founding San Xavier del Bac, he was able to send along seven hundred animals—a large herd for the time. He also originated the idea of building a road around the head of the Gulf in order to shorten the water route for shipping livestock. One historian has credited Kino with establishing the cattle industry in at least twenty places where it still exists today, including Tucson.

Spanish return to New Mexico

In 1692 the Spanish again conquered the Pueblo tribe and began moving back into the Southwest. They resettled Santa Fe the following year. This time they made the town a presidio guarded by one hundred soldiers. In 1695 several Spanish families left to establish Santa Cruz de la Cañada; eleven years later Albuquerque was founded and twenty-one missions were reestablished. By 1749 New Mexico's European population had risen to about forty-three hundred inhabitants. Meanwhile, the Native American population had declined dramatically, from seventeen thousand in 1679 to about nine thousand in 1693, the year the Spanish returned in full force.

French Exploration and Settlement

3

Spain dominated southwestern and southeastern North America until the late seventeenth century. Within twenty years of that time, however, Spanish influence had gone into decline as a result of English expansion into present-day South Carolina and Georgia (see Chapter 4). Native Americans came to rely on English trade goods and formed alliances with the English settlers against the Spanish. During this time, France had been establishing New France in present-day Canada. Like the Spanish and English, the French were attracted to North America by promises of great wealth in gold, silver, and other precious metals. Like the Spanish, the French also wanted to convert the "pagan" (one who is not Christian, Muslim, or Jewish) Native Americans to Roman Catholicism, thus combining conquest with a Christian mission. (Roman Catholicism is a Christian religion based in Rome, Italy, and headed by a pope who has supreme authority in all church affairs.) Although France did not establish permanent settlements in the territory that became the United States, French explorers extended the frontiers around the Great Lakes (a chain of five lakes along the border of present-day Canada and the United

States), along the Mississippi River valley, and around the Gulf of Mexico. The French presence became an obstacle to English expansion in the seventeenth and eighteenth centuries. Tensions came to a head during the French and Indian War (1754–63), which marked the end of French power in North America.

Verrazano explores Northeast

French efforts at colonizing North America began in the early sixteenth century. In 1523 a group of Italian merchants in the French cities of Lyons and Rouen persuaded the king of France, Francis I, to sponsor a voyage by Italian explorer Giovanni da Verrazano (also spelled Verrazzano; c. 1485–1528) to North America. They hoped to find the Northwest Passage, a direct sea route to Asia via the Pacific Ocean. The king commissioned Verrazano to chart (to make a map of) the entire Atlantic coast of North America, from modern-day Florida to Newfoundland (an island off the coast of Canada). Accompanied by his younger brother Girolamo, a mapmaker, Verrazano set sail aboard the ship *La Dauphine* in early 1524. The expedition reached the coast and sailed south to Florida. Then, turning north, Verrazano anchored at what is now Cape Hatteras on the Outer Banks, a sandbar separated from the mainland by Pamlico Sound. Unable to see the mainland from this vantage point, he assumed the body of water on the other side of

the sandbar was the Pacific Ocean. He concluded he had found the route to China because Girolamo's maps showed North America as a vast continent tapering to a narrow strip of land near the coast of North Carolina.

Discovers New York Harbor

Verrazano could not find a passage to the mainland, so he continued north to the upper reaches of present-day New York Harbor. He anchored *La Dauphine* at the narrows, which was later named in his honor. (Today the Verrazano-Narrows Bridge spans the entrance of New York Harbor from Brooklyn to Staten Island.) Leaving the harbor, he sailed up the coast to the entrance of Narragansett Bay. He found some islands in the bay and named one of them Rhode Island because it was shaped like Rhodes, the Greek island in the eastern Mediterranean. More than one hundred years later, religious dissident Roger Williams would take the name Rhode Island for new colony he founded on the mainland off Narragansett Bay (see Chapter 4). Verrazano's exploring parties went as far inland as the site of modern Pawtucket. From Rhode Island, Verrazano led his expedition up the coast of Maine to Nova Scotia and Newfoundland before returning to France in July 1524.

Meets death in West Indies

Immediately after landing in France, Verrazano wrote a report on his expedition for King Francis I, in which he gave one of the earliest firsthand descriptions of the eastern coast of

Giovanni da Verrazano

Giovanni da Verrazano was born in 1485 into an aristocratic family in the Chianti region of Tuscany, Italy. Pursuing a career as a seaman, he moved in 1506 or 1507 to Dieppe, a port on the northwestern coast of France. From Dieppe he sailed to the eastern Mediterranean Sea and may have traveled to Newfoundland in 1508. In 1523 a group of Italian merchants in the French cities of Lyons and Rouen persuaded the French king, Francis I, to sponsor Verrazano's voyage to North America. They hoped to find a more direct sea route to Asia, which was becoming a profitable trading partner. Although Verrazano did not fulfill this mission, in 1524 he became the first European to sight New York Harbor as well as Narragansett Bay and other points along the northeastern Atlantic shore. He made two other voyages to North America. On the final trip, he was killed by members of the hostile Carib tribe

Giovanni da Verrazano. *Reproduced by permission of Archive Photos, Inc.*

in the West Indies. Verrazano did not found any permanent settlements, but he opened the way for French explorers who came to the northeast part of North America in the early seventeenth century.

North America and the Native Americans who lived there. Verrazano's next expedition in 1527 was sponsored in part by Philippe de Chabot, admiral of France, because the king was preparing for war in Italy and could not spare any ships. On this trip Verrazano traveled to the coast of Brazil and brought back a valuable cargo of logwood for use in making textile (cloth) dyes. In 1528 he

undertook another voyage to North America to renew his search for a passage to the Pacific, which he still thought could be found just south of Cape Fear, North Carolina. Leaving France in the spring of 1528, his party apparently reached the West Indies (a group of islands in the Caribbean Sea), where they followed the chain of islands north. After landing on one of

"the greatest delight on beholding us"

After heading an expedition along the eastern coast of North America in 1524, Giovanni da Verrazano wrote a letter to King Francis I of France about his discoveries. The letter is considered an important document in the story of the exploration of North America. In his account Verrazano gave one of the earliest firsthand descriptions of native peoples living in North America. The excerpt below describes his party's initial encounter with Native Americans, near Cape Fear, North Carolina.

Captain John de Verrazzano [Giovanni da Verrazano] to His Most Serene Majesty, the King of France, Writes:

. . . .[Around January 18, 1524] we reached a new country, which had never before been seen by any one, either in ancient or modern times. . . . Many people who were seen coming to the sea-side fled at our approach, but occasionally

stopping, they looked back upon us with astonishment, and some were at length induced, by various friendly signs, to come to us. These showed the greatest delight on beholding us, wondering at our dress, countenances and complexion. They then showed us by signs where we could more conveniently secure our boat, and offered us some of their provisions. That your Majesty may know all that we learned, while on shore, of their manners and customs of life, I will relate what we saw as briefly as possible. They go entirely naked, except that about the loins they wear skins of small animals like martens [carnivorous animals related to the weasel] fastened with a girdle of plaited grass [a type of belt made with braided grass], to which they tie, all around the body, the tails of other animals hanging down to the knees; all other parts of the body and the head are naked. Some wear garments similar to birds' feathers.

Reprinted in: Elliott, Emory, ed. American Literature: A Prentice Hall Anthology. Englewood Cliffs, N.J.: Prentice Hall, 1991, pp. 48–49.

---

the islands, probably Guadeloupe, Verrazano was captured and killed by members of the hostile Carib tribe. His ships then sailed south to Brazil, where they obtained another cargo of logwood and returned to France.

Cartier continues search for passage

Although Verrazano did not find the Northwest Passage, he opened

the way for other French explorers in North America. The first was Jacques Cartier (1491–1557), who was determined to find a natural waterway to Asia. In 1532 the bishop of Saint-Malo proposed to Francis I that the king sponsor an expedition to the New World (a European term for North and South America) and that Cartier, who had already been to Brazil and Newfoundland, be chosen to lead it. In April 1534 Cartier set off from Saint-

Malo with two ships and sixty-one men. His mission was "to discover certain islands and lands where it is said that a great quantity of gold, and other precious things, are to be found." Cartier's fleet sailed to the northern tip of Newfoundland, entering the Strait of Belle Isle, which was known to lead to a large gulf. In order to avoid the barren northern coast in reaching the gulf, Cartier headed south along the western shore of Newfoundland, naming many rivers and harbors. The party continued along the western coast until they came to the channel (strait) that is now called Cabot Strait (in honor of Italian explorer John Cabot, who claimed the area for England; see Chapter 4).

Sailing through the Strait of Belle Isle, Cartier became the first European to explore the Gulf of Saint Lawrence. He was also the first European to report on the Magdalen Islands (Îles de la Madeleine) and Prince Edward Island. He then sailed on to the coast of New Brunswick, where he explored Chaleur Bay. Heading north along the coast to Gaspé Bay, he claimed the Gaspé Peninsula for France. From Gaspé, Cartier continued as far as Anticosti Island. After he went ashore in present-day Canada, he claimed the land for France. He also encountered the Iroquois chief Donnacona. When Cartier left, he took two of the chief's sons with him as guests (some historians say as prisoners) on the return trip to France.

Begins second voyage

Upon arriving in Saint-Malo in September 1534, Cartier received a grand welcome. Although he had not found gold, he brought reports of a warm climate and fertile land in New Brunswick and the Gaspé Peninsula. The region had previously been considered suitable for fishing but certainly not for settlement or commercial trade. Intrigued by Cartier's report, the king began planning a second voyage. The following year he provided Cartier with three ships for a return trip to North America. Cartier left Saint-Malo in 1535, taking with him Donnacona's two sons, who had learned French in order to serve as translators.

This proved to be Cartier's most important voyage. Guided by the two Iroquois, he sailed west from Anticosti and entered the great river, which the French later called the River of Canada (now the Saint Lawrence River). It became the main gateway for French exploration of Canada for the next two centuries. Cartier went up the Saint Lawrence past the Saguenay River to the village of Stadacona, on the site of present-day Quebec City. After meeting with Donnacona he traveled on to the village of Hochelaga, where the city of Montreal is now located. When Cartier encountered rapids, he did not travel any farther. He was informed by the Iroquois, however, that the Saint Lawrence River extended west to a region that contained gold and silver.

Iroquois help cure epidemic

During his stay in New France, Cartier climbed Mont-Royal to view the Saint Lawrence valley. He also sighted the Lachine Rapids and the

Constitution Embraces

Jacques Cartier was born in 1491 in the French port of Saint-Malo in the province of Brittany. Little is known about his early life, but it is clear that he made several sea voyages. According to some accounts, he may have been a crew member on expeditions led by Giovanni da Verrazano (sailing for France) to North America in 1524 and the West Indies in 1528. Cartier headed three expeditions to North America (1534, 1535, and 1541), during which he discovered the Gulf of Saint Lawrence and the Saint Lawrence River. Although he is one of the best-known explorers in American history, historians cite three factors that could diminish his stature. First, Cartier did not thoroughly explore the Saint Lawrence River valley, thus failing to recognize the potential of rich natural resources such as fur-bearing animals. He also had questionable dealings with the Iroquois, whom he reportedly mistreated. For instance, it is debatable whether he took members of the tribe back to France as guests or as prisoners. Finally, Cartier deserted Jean-François de La Rocque, sieur de Roberval, a French nobleman and explorer, who had been commissioned to found a colony in present-day Canada. When Cartier met Roberval in Newfoundland in 1542, he was instructed

Jacques Cartier. *Reproduced by permission of Archive Photos, Inc.*

to join Roberval's expedition. Instead, Cartier secretly returned to France, where he apparently hoped to get rich from "precious" metals he had found (the metals proved to be of little value). Even though he was not punished for leaving Roberval behind, France never again granted him an exploring commission. Cartier spent his remaining years in Saint-Malo as a prosperous businessman. His book about his second voyage to Newfoundland was published in 1545. He died in Saint-Malo in 1557.

Ottawa River. Cartier's party then returned to Stadacona, where they settled for the winter. They were the first Europeans to spend the winter in Canada, and they were surprised at the extreme cold. Although the Iroquois were becoming less friendly, they nevertheless helped the Frenchmen survive an epidemic of scurvy (a disease caused by a lack of vitamin C). In February 1536, Cartier wrote an account of the difficult winter, describing the rapid decline of his men:

> In the month of December we understood that the pestilence [a devastating contagious disease] was come among the people of Stadacona [the Iroquois], in such sort that before we knew it, according to their confession, there were dead above 50; whereupon we charged them neither to come near our fort, nor about our ships, or us. And albeit [even though] we had driven them from us, the said unknown sickness began to spread itself amongst us after the strangest sort that ever was either heard of or seen, insomuch as some did lose all their strength and could not stand on their feet; then did their legs swell, their sinews [tendons] shrink as black as any coal. Others also had all their skins spotted with spots of blood of a purple colour; then did it ascend up to their ankles, knees, thighs, shoulders, arms, and neck; their mouth became stinking, their gums so rotten that all the flesh did fall off, even to the roots of the teeth, which did also almost all fall out.

Fortunately, there was good news for the survivors of the epidemic. During a meeting with the Iroquois, Cartier obtained a cure—the juice and sap of the ameda tree (possibly a sassafras tree)—and all of the men recovered.

Iroquois Cure for Scurvy

After many men in Jacques Cartier's party had died from scurvy, Cartier met an Iroquois named Domagaia, who appeared to be cured of the disease. When questioned, Domagaia responded "that he had taken the juice and sap of the leaves of a certain tree and therewith had healed himself, for it is a singular remedy against that disease." The ingredients of the remedy are the bark and leaves of the ameda tree, boiled together into a concoction to be consumed every other day. After cutting down a huge tree, the Frenchmen were able to prepare enough of the remedy to cure all of them. Cartier remarked on the effectiveness of the simple cure, observing that all the doctors in the modern world could not "have done so much in one year as that tree did in six days."

Embarks on final voyage

When Cartier left Stadacona for France in May 1536, he took Donnacona back with him. They arrived in France in July.

Cartier's second voyage had been a great success. He had found a major waterway that might be the sought-after route to Asia, and he even brought back a few pieces of gold. Francis I wanted to send Cartier back to New France, but a war between France and the Holy Roman Empire prevented any plans for exploration. In the meantime, the rights to colonize New France had been granted to a nobleman, Jean-François de La Rocque, sieur de Roberval (1500–1561). Finally, in 1540, Cartier was assigned to conduct reconnaissance (survey of a land's terrain) work for Roberval's voyage the following year.

The expedition reached Stadacona in August 1541. While building a camp at the present-day town of Charlesbourg, north of Quebec, Cartier found some stones he thought were diamonds. After spending a harsh winter at Hochelaga, Cartier decided to head back to France. He had not seen Roberval on the entire trip, but the two men finally met as Cartier was preparing to sail from Saint John's, Newfoundland. Cartier received instructions to return to New France with Roberval and help him found the new colony. However, he ignored the orders and sailed for France. When he arrived in Saint-Malo, he found that the "gold" he was carrying was iron pyrite and the "diamonds" were quartz crystals. Cartier was not punished for deserting Roberval, but when Roberval returned without starting a new colony, the king decided to abandon plans for settling New France.

Huguenot settlement fails

Twenty years later French Protestants, called Huguenots, attempted to start a settlement off the coast of present-day South Carolina. (Protestants are members of a Christian faith that formed in opposition to Roman Catholicism.) At that time the Huguenots and Roman Catholics were engaged in a bitter struggle over such issues as Protestant freedom of worship and the power of the Catholic nobility. In 1562 the Protestant leader Gaspar de Châtillon, comte de Coligny sent five ships carrying 150 male settlers under the command of Jean Ribault (c. 1520–1565) to the Carolina coast. Their plan was to start a refuge for Huguenots. They sailed into the Saint Johns River, which Ribault called the River May, and went ashore in Florida (at present-day Brevard County). Ribault claimed the land for France and then led the party north to Port Royal Sound, off the coast of South Carolina. On an island in the sound (now Parris Island) they built Charlesfort, a small fort. Shortly afterward Ribault left for France, expecting to return to Charlesfort. Instead, he fled to England when he found France engulfed in the first of the Wars of Religion (also known as the Huguenot Wars; 1562–98), which lasted for the rest of the century.

While Ribault was in England, Queen Elizabeth I tried to persuade him to join an English colonizing expedition to Florida. She then accused him of planning to escape to France on English ships and imprisoned him in the Tower of London. In the meantime, the stranded colonists deserted Charlesfort and made their way back to France. In 1564 another Huguenot leader, René Goulaine de Laudonnière (d. 1682), led a second expedition to the Atlantic coast, founding Fort Caroline near the mouth of the Saint Johns

River. Shortly before Laudonnière was to return to France, Ribault showed up with supplies and reinforcements for Fort Caroline. By now the Spanish had become aware of the French presence, and Pedro Menéndez de Avilés arrived from Saint Augustine with ships to drive them out. Ribault's fleet pursued the Spanish, planning to attack their fort at nearby Saint Augustine. This move left Fort Caroline undefended, so Menéndez led his troops overland and slaughtered most of the French colonists. Laudonnière managed to survive, however, and escaped to France. During this time Ribault's ships wrecked on an island south of Saint Augustine, where he and his men were captured by Menéndez. Nearly all of the Frenchmen, including Ribault, were killed.

Champlain sees potential in New France

The Protestants were ultimately victorious in the Wars of Religion, bringing an end to the conflict in 1598. The Protestant king, Henry IV (1553–1610), once again turned France's attention toward North America. In 1603 he commissioned an expedition, headed by François Gravé Du Pont, to the Saint Lawrence River. The navigator on the voyage was Samuel de Champlain (c. 1567–1635), who had been loyal to Henry IV during the war. The expedition landed at Tadoussac, a summer trading post where the Saguenay River runs into the Saint Lawrence. Champlain sailed up the Saint Lawrence past

the sites of present-day Quebec, Trois-Rivières, and Montreal. He immediately realized that these lands could be colonized and made a source of wealth for the French king. Champlain also learned of the existence of the Great Lakes. The French found the land sparsely inhabited by Native Americans, some of whom were friendly while others were often hostile. Champlain wrote about the customs of the Native Americans he encountered in *Voyages de la Nouvelle France* (*Voyages of New France*), a report that was later published in France in 1632.

Returning to Tadoussac in July, the expedition sailed around the Gaspé Peninsula into a region Champlain called Acadia (probably named for Arcadia, the mythical paradise of the ancient Greeks). Champlain urged the French government to explore Acadia, now known as Nova Scotia. The region reportedly had rich mines, and some speculated it might even be the key to finding the elusive Northwest Passage.

Explores present-day New England

As a result of his efforts in New France, Champlain was chosen in 1604 to be the geographer on an expedition to Acadia. It was led by Lieutenant-General Pierre du Gua, sieur de Monts, who had been granted the rights to fur trade in the region. Traveling down the coast of New Brunswick, they stopped at the Saint Croix River and built a small fort on a site that is now almost exactly on the border between the United States and Canada. The first

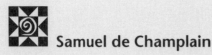

Samuel de Champlain

Samuel de Champlain was born in the small seaport town of Brouage on the west coast of France in about 1567. It is thought that he was born a Protestant and at some point converted to Roman Catholicism; this was during the period of bitter rivalry between Protestants and Catholics over which religion would control the French government. Champlain went to sea at an early age, learning navigation and cartography (mapmaking). Until 1598 he fought as a sergeant on the side of Protestant King Henry IV in the Wars of Religion. He then made a voyage to the West Indies. Although Champlain was born a commoner, his reputation as a navigator earned him an honorary title in Henry's court. In 1603 and 1608 he went to New France. Within four years he had convinced the French government that the land in North America had potential for settlement and commercial development. Now considered the father of New France and the founder of Quebec, Champlain made

Samuel de Champlain.

twelve journeys to New France to explore and consolidate French holdings in the New World. He wrote six books about his expeditions and the importance of the new French settlement. Serving for a time as the king's lieutenant in New France, Champlain lived to see Quebec established on both shores of the Saint Lawrence River. He died in Quebec in 1635.

winter was disastrous; ten of the eighteen men in the party died of scurvy. The following year they moved across the Bay of Fundy to Port Royal, now called Annapolis Royal, in Nova Scotia. This was to become the center of settlement for the French Acadians.

During the next three years Champlain traveled on his own, trying to locate an ideal site for colonization. He sailed along the coast of present-day Maine and journeyed 150 miles inland. On another trip, he sailed down the coast of New England to the island that is now Martha's Vineyard, off Cape Cod. Although the English were exploring in the same area and eventually established the Plymouth Colony in 1620, Champlain was the first European to give a detailed account of the region. He is credited with discovering Mount Desert Island as well as most of the major rivers in Maine. Since the Frenchmen could not find a suitable area for settlement, they returned to Acadia to build a more permanent fort at Port Royal. Monts returned to France, and Champlain stayed with the settlers in Acadia. In 1607, when Henry IV canceled Monts's trading privileges, the entire colony was forced to return to France. Before he left, Champlain had accurately charted the Atlantic coast from the Bay of Fundy to Cape Cod.

Founds Quebec City

By 1608 Champlain had secured backing for his most ambitious project in the New World, the founding of a permanent settlement called Quebec. Arriving in July, the party, which included thirty-two colonists, built a fort and prepared to face their first hard winter. Only nine people survived to welcome the reinforcements who arrived the following year. Champlain continued his exploration of New France by traveling up the Saint Lawrence and Richelieu Rivers to the lake that now bears his name. In 1609 he joined the Huron tribe and their allies in a great battle against a band of Iroquois raiders on Lake Champlain near present-day Crown Point, New

York. The French and Hurons defeated the Iroquois, thus turning the Iroquois, one of the most powerful tribal nations in North America, against the French.

Named lieutenant in New France

In 1612 Champlain returned to France. On the basis of his report, the king decided to make Quebec the center for French fur trading in North America. During the next few years, Champlain frequently traveled back and forth between New France and France. While in New France he pursued his explorations and tried to nurture the colony of Quebec, but political schemes in France demanded most of his attention. When the fur trade faltered, he had to gain new support for the colony. He came out of this predicament the victor, having been made a lieutenant in New France by the new king, Louis XIII.

When Champlain returned to New France in 1613, he explored the Ottawa River to present-day Allumette Island, opening what would become the main river route to the Great Lakes for the next two centuries. By this time the French had made favorable treaties with many Native American tribes, and the fur trade was prospering. Champlain then concentrated on governing the colony. In 1615 he returned from France with the first Roman Catholic missionaries, who came to convert the Native Americans to Christianity. During that summer he saw the Great Lakes for the first time.

Champlain Describes Torture

In *Voyages of Samuel de Champlain, 1604–1618* Champlain provided a detailed account of the aftermath of the battle the Hurons and their allies waged against the Iroquois in 1609. He wrote about the torture of an Iroquois prisoner by the Hurons, a common practice among Native Americans in the seventeenth century. Champlain listed the various techniques they used, including branding, scalping, and mutilation. He admitted that it was difficult to watch another human being suffer, but he also spoke of the strength of the victim, who displayed "such firmness that one would have said, at times, that he suffered hardly any pain at all."

When Champlain turned his back on the torture, the Hurons allowed him to kill the prisoner with a shot from a musket. Afterward, they performed ritualistic mutilations of the dead body, including cutting off the head, legs, and arms. Champlain noted that following the ritual "we set out on our return with the rest of the prisoners, who kept singing as they went along, with no better hopes for the future than he had had who was so wretchedly treated." Champlain concluded his account by saying that when the French, Iroquois, and Hurons went their separate ways, they parted "with loud protestations of mutual friendship."

Position threatened by politics

The Iroquois presence continued to be troublesome to the French colonists. When the French, in alliance with the Hurons and Algonquians, unsuccessfully attacked an Iroquois stronghold at a site in modern-day New York State, Champlain was seriously wounded. He spent the winter recuperating among the Hurons. When he returned to France in 1616 he found his position once again weakened, and he lost the rank of lieutenant in New France. In order to regain his status he proposed an ambitious plan to colonize Quebec, establish agriculture, and search for the Northwest Passage. He gained the king's support and spent part of 1618 in Quebec.

But Champlain's problems in France were not yet over. Plagued by lawsuits and political manipulations, he again appealed to the king. This time he was appointed commander and spent the following years trying to strengthen the colony. His authority gained momentum when Armand Jean du Plessis, duc de Richelieu, the king's chief minister and the most powerful man in the French government, formed the company of One Hundred Associates to rule New France with Champlain in charge.

A drawing of Quebec, the capital of New France. *Reproduced by permission of The Granger Collection.*

Quebec becomes stable

In 1629 Quebec was attacked by a party of English privateers (pirates licensed by the government) and forced to surrender. Champlain sought refuge in England, where he spent the next four years defending the importance of New France and writing accounts of his life. Champlain regained his position in 1632 when a peace treaty with the English returned the province to France. Two years later he sent Jean Nicolet (1598–1642), a French trapper and trader, west to extend French claims in the region that is now Wisconsin. Westward expansion was made possible through Champlain's friendly relations with the Hurons. Even though expansion to the south was still impossible, Quebec was a stable French settlement. It was stronger, in fact, than the English colony at Jamestown (see Chapter 4). Before Champlain died in 1635 he was able to witness the success of his efforts as an explorer and diplomat.

Jolliet and Marquette explore Mississippi River

The Catholic missionaries who accompanied Champlain to New France were Jesuits (members of the

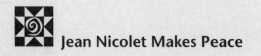

Jean Nicolet Makes Peace

Jean Nicolet was a Frenchman who had been living among the Huron, Algonquian, and Nipissing tribes since 1618. He was an interpreter and negotiator between Native American fur traders and French companies. In 1634 French explorer Samuel de Champlain sent Nicolet on a diplomatic mission to the Winnebago tribe, who lived on the shores of Green Bay in the present-day state of Wisconsin. Because the Winnebago were enemies of the Algonquians, the French feared that they would begin trading with the English. Since the theory was that the route to the Great Lakes might also lead to China, Nicolet wore a Chinese robe embroidered with flowers and birds.

Nicolet began his journey in July 1634 and traveled via the Ottawa River, Lake Nipissing, and the French River to Lake Huron, where he passed through the Straits of Mackinac to Lake Michigan, then proceeded southwest to Green Bay. He was the first European to follow this route, which eventually became the passage to the west for French fur traders. One of the great scenes of North American exploration is Nicolet coming ashore in Green Bay dressed in his flowery Chinese robe. Impressing the tribe with his elaborate costume, Nicolet successfully completed his mission by signing a peace treaty between the Winnebago and the French.

Society of Jesus). They were known throughout the world for their ability to adapt to foreign cultures and thus draw in converts to Catholicism. Attired in distinctive black tunics, the priests were called the "Black Robes" by the Hurons. The Jesuits ministered to French settlers and Hurons until the fall of Quebec in 1629. They then moved south into territory around the Great Lakes, which is now the United States.

As the French combined colonization with religion, some of the Jesuits became explorers themselves. One of the most prominent was Father Jacques Marquette (1637–1675), who had settled in New France in 1666. Becoming proficient in six Native American languages, he founded a mission at Saint Ignace (in present-day Michigan) in 1671. The following year the governor of New France, Count of Frontenac (Louis de Buade; 1622-1698), announced plans to send an expedition through Native American country to discover the "South Sea [Gulf of Mexico]" and to explore "the great river they call Mississippi, which is believed to discharge into the sea of California [Gulf of California]."

Frontenac chose Marquette to accompany the leader of the expedition, the French-Canadian explorer Louis Jolliet (1645–1700). Jolliet had studied for the Jesuit priesthood in France, but by 1671 he had returned to New France and entered the fur trade. He was also one of the signers of a document in which the French claimed

A Jesuit missionary preaching to the Hurons. The Jesuits ministered to the French settlers and the Native Americans until the fall of Quebec in 1629.

Reproduced by permission of The Granger Collection.

possession of the Great Lakes region. Jolliet's party, which included five Native American guides, left Quebec in October 1672. By early December they reached Saint Ignace, where Marquette joined them. The following May the seven men embarked in two canoes, going west along the north shore of Lake Michigan to present-day Green Bay, Wisconsin, then up the Fox River.

Louis Jolliet

Louis Jolliet was born in the town of Beauport, in the colony of New France, in 1645. He was the son of a craftsman who died while Jolliet was still a child. At the age of eleven Jolliet entered the Jesuit college in Quebec, where he studied philosophy and prepared to enter the priesthood. He also studied music and played the organ at the cathedral in Quebec for many years. In 1666 he defended a thesis before Bishop François Xavier de Laval of Quebec, who was so impressed by Jolliet's work that he became one of the young man's principal patrons (financial supporter). In 1667 Jolliet gave up his seminary studies and borrowed money from Laval to spend a year in France. During his stay he studied hydrography (mapping bodies of water). Upon his return to Quebec he entered the fur trade, which was the main business in New France. In 1673 he and Jesuit missionary Jacques Marquette were the first Europeans to travel down the Mississippi River. Jolliet also conducted extensive explorations of Labrador. In 1692 he was named royal professor of hydrography at the Jesuit college in Quebec, where he died in 1700.

From there they portaged (carried boats overland) to the Wisconsin River and descended to the Mississippi on June 15, 1673.

First Europeans to explore Mississippi River

During the voyage Jolliet and Marquette traveled down the Mississippi past the Missouri and Ohio Rivers. They stopped at the mouth of the Arkansas River, about 450 miles south of the mouth of the Ohio and just north of the present boundary between Arkansas and Louisiana. Here they stayed among the Quapaw tribe, from whom they heard reports of the Spanish approaching from the west. Fearing the Spanish and concluding that the Mississippi must run into the Gulf of Mexico, the explorers turned back before reaching the mouth of the Mississippi.

"monstrous fish" and "hideous monsters" During the journey Marquette kept a detailed journal. The following excerpts describe some of the sights they encountered along the way:

> We met from time to time monstrous fish, which struck so violently against our canoes, that at first we took them to be large trees, which threatened to upset us. We saw also a hideous monster; his head was like that of a tiger, his nose was sharp, and somewhat resembled a wildcat; his beard was long; his ears stood upright; the color of his head was gray; and his neck black. He looked upon us for some time, but as we came near him our oars frightened him away. . . .

> As we were descending the river we saw high rocks with hideous monsters painted on them, and upon which the bravest Indians dare not look. They are as large as a calf, with head and horns like a goat; their eyes red; beard like a tiger's; and a face like a man's. Their

A depiction of Louis Jolliet and Jacques Marquette with their Native American guides during their exploration of the Mississippi River. They were the first Europeans to explore the river. *Reproduced by permission of The Granger Collection.*

tails are so long that they pass over their heads and between their fore [front] legs, under their belly, and ending like a fish's tail. They are painted red, green, and black. They are so well drawn that I cannot believe they were drawn by the Indians. And for what purpose they were made seems to me a great mystery.

Make important contribution

The explorers had made an important contribution to knowledge about North America, and their discoveries opened the way for future expeditions. Jolliet and Marquette, however,

went their separate ways after the Mississippi trip. Jolliet returned to Montreal to report on their discoveries. Marquette had become ill, so he made his way back to Saint Ignace. On the Thursday before Easter 1673, Marquette preached a sermon to a gathering of two thousand. members of the Illinois nation. He died shortly thereafter, never reaching Saint Ignace. He was buried at the mouth of the river that was named for him, on the site of present-day Ludington, Michigan. Marquette had partially fulfilled his goal of establishing missions around the Great

René-Robert Cavelier, sieur de La Salle

René-Robert Cavelier, sieur de La Salle, was born into a well-to-do family in Rouen, the capital of the French province of Normandy. He chose a religious calling as a boy, but as an adult he became an explorer and was later vital as a builder of New France. After the French government granted La Salle permission to explore, trade, and construct forts in New France, he and his men set out across the Great Lakes in a specially built ship called the *Griffon*. During their journey between 1679 and 1681 they established the sites of many present-day cities in the Midwest, and La Salle became the first European to sail down the Mississippi River to its mouth. He also established the only French settlement in Texas. Yet in spite of La Salle's success, he was responsible for several misadventures and disasters that led directly to his being killed in cold blood by his own men in 1687.

Lakes and in the Mississippi valley. Yet modern historians conclude that the Jesuits ultimately had little impact on Native American life.

Jolliet continued his explorations. In 1679 he led an expedition on an overland route to the rich fur-trading regions of Hudson Bay, which the English were exploiting. When he reached Hudson Bay he encountered English traders and learned the extent of their activities. Upon his return to Quebec, Jolliet wrote a report warning that the French risked losing the fur trade if they allowed the English to remain in the area. As a reward for his success, Jolliet was given trading rights and land on the north shore of New France. He was also awarded the island of Anticosti. In 1694 Jolliet was commissioned to map the coastline of Labrador. He drew the first maps of the area, described the landscape, and gathered information about the Inuit (Eskimo) inhabitants. In October 1694 he returned to Quebec, only to discover that the British had seized Anticosti during his absence.

La Salle begins explorations

French explorer René-Robert Cavelier, sieur de La Salle (1643–1687), continued exploring the Mississippi valley, eventually reaching the Gulf of Mexico. He made important discoveries in the Great Lakes region, but he was constantly involved in controversies that overshadowed his accomplishments. La Salle began his exploring career when he left the Jesuit priesthood in France and moved to New France in 1667. Through family connections, he was granted land on the island of Montreal (located on the Saint Lawrence River in Canada), which he sold two years later for a profit. With this money La Salle organized an ill-fated expedition to find the Ohio River, which he thought would lead to the South Seas and eventually

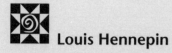

Louis Hennepin

Louis Hennepin was a Franciscan priest who served as a chaplain to René-Robert Cavelier, sieur de La Salle, on an expedition down the Mississippi River in 1678. Like many other French priests who came to North America, Hennepin was also an explorer. In addition to being the first European to describe the Niagara Falls, he claimed to have traveled the length of the Mississippi River in 1680—two years before La Salle's historic voyage. Although evidence proved Hennepin's claim was false, he stood by his story. When he returned to Europe he published an account of his adventures in *Description de la Louisiane* (*Description of Louisiana*; 1682). It was an immediate success, becoming a best-seller in several languages. His career flourished until 1687, when he was expelled from his monastery and forced to go to Holland. Hennepin blamed these events on a plot by La Salle, who supposedly feared what the priest would reveal about the discovery of the Mississippi. The rest of Hennepin's life was filled with turmoil, as he became involved in various disputes in Holland, France, and Rome.

to China. There is no record of his travels from 1669 to 1670, but many supporters claimed he discovered the Mississippi River. Evidence shows, however, that Jolliet and Marquette first found the Mississippi in 1673.

Explores Great Lakes

La Salle made other unknown trips from 1671 to 1673. In the fall of 1673 he returned to Montreal, where he took the side of Frontenac, the governor of New France, in a dispute that was then going on in the colony. As a result La Salle was rewarded with a title of nobility (sieur de La Salle) and command of Fort Frontenac at the site of present-day Kingston, Ontario. In 1677 he went back to France, and the following year he received permission from King Louis XIV to explore North America between New France and Mexico.

La Salle started the expedition by constructing a fort on the Niagara River, on the border between present-day Ontario, Canada, and New York State. He was accompanied by several other notable explorers, including Italian adventurer Henry de Tonti (1650–1704) and Franciscan priest Louis Hennepin (1626–after 1701). After spending the winter of 1678 to 1679 at Fort Frontenac, La Salle discovered that his men had built a ship, the *Griffon,* especially for exploring the Great Lakes. They sailed in August 1679, traveling across Lake Erie into Lake Huron and then to Mackinac, a strip of land that separates Lake Huron from Lake Michigan. They went south on Lake Michigan in canoes. In the middle of winter they reached a village of the Illinois tribe near the present-day city of Peoria, Illinois. Discouraged by Native Americans from continuing, several of La Salle's men deserted the expedition. But La Salle built a fort called Crèvecoeur in the area to serve as a supply center for future explorations. He sent Hennepin to lead an advance party to the Mississippi and then headed back to New France.

Sights Ohio River

La Salle's return trip to New France was beset by several disasters. The *Griffon* got lost; then La Salle discovered that the fort on the Niagara had been burned down and a supply ship had sunk. At Fort Frontenac he learned that Crèvecoeur had also been burned. Making matters even worse, many of his men had deserted and were making their own way back to New France, robbing his supply posts along the way. Setting an ambush, La Salle managed to capture them. In 1681 he finally returned to Montreal, where he tried to calm his creditors as well as his enemies, who were spreading rumors about his mismanagement of the expedition. He then headed into the wilderness with a party of forty men, reaching Crèvecoeur in January 1682. From Crèvecoeur they descended the Illinois River onto the Mississippi, passing the mouth of the Missouri. La Salle finally sighted the Ohio River, which had been his goal

when he set out on his first expedition thirteen years earlier. On the site of present-day Memphis, Tennessee, he also built a fort called Prud'homme.

Reaches Gulf of Mexico

In March a war party from the Arkansas tribe threatened to attack La Salle and his men. He managed to avert a conflict and took possession of the country in the name of Louis XIV. The Frenchmen then continued down the river and passed the farthest point reached by Jolliet and Marquette. La Salle and his men spent time among the Tensas and Natchez tribes before reaching the Gulf of Mexico. He claimed the territory for France, calling it Louisiana. In the meantime Frontenac had been replaced by a new governor, who believed the charges that La Salle had mismanaged his expedition and mistreated his men. On the governor's orders, La Salle was sent back to France in 1683 to report on his conduct. He found little support in France for his ideas on developing the Mississippi valley. He did learn, however, that an influential group was trying to interest the French government in sending an expedition to the mouth of the Rio Grande on the Gulf of Mexico. Their plan was to seize valuable mines in New Mexico and New Spain (Mexico). In order to be a part of these schemes, La Salle purposely falsified his discoveries, making a map that moved the Mississippi River much farther to the west so that it emptied into the Gulf of Mexico from Texas rather than Louisiana.

Misses mouth of Mississippi River

La Salle succeeded in convincing the king and rich French merchants to sponsor an expedition to the Gulf of Mexico. He left France in 1684, heading a party of four ships and 327 men and women. As a result of bad planning and La Salle's ongoing quarrel with the naval captain, the ships were overloaded, and there was not enough water. The party was forced to stop at the French colony of Haiti (an island in the Caribbean Sea). There they learned that one of their ships, which had been following with most of their supplies, had been captured by the Spanish. Leaving Haiti with the three remaining ships in November, La Salle headed toward the Mississippi delta (a deposit of sand, gravel, clay, and similar material). On December 27 and 28, they saw muddy waters that indicated they were near the mouth of the great river. La Salle had made miscalculations in his navigation, however, and chose to believe unreliable Spanish charts. Therefore, instead of investigating, he headed west.

Sails off course to Texas

By the time La Salle realized his mistake, the ships were off Matagorda Bay, south of the site of present-day Houston, Texas. After one of the ships ran aground while sailing into the bay, local Native Americans tried to ransack the wreckage. The Frenchmen shot at them, and from then on the two groups were enemies. In March 1685 the naval captain returned to France

René-Robert Cavelier, sieur de La Salle's ship arriving in Texas. *Reproduced by permission of Archive Photos, Inc.*

with one of his ships, leaving La Salle with only one vessel.

In May 1685 La Salle constructed a fort at the mouth of the Lavaca River on Matagorda Bay. It was

Mississippi Bubble

In 1717 John Law (1671–1729), a Scottish adventurer and financier, started the French Company of the West. It was granted exclusive development rights in the Mississippi River valley and around the Gulf of Mexico. Soon Law and his partners controlled the tobacco and African slave trades in the Louisiana Territory. A year later they requested that Louisiana Governor Jean Baptiste Le Moyne, sieur de Bienville, establish the city of New Orleans. In 1719 the company changed its name to Company of the Indies and embarked on an elaborate program called the Mississippi Bubble to encourage settlement in Louisiana. Promoters brought in German and Dutch immigrants, promising them property and supplies if they agreed to farm the land. The plan attracted thousands of immigrants to New Biloxi, Natchez, and other settlements. The company also managed to monopolize French trade in the colonies, but by 1720 the scheme had triggered a buying frenzy that inflated company shares to more than thirty times their actual worth. Profits could not keep pace with stock values, causing a stock-market crash in France. As a result, nearly everyone involved in the company was financially ruined. Although the Mississippi Bubble was a failure, it had boosted the population of Louisiana and prevented England or Spain from gaining a foothold in the region.

the only French colony to be established in the Southwest. With the fort as a base, La Salle and several members of the party made exploring trips into the surrounding countryside. In April 1686, when a drunken captain wrecked the last ship, the little colony was left with no means of escape. La Salle decided the only way out was to travel overland to the Mississippi and then head up the river to the Great Lakes, where they could find French missions and traders. The party of twenty men left at the end of April. As a result of various mishaps, the number was reduced to eight by October. La Salle was forced to return to the fort on the Lavaca.

Killed by his own men

La Salle set out again in January 1687 with seventeen companions, leaving twenty-five behind at the fort. By this time the men hated La Salle for causing them such misery. On the night of March 18, 1687, a mutinous (rebellious) group killed his nephew, servant, and guide. The next morning, at a spot just north of the present-day town of Navosta, Texas, they shot La Salle in cold blood and left his body to be eaten by wild animals. The remaining members of La Salle's expedition reached Montreal in July 1688.

Le Moynes settle Louisiana province

The Mississippi valley was now opened to French settlement in two principal areas: Illinois country (*le pays des Illinois*) around the Great Lakes and Louisiana on the Gulf of Mexico. The Illinois country stretched from a French settlement at Cahokia (across the river from present-day Saint Louis, Missouri) fifty miles downriver to another settlement at Kaskaskia. Cahokia was founded in 1699 as a mission for the conversion of Native Americans, and Kaskaskia was a fort established in 1703. Both attracted *coureurs de bois* (woods runners), French trappers and traders who lived among the Native Americans.

The French also began settling Louisiana in 1699, under the leadership of Pierre Le Moyne, sieur d'Iberville (1661–1706) and his brother Jean-Baptiste Le Moyne, sieur de Bienville (1680–1747). Along with two hundred French colonists, they established Old Biloxi on the site of present-day Ocean Springs, Mississippi. In 1701 Iberville returned to Montreal, while Bienville remained at Old Biloxi, which had been made the capital of the Louisiana Territory. Bienville was named governor of Louisiana. The French founded other settlements, such as Fort Louis, on the site that is now Mobile, Alabama. In 1718 Bienville established the city of New Orleans, which became the capital of Louisiana in 1722.

The population of Louisiana boomed from 1718 to 1720 as a result of the failed Mississippi Bubble scheme (see box on page 76), which resulted in Bienville being forced out of office. When he began his third term as governor in 1733, more than eight thousand people lived in Louisiana. Over the years the province served as a penal colony (settlement for convicted criminals), a temporary home for indentured servants (laborers contracted to work for a master for a specified period of time), and a slave import center. Yet death rates were high: by 1763, when France surrendered most of Louisiana to the Spanish at the end of the French and Indian War, the inhabitants included 3,654 Europeans and 4,598 African slaves.

France defeated in French and Indian War

The French and Indian Wars, which lasted from 1689 until 1763, were a series of conflicts between the French, their Native American allies, and the British over territories bordering the British colonies in North America. Both sides blocked seaports, attacked forts, and raided frontier settlements. The colonial wars were directly linked to French and British struggles for worldwide dominance. Therefore, three major European conflicts—King William's War (1689–97), Queen Anne's War (1702–13), and King George's War (1744–48)—are usually considered part of the French and Indian Wars. However, the French and Indian War of 1754 to 1763 had the most direct impact on France. Throughout this complex and prolonged confrontation, the French and Native Americans resisted westward expansion of British settlers. Hostilities began at the end of King George's War, in 1748, when the British-owned Ohio Company wanted to claim the area around present-day Pittsburgh, Pennsylvania, where the Monongahela and Allegheny Rivers join to form the Ohio River. The English started building a fort on the spot but were driven out by the French, who then built Fort Duquesne in 1754.

Soon thereafter a young Virginia militia officer, George Washington (1732–1799; later first U.S. president), led a skirmish against the French and their Native American allies. Although Washington and his men were victorious, they withdrew and built Fort Necessity near the site of present-day Uniontown, Pennsylvania. Leaders of British colonies then assembled the Albany Congress at Albany, New York. They coordinated their defense against the French and tried to sign a treaty with the Iroquois, who soon sided with the French. The French

and Indian War began when the British attempted to seize not only Fort Duquesne but also Fort Frontenac in New France and French forts at Niagara and Ticonderoga near the New York colony. The war continued, with victories on each side, for the next five years. A decisive battle took place in 1759 on the Plains of Abraham, a field outside the city of Quebec, between French general Louis Joseph de Montcalm and British military leader James Wolfe. Both Montcalm and Wolfe were killed, and Quebec fell to the British. The following year the British took Montreal, and the war was over. The Treaty of Paris (1763) gave control of Canada and all territory east of the Mississippi to the British (see Chapter 5), thus ending the French presence in North America. Yet the French enjoyed a bit of revenge: in the Treaty of Fontainebleau (1762), France secretly gave the area west of the Mississippi and the "Isle of Orleans" to Spain to prevent the British from gaining control of the entire Louisiana Territory.

The Thirteen English Colonies

E nglish exploration of North America began with the voyages of the Italian-born navigator John Cabot (c. 1450–c. 1499), who, in 1497, reached the region that is present-day New England. By 1502 fishermen were sending cod (a type of whitefish) from Labrador and New England to the port of Bristol, England. As early as 1508 or 1509 Cabot's son Sebastian had explored the Atlantic coast, but the English did not establish a permanent presence on the continent for another one hundred years. Although English explorer Bartholomew Gosnold (d. 1607) briefly attempted to colonize New England in 1602, the settlers were not prepared for life in the New World (a European term for North and South America). Nevertheless, published reports of Gosnold's venture described North America as "the goodliest continent that ever we saw, promising more by farre [far] than we any way did expect." Eager investors formed colonizing companies in hopes of exploiting the New World's bountiful resources.

First English settlement?

In the meantime, other Englishmen were trying to find a Northwest Passage, a natural waterway between the Atlantic

Walter Raleigh and his son. Raleigh organized the failed Roanoke Colony in Virginia. *Reproduced by permission of The Library of Congress.*

Ocean and the Pacific Ocean that would provide more direct access to Asia. In 1576 Martin Frobisher (c. 1535–1594) undertook a series of voyages to Greenland to search for a water route, but each time ice stopped his ships in the Canadian Arctic. In 1578 Queen Elizabeth I (1533–1603) gave English navigator Humphrey Gilbert (c. 1539–1583) a patent (a contract granting specific rights) to explore and colonize North America. On his second expedition, in 1585, he reached Newfoundland and claimed the region for England. Discovering some fishermen

living on the site of present-day Saint John's, Gilbert appointed himself governor of the settlement. According to some scholars, Gilbert established the first English colony in the New World, although most historians give that distinction to Jamestown, Virginia.

During the return trip to England, Gilbert was lost at sea. The patent was then transferred to his half brother, explorer Walter Raleigh (1554–1618), who secured the support of influential noblemen and navigators for a colonizing effort. In 1584 Raleigh appointed Philip Amadas and Arthur Barlowe to head an expedition to explore the mid-Atlantic coast of North America. Reaching the outer banks of present-day North Carolina, the party came in contact with the Roanokes, Native Americans who inhabited Roanoke Island and the surrounding region. After a brief stay, the Englishmen took two Native Americans, named Manteo and Wanchese, back to England. Amadas and Barlowe gave enthusiastic reports about Roanoke, claiming the island offered favorable trading prospects and an excellent location for a military fort. Impressed by the success of the mission, Elizabeth I knighted Raleigh (gave him a special military rank) and named the region Virginia in honor of herself (she was called the "Virgin Queen" because she refused to marry).

Raleigh organizes Roanoke venture

Raleigh immediately organized a venture to establish a permanent colony at Roanoke. He assembled five ships and two boats, which he placed under the command of English navigator Richard Grenville (1542–1591). Among the party of 108 men—mainly soldiers and servants—was Thomas Harriot (1560–1621), a mathematician and Raleigh's tutor, who was given the task of surveying Virginia. (Surveying is a branch of mathematics that involves taking measurements of the Earth's surface.) Manteo and Wanchese were to serve as interpreters, and artist John White (d. 1593) was to make drawings of animal and plant life. Upon arriving at Roanoke in July 1585, the expedition got off to a bad start. First, Grenville determined that the island was not suitable for a permanent military base. When he learned a silver cup was missing, he ordered his men to burn a Native American village because he thought a Native American had stolen the cup.

Later the next month Grenville departed for the Caribbean. Before leaving he placed colonist Ralph Lane (1530–1603) in charge of one hundred men, with orders that they find a better site for the settlement and then construct a fort and other buildings. In spite of Grenville's earlier aggression toward the Native Americans, the Englishmen established friendly relations with the Roanoke (also called Wiroan) tribe and their chief, Wingina. Lane explored the area, White sketched plants and animals, and Harriot conducted a detailed survey of the land. Harriot also recorded his observations of Native American life, language, and customs. As spring approached, the colonists began to run out of food, so Lane took the drastic step of demanding corn from Wingina. Although the chief offered some land and seeds, Lane overlooked his generosity and concluded that the Native Americans were planning an attack. Lane therefore decided to strike first, and in the conflict Wingina and several of his people were killed.

Colony deserted

The murder of Wingina and other Roanokes only contributed to the food shortage at Roanoke settlement by causing neighboring groups to withdraw from contact with the Europeans. The struggling colony was in a desperate situation by June 1586, when English seaman Francis Drake (c. 1540–1596) paid a surprise visit on his way back from the Caribbean, where he had attacked Spanish ships. Along the way he had also made an assault on the Spanish fort at Saint Augustine in Florida. Anxious to go home, all but three of the Roanoke settlers boarded Drake's ship and set sail for England. Soon after the colonists' departure, Grenville returned to Roanoke with a new load of supplies and six hundred additional men. He found the colony deserted—no one knows what happened to the three men who had remained on the island. Eventually Grenville decided to return to England and recruit more settlers. He left fifteen men at Roanoke to plant crops and build dwellings in preparation for the new colonists. By that time, however, Raleigh had lost interest in colonizing

Virginia. John White therefore took over the project and acquired the backing of several investors for another expedition.

White's plan was to start a new colony called the City of Raleigh, which would be located north of Roanoke in the Chesapeake Bay area. White would be the governor. Since this settlement would be devoted to families and farming instead of military defense, the party included seventeen women, nine children, and ninety-four men. When the ships reached North America in late 1587, the captain refused to go any farther than Roanoke. Forced to remain at the old settlement, the colonists discovered that the fifteen men left by Grenville were gone, possibly driven out by unfriendly Native Americans. Consequently there were no crops or suitable housing. The only solution was for White to go back to England for more supplies and additional men. Before departing he told the colonists to move to another location if they had any problems and to leave a message telling him where to find them.

"The lost colony"

In the meantime, war had been brewing between England and Spain. When the conflict erupted in 1588—as White was about to sail back to North America—contact between England and Roanoke was cut off. In 1591, after Drake led the English in defeating the Spanish Armada (a fleet of mighty warships), White was finally able to return to Roanoke. By that time the settlers

had all vanished without a trace—among them White's daughter, son-in-law, and granddaughter, Virginia Dare. White found only two clues to their whereabouts: the word "Croatan" carved on a fence post and the letters "Cro" etched into a tree trunk. The English suspected that the colonists' disappearance was somehow linked with the Croatoans, a friendly Native American tribe that lived on Croatoan Island about 50 miles south of Roanoke.

The Roanoke settlers were never found, and the fate of the "lost colony" remains a mystery. Numerous theories about their disappearance have evolved over the centuries. They could have died as the result of a natural disaster, such as disease, starvation, hurricane, flood, or tornado. They could have tried to return to England and become lost at sea. More outlandish explanations include pirates kidnaping all the inhabitants. The most reassuring conclusion is that the colonists joined a nearby Native American tribe, with whom they intermarried and prospered.

After the failure of the Roanoke Colony, the English made no other attempts to colonize North America for nearly twenty years, realizing they had neither the skills nor the money required to establish permanent settlements in a strange and hostile land. One modern historian has noted that venturing into the wilderness of North America in the sixteenth century was similar to landing on the moon in the twentieth century. Moreover, the Eng-

Von der ankunfft der Engellender in Virginia.

II.

SECOTAN
Dasamonquepen
Pasquenoke
WEAPEMEOC
Trinity harbor
Hatorask

Je Port oder Meerhafen der Landschafft Virginia ist voll Inseln/die da verursachen/ daß man gar beschwerlichen in dieselben kommen kan. Dann wiewol sie an vielen orten weit von einander gescheiden sind/vnd sich ansehen lässet/als solte man dadurch leicht= lich können hinein kommen/so haben wir dannoch mit vnserm grossen schaden erfahren/ daß dieselben offne Plätz voll Sandes sind. Deßwegen haben wir niemals können hin= ein kommen/biß so lang wir an vielen vnnd mancherley örtern mit einem kleinen Schiff die sach versucht haben. Zuletzt haben wir einen Paß gefunden/auff einem sonderlichen ort/der vnsern Engelländern wol bekannt ist. Als wir nun hinein kommen/vnd eine zeitlang darinn on vn= terlaß geschifft hatten/sind wir eines grossen fliessenden Wassers gewar worden/dessen außgang gegen der Inseln/von welcher wir gesagt haben/sich erstrecket. Dieweil aber der Inngang zu demselbigē Wasser deß Sandes halben zu klein war/haben wir denselben verlassen/vñ seyn weiter fort geschifft/biß daß wir an ei= ne grosse Inseln kommen sind/deren Einwohner/nach dem sie vnser gewar worden/haben alsbald mit lau= ter vnd schrecklicher stimm zu ruffen angefangen/dieweil sie zuvor keine Menschen/die vns gleich weren/be= schawet hatten. Deßwegen sie sich auch auff die Flucht begeben haben/vnnd nicht anders dann als Wölffe vnd vnsinnige Leut/alles mit ihrem heulen erfüllt. Da wir ihnen aber freundtlich nachgeruffen/vnd sie wi= derumb zu vns gelocket/auch ihnen vnsere Wahr/als da sind Spiegel/Messer/Puppen/vnd ander geringe Krämeren (an welchen wir vermeyneten sie einen lust haben solten) fürgestellt hatten/sind sie stehen bliebē. Vnd nach dem sie vnsern guten willen vnd freundschafft gespürt/haben sie vns gute Wort geben/vnnd zu vnser ankunfft glück gewündschet. Darnach haben sie vns in ihre Statt/Roanoac genannt/ja daß noch mehr ist/zu ihrem Weroans oder Oberherrn geführet/der vns freundtlich empfangen hat/wiewol er erst= lich sich ab vns entsetzte. Also ist es vns ergangē in vnser ersten ankunfft der newen Welt/so wir Virginiam nennten. Was nun für Leiber/Kleydung/art zu leben/Feste vnd Gastereyen die Einwohner daselbst haben/ das will ich stück für stück nach einander einem jeden vor die Augen stellen/wie nachfolget.

An early map of the failed Roanoke Colony in Virginia. *Reproduced by permission of The Library of Congress.*

lish, like the Spanish, were primarily interested in conquering Native American empires that would yield instant wealth. But by the late 1590s Europeans had seized all of the available riches in the New World.

Virginia charter granted

England again turned its attention to North America in 1604, after signing a peace treaty with Spain. Freed from the burden of waging a war, the government now had funds that could be used for colonization and trade. Since the failure of the Roanoke settlement, English investors had come to realize that North America offered more than gold, silver, and other precious metals. As the Spanish had proved in the Caribbean, sizable profits could be made from plantations that produced cotton, sugar, tobacco, and coffee. Fishing could also be a source of potential wealth. Speculating on new opportunities overseas, several investors received a charter for the "Virginia Company of London and of Plymouth" in 1606. The charter gave them the right to land along the Atlantic coast from the Cape Fear River in North Carolina to present-day Bangor, Maine. This vast territory was divided into two colonies: the northern colony, named Plymouth, was granted to the Plymouth Company, and the southern, called Virginia, was given to the London Company. Each was to be governed by a council in America that took its orders from a royal council in England. The charter

further provided that all colonists and their descendants would enjoy the full rights of Englishmen.

The London Company was the first to organize an expedition. The plan was to build the capital of the Virginia colony on a site that would provide access for sea trade yet protect against Spanish attack. Under the temporary leadership of Christopher Newport (c. 1565–1617), three vessels carrying 105 settlers—all of them men—embarked from England in December 1606. The expedition immediately ran into the first of numerous problems that would nearly doom the venture: winds prevented the ships from making any progress, and for a full six weeks they stayed within sight of England. Finally arriving on the shore of Virginia more than four months later, in April 1607, Newport led the party 50 miles inland along the present-day James River. He spotted an apparently suitable location for a fort and town—a small peninsula surrounded by a marsh—and claimed the land for King James I, naming the new settlement Jamestown.

Jamestown: First English settlement

For a time the situation seemed ideal as the settlers industriously cleared the land and built their town. They erected a fort and a palisade (high fence), constructed one- and two-room cottages inside the fence, and prepared nearby fields for crops. They also made friends with the Powhatans, the local Native Americans, who were initially hostile. But within a few days Chief

Powhatan (d. 1618), the principal leader in the region, had given the settlers food and other assistance. Many of the Englishmen were also exploring the surrounding countryside in search of gold. Although the Virginia project was devoted principally to agriculture and trade, the English government and private investors were still hoping to find instant wealth in the New World. Therefore many settlers had joined the Jamestown venture not to become farmers but to get rich.

Before the settlers departed from England, the London Company had appointed a seven-member council to govern the colony. The names of the councilmen were to be kept secret, however, until the ships reached their destination. By the time the colonists came ashore, the seven men on the council despised and feared one another. The ablest member of the group was John Smith (1580–1631), but he was already under arrest for having a conflict with Newport over an unspecified issue. No doubt unaware that Smith was one of the councilmen, Newport had imprisoned him for the majority of the voyage.

Smith takes control By late summer the colonists discovered they had chosen an unhealthy location for Jamestown: men were falling ill and dying as a result of living beside a swamp. The English had unknowingly brought typhoid (a bacterial disease marked by fever, diarrhea, headache, and intestinal inflammation) and dysentery (severe diarrhea caused by infection) with them. Now,

Under John Smith's leadership, the Jamestown colonists were able to establish a permanent settlement in Virginia. *Reproduced by permission of The Library of Congress.*

because of their own poor hygiene (cleanliness), the river had become an open sewer and a breeding ground for the diseases. In addition, many were suffering from salt poisoning—the force of the water coming down the river from the mountains was not enough to get past the tide rolling up from the Chesapeake Bay, so the settlers were drinking water that contained trapped sea salt.

By September 1608 three of the seven council members had returned to England and three others had died. Smith was the only councilor remaining in Virginia, so he automatically became the leader of the colony. He was confronted with the impossible task of organizing unruly, inexperienced settlers into some sort of workforce. The ships had carried 105 men, but 49 of them were noblemen who had never earned a living with their hands. Only 24 were laborers. The settlers had not planted and harvested enough food—partly because too many men had wasted their time searching for gold. Already 46 settlers had died of disease and lack of food. Smith also had to contend with the well-organized Powhatans, who had again become suspicious of the Europeans. Although Smith was eager to negotiate peaceful relations, he was also willing to force the Powhatans to provide the settlers with grain. Reportedly Powhatan agreed to trade meat and corn at the urging of his daughter Pocahontas (see Chapters 8 and 10). By most accounts, the Jamestown settlers would have perished had it not been for Powhatan and Pocahontas's assistance.

Under Smith's leadership the inexperienced settlers built houses, completed a church, fortified Jamestown, and learned how to farm and fish. While Smith managed to keep the struggling colony from dissolving, however, he did so at the expense of his own popularity. He imposed strict rules and forced the colonists to obey. As a result, he caused much resentment and bitterness. In 1609 another group of settlers arrived from England. Along with

them came several of Smith's old enemies, who plotted against him. The colonists were also still having problems with the Powhatans. Smith might have weathered these difficulties if he had not been severely wounded when a stray spark from a fire lit his gunpowder bag as he lay napping. The explosion and subsequent flames burned him so badly that his life was threatened. The following October he sailed back to England.

From "starving time" to tobacco boom
Although Smith survived his wounds, he never returned to Jamestown. During his stay in North America he had conducted extensive explorations, and he later wrote several books that provide modern historians with information about life in early Virginia (see Chapter 14). In his absence, the colony quickly fell apart, and the winter of 1609 to 1610 became known as the "starving time." The suffering was caused not only by a shortage of food but also by the settlers themselves. Many stole and sold their meager supplies; as a result, some men were fed while others died. Of the 490 settlers remaining in Virginia when Smith left, only 60 survived the winter. Soon the council in Virginia became unworkable, and in 1609 the London Company rewrote the charter, putting one man in charge. The royal council was also eliminated when the company took over the colony and reorganized to keep from going bankrupt. The former London Company was now the Treasurer and Company of Adventurers and Planters of the City of London for the

First Colony in Virginia (usually called the Virginia Company).

In 1610 a new governor, Thomas West (Baron De La Warr; 1577–1618), arrived in Jamestown. The settlement was under a form of martial law (law administered by military force), which Smith had initiated, and the men were being forced to work. Yet the colony's survival was still far from certain. In 1614 John Rolfe (1585–1622), one of the original settlers, took two important steps. First, he married Pocahontas, Powhatan's daughter, thus bringing about a truce between the Powhatans and the colonists. Second, Rolfe experimented with a West Indian species of tobacco and found that he could produce a crop of high enough quality to fetch good prices in England. Soon Virginia was in the midst of a tobacco boom, and the colony moved toward a plantation economy that continued to thrive throughout the colonial period.

First royal colony Yet further problems undermined these efforts. Once tobacco was found to be a profitable crop, laborers sent to work for the company were hired instead by local officials to work on private plantations. By 1616 there were no profits for the original investors. Three years later the Virginia Company reorganized again, this time promising a less rigid government and dividing the colony into four large settlements. At that time the company also authorized the formation of a general assembly, the House of Burgesses, which was the first elected representative body

 James Fort Excavated

In 1994 the Jamestown Rediscovery archaeological project began excavating the ruins at the Jamestown site, and by 1998 12 percent of the fort had been recovered. In 1996 archaeologists discovered the well-preserved skeleton of a white male who had been buried in a wooden coffin near the fort. After extensive investigation and testing, they concluded that the man was probably one of the "gentlemen" mentioned by Smith in his Jamestown account—the skeleton indicates that the man was not accustomed to manual labor. Scientists have further determined that the man, who is known as JR102C (a record number assigned by archaeologists), was nineteen to twenty-two years of age, stood around 5 feet, 5 inches in height, and died of a massive, untreated gunshot wound to the leg.

in America (see "Rise of the colonial assembly" in Chapter 6). Although a steady stream of settlers continued to flow into the colony, high death rates considerably reduced their numbers. Then, in 1622, Powhatan's son Opechancanough led the Powhatans in the massacre of 350 settlers—about one-third of the community. In 1624 James I dissolved the bankrupt Virginia Company, and Virginia became the first royal colony in America.

The Thirteen Colonies: A Brief History

The first permanent English colony was founded at Jamestown, Virginia, in 1607 after King James I approved a charter for the Virginia Colony. The same charter included the Plymouth Colony, which was started in 1620 in Massachusetts. Plymouth was later absorbed into the Massachusetts Bay Colony, which was granted a charter by King Charles I and settled in 1629. Massachusetts colonists then formed Connecticut (1639), Rhode Island (1644), and New Hampshire (1679). In 1632 Charles I awarded George Calvert, First Baron Baltimore, a tract of land on the Chesapeake Bay, which was later named Maryland. In 1663 King Charles II granted the region south of Virginia and north of Spanish territory (present-day Florida) to eight proprietors, who called it Carolina. The colony was divided into North Carolina and South Carolina in 1713. The following year the English took over New Netherland, which the Dutch had founded in 1624. Renaming the colony New York, Charles II awarded it to his brother James, Duke of York (later King James II). New Netherland also included Delaware and New Jersey, parts of which were settled as New Sweden in 1638. Delaware became an English colony in 1674. Two years later New Jersey was divided into East Jersey and West Jersey; it became an independent colony in 1738. William Penn received a proprietary charter in 1681 from Charles II for the Quaker colony of Pennsylvania, a year later annexing Delaware. In 1732 Parliament (the lawmaking branch of the government) granted a charter to James Oglethorpe and others, who established Georgia north of Florida as a penal colony and a buffer against Spanish invasion. Georgia was the last of the original thirteen colonies.

Maine winter defeats settlers

In 1607, a year after the London Company colonists embarked for Jamestown, the Plymouth Company outfitted an expedition to Maine. This was the place that Bartholomew Gosnold had so glowingly praised in the reports of his venture. Gosnold's party had seen the region only in the summertime, however, and the Plymouth group was planning to stay permanently. They were completely unprepared for the long and extremely cold Maine winter. Although most of the settlers managed to survive the harsh climate, one of the leaders died and another was called back to England. Finally the settlement broke up, and the English did not return to the area for another thirteen years.

New England

Colonization of present-day New England came about as a result of the Puritan movement. Puritanism (a Protestant faith that stressed strictness in matters of religion and conduct; see Chapter 11), in turn, was an outgrowth of Protestantism. (Protestantism was founded in 1517 by German theologian Martin Luther [1483–1546] who accused Roman Catholic Church leaders of corruption and misuse of power; see Chapter 11.)

The rise of Puritanism

The Protestant movement began in England in 1531, when King Henry VIII (1491–1547) decided to annul (legally invalidate or void) his marriage to Catherine of Aragon. A staunch Roman Catholic, Henry wanted to marry again because Catherine had not borne him a son and he was determined to father a male heir to the throne. Yet Henry encountered strong resistance from the pope, who had the final authority to nullify marriages. Since Catherine was a Spanish princess and the Catholic Church depended on Spain to fight Protestantism in Europe, the pope (leader of the Roman Catholic Church) could not afford to alienate the Spanish by granting the annulment. Henry therefore broke with the Catholic Church and declared himself head of the Church of England.

Henry's quarrel with Roman Catholicism was political, not religious. Although he closed monasteries (houses for monks, or men who took religious vows) and seized Catholic lands, he did not want to change the church. Therefore he maintained most of the rituals, especially the elaborate ceremonies and fancy vestments (robes) worn by bishops and priests. Henry's daughter, Elizabeth I, also loved the grand processions and dramatic services, so she continued her father's policies. Her successor, James I (1566–1625), was similarly unwilling to make any changes. But by this time, many English Protestants were rebelling against the heavy emphasis on Catholic ritual in the Church of England. They wanted a simpler church, which placed less emphasis on displays of wealth.

Nonconformists go to Netherlands
During the reign of James I, ministers and congregations (groups who worship together) increasingly refused to organize their worship services according to the requirements of the Church of England. Some critics, who became known as Puritans, felt that purifying the national church would solve the problems. At the same time others were contending that the church was too corrupt to be saved; they wanted total separation. Since the king was head of both the church and the government, separation was considered a crime against the state. Nevertheless a congregation in Scrooby, England, declared themselves to be Nonconformists, or separatists. When the Scrooby leaders were

An illustration of the *Mayflower* during its journey to North America. Because of stormy weather, the ship arrived in Plymouth, Massachusetts, instead of Virginia.
Reproduced by permission of The Library of Congress.

persecuted (punished or discriminated against because of their beliefs) in 1607, the congregation resolved to leave England and go to Leyden in the Netherlands (Holland), the most tolerant of the European societies.

Life was pleasant in Leyden, and the Nonconformists were free to practice their religion. Nevertheless they were uneasy because their children were becoming more Dutch than English. Economic opportunities were also lim-

ited, and there were rumors that war would soon break out between Spain and the Netherlands. Many members of the group wanted to relocate to another country where they could speak English and bring up their children in a familiar Christian environment. Calling themselves Pilgrims, they decided to settle at the northernmost end of the land granted to the Virginia Company.

Mayflower **caught in storm** In 1619 the Pilgrims secured financing through Thomas Weston and Associates, an investment company, and the following year they left the Netherlands for the New World. Stopping first in England, they found that only one of their ships, the *Mayflower,* was seaworthy. The party consisted of 102 men, women, and children, but they were not all Pilgrims. Several men called "merchant adventurers" represented the Weston company and did not share the Nonconformists' beliefs. Although no minister had joined the party, one of the members of the Leyden group, William Bradford (1590–1657), became a leader of the venture. On September 5, 1620, they set sail on the *Mayflower.*

Along the way the *Mayflower* encountered stormy weather, and the Pilgrims never arrived in Virginia. Instead they anchored the ship in Cape Cod harbor (off the coast of present-day Massachusetts), which was far north of their original destination. Since they were not on the land that had been legally granted to them, Bradford and forty other free adult males (those with voting rights) drafted and signed a new contract, the Mayflower Compact, in November 1620. The contract, which was based on Nonconformist church covenants (God's promises to man), would allow the Pilgrims to establish a government with binding laws. They had to face the problem that they were only 40 percent of the people aboard the ship. The rest, including men such as Myles Standish (1584–1656), were outsiders whom the Pilgrims called "strangers." The Mayflower Compact was intended to prevent conflict, provide for a government, and form a new religious society. It is considered the first democracy (a government where people elect representatives) established by Europeans in North America.

Pilgrims land at Plymouth Rock While the *Mayflower* was anchored in Cape Cod harbor, Standish led an expedition inland. Leaving the ship in a small boat, they set out for the Hudson River, but bad weather forced then to return to the harbor at Cape Cod. Calling it Plymouth Harbor, they anchored near a rock that is now known as Plymouth Rock. The Pilgrims began settling their new colony on December 25, 1620, and elected John Carver (1576–1621) as their first governor. Although they faced the hazards of winter in the northeast, several factors worked in their favor. Unlike many ships that brought settlers to North America, the *Mayflower* remained at Plymouth and furnished housing until the colonists could build shelters. The colonists' first dwellings were small, one-room houses

The Mayflower Compact

In the Name of God, Amen. We, whose names are underwritten, the loyal subjects of our dread Sovereign Lord King James, by the Grace of God of Great Britain, France, and Ireland King, Defender of the Faith, etc.

Having undertaken, for the Glory of God and Advancement of the Christian Faith and Honour of our King and Country, a Voyage to plant the First Colony in the Northern Parts of Virginia, do by these presents solemnly and mutually in the presence of God and one of another, Covenant and Combine ourselves together into a Civil Body Politic, for our better ordering and preservation and furtherance of the ends aforesaid; and by virtue hereof to enact, constitute and frame such just and equal Laws, Ordinances, Acts, Constitutions and Offices, from time to time, as shall be thought most meet and convenient for the general good of the Colony, unto which we promise all due submission and obedience. In witness whereof we have hereunder subscribed our names at Cape Cod, the 11th of November, in the year of the reign of our Sovereign Lord King James, of England, France and Ireland the eighteenth, and of Scotland the fifty-fourth, Anno Domino 1620.

Source: Bradford, William. Of Plymouth Plantation, 1620–1647. *Samuel Eliot Morison, ed. New York: Knopf, 1966, pp. 75–76.*

made of boards (not logs). The careful selection of a settlement site also gave them an advantage: rather than facing a "howling wilderness," they were nestled into a hillside that had once been inhabited by Native Americans. Fresh water was nearby, and they had access to corn Native Americans had put away for the winter.

Squanto saves Pilgrims Even so, nearly half of the party died, just as the earliest colonists at Jamestown did. Although the Pilgrims and local Native Americans were aware of one another, they did not make contact during that difficult winter. The dying settlers maintained their distance from their neighbors, even though the Native Americans could have helped them. In turn, the Wampanoag, who had had mixed experiences with Europeans, watched the newcomers warily. In the spring the surviving colonists were helped by Squanto (d. 1622), a member of the neighboring Pawtuxet tribe, who had been sent by Chief Massasoit (c. 1590–1661). Years earlier Squanto had been kidnaped and taken to England. During his captivity he had learned to speak English, and as a result, he could communicate with the settlers. Squanto helped them plant corn and other crops, and the next fall there was a plentiful harvest. The colonists invited Massasoit, Squanto, and other warriors to a celebration feast, which has become known as the first Thanksgiving in America (thanksgivings were common in England).

Colonists encounter problems When Carver died in April 1621, Bradford was chosen to take his place as governor. (He would be reelected thirty times between 1621 and 1656.) After solving the initial problems of food and shelter, the Plymouth settlers realized they did not know how to run businesses such as fur trading, which was thriving in other colonies. The colony proved to be a disappointment to Weston and other investors, who were making no profits from Plymouth. In 1622 Weston gave up on the colony. One reason was that Pilgrim leaders paid attention to immediate needs rather than long-term plans. For instance, despite extreme food shortages, they invited other Nonconformists to move to Plymouth from Leyden.

As the colony grew, the Pilgrims benefitted from their alliance with Massasoit. The result was peaceful trading relationships and an increased food supply in Plymouth. Nevertheless this harmony was disturbed when the colonists found themselves in the middle of battles between the Narraganset and the Mohegan. Tensions continued to mount, and in the Pequot War (1637) the New England colonies united with the Narraganset to attack a Pequot fort at Mystic, Connecticut. Four hundred Pequots were killed as they were sleeping. Native Americans were not the only unpredictable elements at Plymouth. The colonists also had to contend with the merchant adventurers, many of whom committed crimes. In 1627 Bradford and seven other Pilgrims bought out the merchant adventurers and divided their property evenly among the colonists.

Pilgrims show intolerance Although the Pilgrims had emigrated (moved from one country to another) to America to practice religious freedom, they

A painting illustrating the first Thanksgiving at Plymouth, Massachusetts.
Reproduced by permission of The Granger Collection, New York.

did not extend the same rights to others. They often had conflicts with members of different religious groups. The most famous incident occurred in 1627 when Bradford led a small party of Puritans into the town of Merry Mount in the neighboring Massachusetts Colony and disrupted a May Day celebration. (May Day was observed in England on May 1, in the tradition of spring fertility rites in Egypt and India. The Puritans had passed strict laws banning "pagan" holidays.) Another problem was that Plymouth did not have a formal government. In 1630 Bradford tried to forge relations with the more

prosperous Massachusetts Bay Colony, but he met resistance from Massachusetts residents. Plymouth finally adopted a formal constitution (plan of government) in 1636. The population grew steadily, reaching seven thousand by the time Plymouth became part of Massachusetts in 1691, thirty-four years after Bradford's death.

The "great migration"

The survival of the Plymouth Colony spurred others to think about settling in the same area. One of the early promoters of emigration to North

Families Settle New England

Like the Plymouth colonists, the Puritans who came to New England in the great migration intended to settle permanently in America. This meant they often came as families, or, if single, they were placed in family groups. For example, in 1635 forty-year-old Joseph Hull sailed from Weymouth, England, for New England with his wife, Agnes, and his two sons, five daughters, two male servants, and one female servant. Although most passengers on the ship were under the age of fourteen, Richard and Elizabeth Wade were in their sixties, the oldest people onboard. Members of the wealthiest and poorest classes generally did not leave England, but there were some exceptions, such as wealthy landowner John Winthrop. These people established towns that filled quickly; later waves of settlers fanned out into the wilderness. Forming corporations, the new colonists bought land from Native Americans, petitioned the legislature for the right to build a town, then moved in and set up housekeeping.

America was Robert Cushman, who had gone to Plymouth aboard the *Mayflower* but then returned to England as the colony's business agent. He published a pamphlet outlining the reasons English people, "here born and bred, and hath lived some years, may remove [themselves] into another country." After assuring would-be settlers that God was not opposed to such a move, he went on to say, "[A] man must not respect only to live and do good to himself, but he should see where he can live to do most good to others." Cushman listed several ways English settlers could do good to others. Not only would they bring Christianity to the Native Americans, but they would also make use of the vast, empty land. Moreover, now was the time to leave England: the country was overpopulated—young tradesmen could not find jobs, beggars filled the streets—and religious strife was pitting neighbor against neighbor. With times so hard, there was no hope of leaving a legacy to one's children. Yet in the New World things could be different.

People became enthralled with the promise of a new life in the colonies, and they started making plans to leave their worries behind. Thus began the "great migration" of more than ten thousand English men, women, and children to New England between 1630 and 1640. The movement began slowly. In 1622 Thomas Weston, the backer of the Pilgrims' expedition, financed a group that settled at Wessagusset on present-day Boston Harbor. The next year the Dorchester Adventurers, investors who wanted to start a cod-fishing industry, founded a small settlement called Naumkeag. In 1628 the New England Company for a Plantation in Massachusetts-Bay received a grant that included some of the lands that had been awarded to another company. In June 1628 John Endecott

(1588–1665) led fifty Puritan colonists to Naumkeag, which would become Salem, Massachusetts. They were preparing the way for seven hundred settlers, the first wave of the great migration.

Massachusetts Bay: An "ideal community" The first wave was led by John Winthrop (1588–1649), a wealthy lawyer and prominent Puritan. In 1629 Winthrop joined the New England Company, a group of investors who planned to start a settlement near the Plymouth Colony in Massachusetts. King Charles I (1600–1649) had granted the company a portion of land between the Charles and Merrimack Rivers in Massachusetts, which was owned by the Council for New England (a private organization that promoted trade and settlement in New England). Winthrop and his associates received a royal charter (the right to found a colony that would be ruled by the king) under the new name of "Governor and Company of the Massachusetts Bay in New England."

Although the settlers had initially planned to concentrate on trade, their emphasis soon shifted to religion. Like the Pilgrims at Plymouth, they were fleeing persecution in England. At that time the Puritans and Parliament were engaged in a struggle against the king and the Church of England. The Massachusetts Bay Puritans saw their venture as an opportunity to enjoy religious freedom and to establish an "ideal community" that would serve as a model for Puritans in England. In the

John Winthrop leader of the Massachusetts Bay Colony. *Reproduced by permission of The Library of Congress.*

ideal community, inhabitants would form separate congregations devoted to strict adherence to Puritan doctrines (see "Puritanism" in Chapter 11). Guided by ministers and members of the "elect" (certain people who had been chosen by God for salvation, or forgiveness of sins), they would live in harmony and glorify God.

Winthrop's first step was to organize the signing of the Cambridge Agreement. It stated that, once the Puritans reached North America, they would buy out the company, take over the charter, and govern the colony independently. Thus the Massachusetts Bay Company was the only colonizing venture that was not controlled by governors in England—a situation that would lead to serious problems within a few years. In 1629 Winthrop, as a member of the "elect," was chosen to head the company, and he began assembling the fleet of eleven ships that would take the settlers to America. To help meet expenses he sold his family estate. After arranging for his wife and children to join him in 1631, he set out with the first Massachusetts Bay settlers on the lead ship *Arbella.*

Colonists challenge Winthrop The Puritans arrived at Salem in 1630. As head of the Massachusetts Bay Company, Winthrop took the position of governor from Endecott, who had been serving temporarily. The Puritans organized their settlement on the basis of separate religious congregations that chose their own ministers. This decision set the stage for later unwanted religious diversity. Winthrop also established a government, keeping power in his own hands with the aid of a few assistants. He gave some authority to freemen (men with the full rights of citizens; women had no rights), who served on a general assembly (lawmaking body). After Winthrop had been governor for four years, the freemen challenged him to show them the company's charter. Upon discovering they were entitled to more power than he had allowed them, the freemen formed a new assembly. They elected members from each town and voted Winthrop out of office in 1635. He was replaced by colonist John Haynes.

Winthrop's political fortunes over the next several years reflected the chaos in the Massachusetts Bay Colony. Although he was continually voted in and out of office, he kept his seat on the council and continued to be a powerful force. Along with Endecott and others, Winthrop supported a strict theocracy (control of the government by the church) and bitterly opposed the activities of religious dissidents (those who disagree with church practices). The separate congregations had opened the way for religious diversity, and many colonists were now refusing to conform to Puritan doctrines (established opinions). Puritan leaders would not tolerate any views but their own, and they were greatly disturbed by the protests of such dissidents as the Anabaptists (those who oppose the baptism of infants), Presbyterians (those who advocate a centralized church organization), and Quakers (those who believe in direct communication with God).

Conflicts in the "ideal community" In 1636 the Massachusetts Bay Colony was facing yet another crisis: Native American resistance to English settlement. As a result of the vast influx of settlers, the New England population was rising rapidly (it was four thousand in 1634 and would reach eleven thousand in 1638). The Puritans had begun moving west onto land controlled by the Pequots, a neighboring Native American tribe. This led to the Pequot War, in which the tribe was nearly annihilated.

Making matters even worse was the fact that the English government was trying to gain control of the colony. Ferdinando Gorges (c. 1566–1647), head of the Council for New England, had belatedly realized Charles I had permitted the colonists to settle on land that was still in the possession of the council. Gorges did not approve of their independent charter, and he wanted them to abide by the New England Council's plan of government. In 1634 William Laud (1573–1645), the archbishop of Canterbury (the highest official in the Church of England), was appointed head of a committee to investigate the charter. Laud had been instrumental in removing Puritans from positions of power in England, so he was interested in keeping American congregations under the control of the English church. All Puritans, except the Nonconformists in the Plymouth Colony, had remained members of the Anglican Church (another name for the Church of England), which ordained (officially appointed) Puritan ministers. (The Puritans were certain they could reform the church from within.)

When the committee discovered that the charter was not tied to any governing body in England, they began proceedings to terminate the Massachusetts Bay Company. In 1637 Charles I announced that he would rule Massachusetts through a royal governor and council, and that Gorges would be his deputy (representative). The new royal government was never put in place, however, since England was also in turmoil at the time. Charles I had dismissed Parliament to prevent Puritans from holding office and was

unsuccessfully trying to manage his empire alone. Gorges was instead granted wilderness territory in Maine, north of Massachusetts Bay.

Dissidents banished In the meantime, traditional Puritan leaders had been struggling to maintain harmony in Massachusetts Bay. They thought they might solve some of their problems by getting rid of religious dissidents. Their strategy involved trying to guide the rebels toward accepting traditional Puritan doctrine. If that method failed, they banished the troublemakers (forced them to leave) from the colony. For instance, in 1635 Haynes banished Roger Williams (c. 1603-1683), an advocate of the separation of church and state, who later founded the Rhode Island colony. In 1636 Massachusetts officials confronted Anne Hutchinson (1591–1643), a prominent figure in the community who was challenging basic Puritan teachings (see "Religious dissent: The Anne Hutchinson trial" in Chapter 5). Some of Hutchinson's supporters were anxious for political as well as religious change. Among them were merchants who opposed the tax and trade policies of the council. They scored a victory in the election of 1636, replacing Haynes with a new governor, Henry Vane (1613–1662), who was a member of Hutchinson's congregation.

Winthrop was returned to office as governor in 1637, and he immediately convened the Massachusetts General Court (the Massachusetts government) to review dissident

Henry Vane, one of Anne Hutchinson's followers, replaced John Haynes as governor of the Massachusetts Bay Colony in 1636.
Reproduced by permission of The Library of Congress.

from churches and the guardians of strict morality. Merchants and wage workers were putting their individual needs above the welfare of the community. Non-Puritans arrived in greater numbers, seeking economic opportunity rather than religious freedom. Church membership was declining rapidly, and soon there were few people who could claim to be saved (having been forgiven their sins). In desperation, some Puritan churches adopted the Half-Way Covenant, whereby the children of any baptized person could be admitted to the church regardless of whether their parents were members. Others took the Presbyterian position that anyone who led a moral life could join the church (see "Presbyterianism" in Chapter 11).

Charter withdrawn Puritan officials were still fighting English threats to place them under royal control. Finally, in 1686, King James II united Massachusetts Bay, Plymouth, Connecticut, Rhode Island, New Jersey, and New York into the Dominion of New England. He appointed Edmund Andros (1637–1714), an Anglican, as the royal governor. Andros, however, was an unpopular leader who suppressed colonists' rights. After James II was overthrown in 1688, Protestant monarchs William III and Mary II took the throne in a transition called the Glorious Revolution. Now that Andros had no backing in England, the colonists sent him and other officials to England as prisoners. Although the Dominion of New England had been dissolved, William and Mary did not

cases. When the court ruled in favor of the traditional Puritans, government leaders put Hutchinson and others on trial for sedition (resistance to lawful authority). Winthrop was actively involved in the trials.

Winthrop was elected governor for the final time in 1646, and he was still in office when he died three years later. Challenges to Puritan control of New England then gained momentum. By 1660 more people were settling on isolated farms, away

restore the colonies' original charters. Instead, in 1691, Massachusetts Bay was placed under a royal charter with Plymouth, forming the single colony of Massachusetts. The following year Massachusetts was involved in the Salem witch trials, one of the most infamous events in American history (see "The Salem Witch Trials" in Chapter 5).

During the eighteenth century the population of Massachusetts did not grow substantially. In fact, migration to New England slowed to a virtual halt after the end of the English Civil War (1642–48; a conflict that pitted Parliament and the Puritans against Charles I and the Church of England). Once Puritans controlled England under the Commonwealth and Protectorate headed by Oliver Cromwell (1599–1658), they felt no need to leave the country. Massachusetts soil was relatively poor and its growing season short, so there was no incentive for families to start farms in America. Most of the population growth was due to high birth and low death rates. The colony remained almost totally English, although a small number of African slaves worked in cities and on farms. At the time of the American Revolution (1775–83), 330,000 whites and about 5,200 Africans lived in Massachusetts (which then included Maine).

New Hampshire

Many settlers left Massachusetts to find more fertile land or to start their own Puritan congregations. In 1629 New Hampshire was established between the Merrimac and Kennebec Rivers in Maine territory. A year later farmers and fishermen founded the town of Portsmouth. In 1641 and 1643 Massachusetts claimed the southern part of New Hampshire, initiating a boundary dispute that lasted until the American Revolution. Although New Hampshire became a royal colony in 1679, England appointed a single governor to oversee both New Hampshire and Massachusetts until 1741. That year Benning Wentworth (1696–1770) was named governor of New Hampshire alone, and he expanded the colony's territory to an area east of the Hudson River. This provoked conflicts over land rights with New York. Struggles between frontier settlers and Native Americans allied with the French during the French and Indian Wars (see Chapter 3) prevented expansion onto this land until the late eighteenth century.

Connecticut

In 1634 and 1635 settlers from Massachusetts moved into the Connecticut River valley and founded the towns of Wethersfield, Windsor, and Hartford. Puritan minister Thomas Hooker (1586–1647) brought members of his congregation to the area in 1636. Three years later the towns were united as the colony of Connecticut, adopting the Fundamental Orders "to maintain and preserve the liberty and purity of the gospel [the word of Jesus of Nazareth]." Disputes between the English settlers and the local Pequot tribe

Roger Williams founder of the colony at Rhode Island. He began the colony after his banishment from the Massachusetts Bay Colony. *Engraving by F. Halpin.*

led to the Pequot War. As a result, the Native Americans were nearly annihilated and the land was free for colonization. In 1638 minister John Davenport (1597–1670) and merchant Theophilus Eaton (1590–1658), acquired land from Native Americans along the coast. They founded a colony called New Haven. They felt the Puritans in Massachusetts were not strict enough, so they adopted a government based on Mosaic law (the ancient law of the Hebrews originated by the prophet Moses and contained in the

first five books of the Old Testament, called the Pentateuch).

Connecticut and New Haven remained on fairly friendly terms until 1665, when the English government granted a charter that allowed Connecticut to incorporate New Haven against its will. Without a major harbor, Connecticut did not grow as rapidly as Massachusetts. Most colonists relied on farming and raising livestock for their living. Called "the land of steady habits," Connecticut had neither the wealth nor the poverty of its neighbor. Most settlers came from Massachusetts and so shared its English orientation. An exception were the few African slaves who helped work the farms of wealthy colonists. In 1774 the Connecticut population numbered 191,000 whites and 6,450 nonwhites (including Native Americans).

Rhode Island

Like Connecticut, Rhode Island began as a number of small settlements. Unlike Connecticut or any of the other New England colonies, however, Rhode Island served as a refuge for religious and political dissidents. The Dutch called it the "latrina [sewer] of New England," while Puritans labeled it "Rogues Island." The most famous of Rhode Island's founders were Roger Williams and Anne Hutchinson. Williams was a young minister who arrived in Massachusetts in 1631. He was admired by the Puritans, including John Winthrop, but Williams soon began expressing unacceptable ideas. He accused Massachusetts leaders of unlawfully taking land from Native Americans. As a separatist Williams also believed that Puritans should make a complete break from the Church of England. He further argued that church and state in Massachusetts should be separate because the state would corrupt the church. He maintained that since it was unclear who among the Puritans was actually saved—he said he could be sure only of himself and his wife—the church should be open to everyone. In 1635, Winthrop informed him that he was about to be arrested, so Williams fled Massachusetts and lived with the Narraganset tribe. He bought land from the Narraganset and was joined by some of his followers in founding the town of Providence.

Hutchinson's beliefs were different from Williams's but just as dangerous to Massachusetts. She held that some Puritan ministers were preaching Arminianism, a covenant of works that held that people could influence God's will about their salvation through good behavior (see "Puritanism" in Chapter 11). She also felt that those who were saints (a term the Puritan "elect" used to describe themselves) should not obey laws that were made by those who might not be saints. Her final heresy (violation of church teachings) came out in a lengthy trial when she claimed to know through direct revelation from God who was saved. Puritans were greatly threatened by Hutchinson's views because she was challenging the basis of their government. Hutchinson and her followers were banished on November 7, 1637, and founded the town of Portsmouth soon afterward. Hutchinson did not stay long in Portsmouth because religious squabbles plagued the community. Controversy centered on William Coddington (1601–1678), a political leader and former Hutchinson advocate, and Samuel Gorton (1592–1677), who were not welcome in Plymouth and Massachusetts. Gorton believed in the divinity of all human beings and rejected both a church restricted to saints and any form of social hierarchy (class system). His views proved too much for Coddington, who left in 1639 to found Newport. Gorton finally left in 1641 and established the town of Warwick, the last of the original Rhode Island towns, in 1643.

Charter granted Meanwhile, Williams had traveled to England to secure a charter for this group of quarrelsome settlements. A skillful politician, he succeeded with both the Puritan Parliament in 1644 and the newly restored Charles II in 1663. (The monarchy was restored in 1660 after the collapse of the Commonwealth and Protectorate that Oliver Cromwell established at the end of the English Civil War.) The charter gave Rhode Island more independence than other colonies and was the most tolerant in New England. Quakers found acceptance there, and a small Jewish community emerged. Although Rhode Island never had a large ethnic population, it was the most diverse colony in the region. Newport was a port town with Scots, French, Dutch, Germans, Portuguese, and Italians.

Rhode Island also had the largest percentage of nonwhites in New England. Nevertheless, the numbers of people involved were small since Rhode Island contained only 1,214 square miles, about one-eighth the size of Massachusetts. In 1755 there were thirty-six thousand whites and forty-seven hundred Africans and Native Americans living in the colony.

The middle colonies

Although a part of the original thirteen English colonies, New York, Pennsylvania, Delaware, and New Jersey are also known as the middle colonies.

Dutch start New Netherland

While the English were establishing colonies along the Atlantic coast and in New England, the Dutch (people from the Netherlands) had been settling New Netherland, the region that is now New York State. Following other European nations to North America in search of a Northwest Passage, the Dutch sent English navigator Henry Hudson (d. 1611) to the region that John Cabot had explored for the English. In 1609 Hudson led an expedition to New York Bay and up the river that now bears his name. Instead of finding the Northwest Passage, Hudson and his men discovered an equally profitable resource: native peoples who had an abundance of animal skins and furs. Thus the Dutch, in competition with the French, started a thriving fur trade with the Iroquois (see Chapter 3). Over the next decade the trading business was conducted by independent trappers who roamed the wilderness, lived among the Native Americans in the winter, and then sold their furs to Dutch merchants in the spring. Trading procedures became more commercialized in 1621 with the formation of the Dutch West India Company, which was also granted a charter for the colony of New Netherland.

At first the company set up trading posts, which also served as forts for protection of trade routes. The posts at Fort Orange (present-day Albany, New York) and on "the Manhates" (Manhattan Island) soon grew into small settlements surrounded by farms. Beavers were the most important fur-bearing animals, and since they were less plentiful around Manhattan, Albany became the center of Dutch trade. During the spring fur-trading season, merchants swarmed to the trading post to await the arrival of traders bringing pelts (animal skins). Albany was a booming place, and even local settlers tried to buy and sell furs—they needed an income to support themselves through the winter, when the trading post was virtually deserted.

Colony supports fur trade Actual colonization of New Netherland began in 1624, when the Dutch West India Company paid thirty Walloon families (people from southern and southeastern Belgium and adjacent parts of France) to emigrate to the New World. They settled on farms around Manhat-

An illustration of City Hall and the Great Dock of New Amsterdam. The city became the center of Dutch control for New Netherland. *Reproduced by permission of The Granger Collection.*

tan and Fort Orange and in the Connecticut River valley, where the company had built another fort. The settlement on Manhattan, which was named New Amsterdam in 1626, became the center of Dutch control for New Netherland. Within forty years the population of New Amsterdam had reached nearly two thousand. Fort Orange, however, remained a struggling outpost until the 1630s, when the Dutch West India Company authorized one of its directors, Kiliaen van Rensselaer (1595–1644), to bring settlers from the Netherlands. Called a patroon (proprietor), van Rensselaer founded Rens-

selaerswyck, a patroonship (vast private estate) that surrounded Albany and extended along both sides of the Hudson River. In the 1640s and 1650s the Dutch started villages that became the present-day New York cities of Schenectady and Kingston. They also expanded onto Long Island and into New Jersey (the Dutch town of Pavonia is now Jersey City), which were also part of New Netherland. Finally, the Dutch took over New Sweden, which immigrants from Sweden and Finland had settled in 1638 on the Delaware River near present-day New Castle, Delaware.

Problems plague New Netherland By the early 1660s New Netherland was having serious economic and political problems. The main reason was that the Dutch West India Company had appointed the director general (governor) and his council primarily to oversee the fur trade. Governing was therefore only a secondary role. Their main responsibility was to rent company lands to farmers and give settlers approval to start towns. They also established contacts with Native American fur traders, which almost immediately entangled the company in a conflict between the Mahican (an Algonquian tribe) and the Mohawk (one of the Five Nations of the Iroquois) over control of trade. At first the Dutch tried to remain neutral, but they finally aligned themselves with the Mahican in 1642. An even greater issue was farmland: New Netherland officials initially insisted on acquiring land through treaties with the Native Americans. But peaceful relations broke down when, between 1643 and 1645, the Dutch killed more than one thousand Native Americans over alleged treaty violations.

Another explosive situation was created by the diversity of European settlers in the area: half of the inhabitants of New Netherland and adjoining New Sweden were Germans, Swedes, Finns, Norwegians, French, English, Jews, and Africans. With the exception of African slaves, all had been attracted to the area by the promise of religious freedom. They therefore presented a threat to the Dutch, who were accustomed to the Dutch Reformed Church being the official state religion (see "Dutch Reformed Church" in Chapter 11). Also the New Netherland government had no better success in controlling the Dutch settlers, who could bypass the council and take their grievances directly to the Dutch West India Company. Another problem was that the company was losing money. In 1629 ownership of land had been opened to patroons like van Rensselaer, and ten years later merchants with no connection to the company were allowed to participate in the fur trade. This new system failed to attract immigrants and increase profits.

Stuyvesant put in charge The Dutch West India Company attempted to control the situation by appointing Peter Stuyvesant (1610–1672), a Dutch military leader, as governor of New Netherland. Stuyvesant took his post in 1647, and during the next seventeen years he caused considerable unrest by imposing heavy taxes and passing laws that prohibited religious freedom. For instance, Stuyvesant outlawed meetings and gatherings of people who were not members of the Dutch Reformed Church, making it nearly impossible for other religious groups to assemble and worship. When the directors at the Dutch West India Company headquarters in Amsterdam asked Stuyvesant to be more lenient, their plea landed on deaf ears. The ordinance stayed in place throughout the Dutch regime in New Netherland.

New Netherland becomes New York

Stuyvesant also made progress in the colony, improving relations with nearby English settlements and promoting commerce. Nevertheless, in 1649 the irate citizens of New Amsterdam forced him to declare the city a municipality (a self-governing political unit). Stuyvesant's mismanagement and harsh rule eventually led to New Netherland's downfall. In 1664, after the English victory over the Netherlands in the Second Anglo-Dutch War, England asserted its rights to New Netherland (which was part of the territory claimed by Cabot in 1497). The Dutch quickly surrendered, and King Charles II awarded the colony to his brother James, Duke of York (later King James II). New Netherland was renamed New York, and New Amsterdam became New York City.

The English guaranteed that New Netherland inhabitants, whatever their nationality or religion, could remain in the colony. But this open-minded policy only resulted in the continuation of political and religious strife in New York. In the late 1600s the British attempted to unite New York, New Jersey, and New England under the rule of royal governor Edmund Andros, but the colonists turned against him. Nevertheless, Andros succeeded in negotiating the Covenant Chain (1677), an alliance between the English and the Iroquois. The Covenant Chain protected New England against the French—who had always been a threat to both the Dutch and the English—during the French and Indian Wars (1689–1763). Spanning into the latter half of the eighteenth century, the wars hindered settlement of the western part of the colony, while the more populous areas of New York continued to attract various ethnic and religious groups. Religious tensions came to a head during Leisler's Rebellion of 1689 (see "Leisler's Rebellion" in Chapter 5).

Despite being a multicultural society that was headed by the English, New York was dominated by the Dutch. They still held most of the property and wealth, and real change did not take place until the early 1750s, when the Dutch and English had intermingled to form a new aristocracy (small privileged class) and political power structure. Thus the language and social customs of the English began to replace Dutch culture.

Pennsylvania

After the English colonized the mid-Atlantic coast and New England, they expanded westward with the founding of Pennsylvania. In 1681 King Charles II gave a tract of land, which he called "Pennsylvania" (Penn's Woods) to English admiral William Penn (1621–1670) to repay a debt. Charles granted the land under a proprietary contract, which gave Penn the right to establish and govern a colony with almost complete independence from England. Penn decided to give Pennsylvania to his son William Penn Jr. (1644–1718), who was a close friend of the king. By that time the younger Penn had become a member of the Society of Friends, or Quakers, a religious sect that was greatly feared in England.

The Society of Friends had been founded in the early 1650s by George Fox (1624–1691), an English cobbler (shoemaker) and shepherd. Fox believed he had been awakened to the "Inner Light," or truth, which enabled him to communicate directly with God. He was convinced that everyone possessed an Inner Light. Fox and his followers became evangelicals (those who emphasize salvation by faith, the authority of the scripture, and the importance of preaching), spreading word of their beliefs and calling on other Protestants to renounce the Church of England. Like the Puritans and Nonconformists, the Friends felt the national church relied too heavily on priests and worship services. The Friends were given the nickname "Quakers" by critics who ridiculed their beliefs, but they eventually adopted the name themselves.

Penn founds colony for Quakers The English considered the Quakers a threat to both church and state. Quakerism was soon outlawed, and many Friends, including William Penn Jr., spent time in jail. Penn and other wealthy Quakers began to look for a place that would permit them to worship freely and make a decent living for their families. At first they considered West New Jersey, part of the holdings of the Duke of York, where some Quakers had already settled. Since Penn had been granted land in America, however, he decided to start a new colony where they would have greater freedom.

Penn began making plans for Pennsylvania. In April 1681 he sent his cousin, William Markham, to America to form a governing council. Markham also met with Native Americans and Europeans who lived in the territory to inform them of Penn's authority over the land. The following October, Penn dispatched a group of commissioners to choose a site for a port city, which would be called Philadelphia (a Greek word for "brotherly love"). Since Penn could not fund the entire venture himself, he organized the Free Society of Traders, a group of wealthy Quaker investors. Each investor purchased 10,000 acres and assumed a seat on the governing council. Between 1682 and 1683 they sent fifty ships to America, thus guaranteeing rapid settlement of the colony. Penn's next step was to advertise Pennsylvania among Quakers in England, Wales, Holland, and Germany. He also welcomed non-Quakers. When Penn went to Pennsylvania to take his post as governor in 1682, farms had been established, the city was being built, and new settlers were arriving from Ireland and Wales. The population had already reached four thousand.

The Pennsylvania plan The most important features of the Pennsylvania plan were the frame of government and charter of liberties. Penn envisioned a generous, free society in which taxes were low, no limit was placed on landholdings, and Native

William Penn signing a treaty with the Native Americans for the land that would later become Pennsylvania.

Americans were treated as equals with Europeans. Moreover, he promoted complete religious tolerance, and he gave freedman (citizens with voting rights) status to any male who owned fifty acres of farmland or paid taxes. The colony would be administered by the governor and the general council, which proposed and passed laws. All citizens, including servants, would have certain rights and privileges, and there would be no established church.

Penn insisted on buying land from Native Americans, rather than simply seizing it or using the "whiskey treaty" trick. (Colonists routinely got Native Americans drunk on whiskey and then had them sign treaties that gave away vast amounts of land.) In 1682 the Native Americans and Quakers signed a treaty at a council meeting, in which they agreed to "live in love as long as the sun gave light," thus forming one of the longest-lasting peace treaties between Native Americans and European settlers. Penn stayed in Pennsylvania for only two years. During that time conflict broke out among various religious groups in the colony, disturbing the spirit of harmony and tolerance. Political squabbles also arose between poor landowners and the more privileged members of the Free Society of Traders. In 1684 Penn returned to England to fight the persecution of Quakers and to settle a dispute over the southern boundary of his colony, which bordered Maryland. In the meantime, Protestant monarchs William III and Queen Mary II had ascended the throne, so Penn no longer had a personal relationship with the monarchy. During his absence, he lost his authority in Pennsylvania as well.

Penn financially ruined In 1692 the English government withdrew Penn's proprietorship because the colony was poorly managed during his absence. William III appointed a new governor, Benjamin Fletcher, who immediately faced problems of his own. For example, the pacifist (people who do not believe in war to settle disputes) Quakers were opposed to using Pennsylvania funds for military purposes. In hopes of compromising with the Quakers, the king finally restored the charter to Penn, but this did not settle the problem. Many colonists wanted a royal charter because disagreements between the governing council and the assembly (elected representatives) were causing political chaos and people were losing their rights.

Penn went back to Pennsylvania in 1699, only to face growing opposition from settlers who wanted the English government to take over the colony. Staying for another two years, he helped draft the Charter of Privileges (1701), legal reforms that increased the power of the elected assembly. Affairs in England called Penn home later that year, and he never again saw his colony. Although Pennsylvania was a success, the colony yielded very little profit for Penn. When renters and landowners did not pay their bills, Penn himself became responsible for the debts. He was also swindled by one of his agents. Crushed by the financial burden, he went to debtor's prison in 1707. Five years later he began negotiating with the English government to sell Pennsylvania. During these discussions he suffered a series of disabling strokes. Upon his death in 1718, the proprietorship passed to his son Thomas.

After 1718 Scots-Irish settlers began expanding westward into the Cumberland Valley, pushing the frontier of Pennsylvania into Native American territory. These new colonists resisted the authority of the government, however, and they showed no interest in preserving the spirit of cooperation with Native Americans that was stated in the Pennsylvania plan. At this time the French and Indian Wars had been going on for nearly thirty years. Settlers on the frontiers of New York and Pennsylvania were having regular conflicts with Native Americans, who had allied with France in preserving French claims to land and fur-trading routes to the west along the Mississippi River. This situation continued until 1754, when colonial officials formed the Albany Congress in Albany, New York. Although Pennsylvania signed a treaty with the Iroquois to purchase more land, Native Americans in Pennsylvania were resentful and sided with the French against the British. Soon the British began attacking French forts on the Pennsylvania and New York frontiers and in Canada (then New France), igniting the French and Indian War (1754–63).

Diverse society in eighteenth century Pennsylvania continued to thrive in spite of its internal problems. The Quaker philosophy of tolerance attracted increasing numbers of European ethnic and religious groups. During the eighteenth century Pennsylvania was the fastest-growing colony in America, and Philadelphia was one of the most ethnically diverse cities in colonial America. Ethnic diversity created the audience and the market for a German-language press. Pennsylvania was also home to many African slaves. Although Quakers became increasingly uncomfortable with slavery from the 1750s onward, they remained slave owners until the American Revolution in 1776. Estimates from the 1770s and data from the first federal census indicate that three hundred thousand whites and ten thousand African Americans lived in Pennsylvania.

Delaware

Delaware became an English colony with the takeover of New Netherland in 1664. The Dutch recaptured Delaware in 1673, creating three district courts that were converted into three counties when the English took

 "a very mixed company"

In 1744 Maryland physician Alexander Hamilton stopped in Philadelphia as he was traveling north. Later he reported that he "dined att [at] a tavern with a very mixed company of different nations and religions. There were Scots, English, Dutch, Germans, and Irish; there were Roman Catholicks, Church men [Church of England], Presbyterians, Quakers, Newlightmen [evangelicals], Methodists, Seventh day [Adventist] men, Moravians, Anabaptists, and one Jew. The whole company consisted of 25 planted round an oblong table in a great hall."

the colony back within a year. The Duke of York then annexed Delaware to New York before transferring his claim to William Penn in 1682. This agreement gave Pennsylvania a water route to the Atlantic Ocean for trading vessels. Delaware was then called the Three Lower Counties (or Territory) of Pennsylvania, and the counties were named New Castle, Kent, and Sussex. The proprietors of the Maryland Colony immediately contested Penn's rights to the land, and the dispute was not settled until 1750. At first Delaware colonists were unhappy about joining Pennsylvania because they considered the Quakers "radicals." They came to terms with their status, however, when the Penn charter of 1701 gave the Lower Three Counties a separate assembly (representative government), which convened for the first time in 1704.

New Jersey

After the English took over New Netherland, the Dutch challenged claims to lands between the Hudson River and the northern point of the Delaware River. The region was divided between English noblemen John Berkeley and George Carteret and then split into East Jersey and West Jersey in the Quintipartite Deed of 1676. Carteret owned East Jersey. In 1681 the Quaker founders of Pennsylvania bought East Jersey from Carteret's widow, unleashing disputes over land rights in both Jerseys. Finally the proprietors surrendered their governing powers to England in 1702. In 1738 the two Jerseys became the colony of New Jersey. Yet problems did not end there: squabbles over land and resentment of royal governors led to riots in the 1740s. Tensions were ongoing until the end of the colonial period. East Jersey was dominated by Scots-Irish immigrants and New Englanders who were strict Calvinists (followers of French Protestant reformer John Calvin; [1509–1564]), while Quakers in West Jersey became increasingly prosperous and politically powerful.

The southern colonies

The southern colonies consisted of Virginia, Maryland, the Carolinas (later known as North and South Carolina), and Georgia.

Virginia

The emergence of tobacco as a cash crop changed the destiny of Virginia. Whereas in 1616 the colony exported 2,300 pounds of tobacco, in 1626 planters sent 260,000 pounds of tobacco to England. (Tobacco was dried and cured and then exported for use in pipe smoking. The practice had long been popular among Native Americans.) The "stinking weed" that James I had once threatened to outlaw now produced such high tax revenues that the king quickly came to rely upon the Virginia tobacco industry. The economic boom also dramatically changed the labor situation in Virginia (see Chapter 7). The Virginia Company had already been sending over indentured servants, who usually worked four to seven years in exchange for free passage to Virginia, room, board, and perhaps a plot of land at the end of their service. Tobacco's success intensified the need for indentured servants.

Tobacco growers also required more land for plantations, so settlers fanned out along the James River. Many of the plantations were crude, and life was harsh and often short. Indentured male servants aged fourteen to forty labored on meager rations with little or no protection against dreadful working conditions and Native American raids. For the first fifty years or so, Virginia plantation owners used indentured workers almost exclusively. Beginning in the 1660s, how-

A depiction of workers harvesting tobacco. The emergence of tobacco as a cash crop led to an economic boom for Virginia. *Reproduced by permission of The Granger Collection.*

ever, African slaves and servants largely replaced white servants, although a few slaves had been working in Virginia since 1619. Conditions for slaves were even worse than those for servants (see Chapters 7 and 8). There were many reasons for this shift. As time went on, Virginia gained a reputation as a death trap and attracted fewer indentured servants. Many Englishmen were finding better job prospects in their own country, and recently founded colonies in America competed with Virginia for workers. Another factor was the increasing availability and decreasing cost of slaves.

By this time, however, the huge number of servants had created wide class divisions and social instability in Virginia. An imbalance between men and women produced an underclass of males who married late and had little family life (see Chapters 7 and 8). Problems with Native Americans also increased. As indentured servants gained their freedom, they acquired land on the frontier, where they lived in isolated areas that were vulnerable to Native American attacks. Tensions soon arose between English government officials and unsophisticated property owners who were gaining seats in the House of Burgesses. The situation spilled over into a crisis with Bacon's Rebellion of 1676, when Nathaniel Bacon organized a militia (citizens' army) and confronted the royal government of William Berkeley (see "Bacon's Rebellion" in Chapter 5).

Little diversity, high mortality Virginia did not attract many nationalities other than the English until after the 1740s, when the Great Wagon Road from Pennsylvania brought in Scots-Irish and Germans (see "Commercial and private transportation" in Chapter 7). For the tidewater region (area near the coast) the chief diversity was racial. Close ties to England forged by the tobacco industry also affected the religious diversity of the colony. Most were members of the Church of England, although Quakers were tolerated. In the eighteenth century Presbyterians and Baptists moved into the backcountry.

The history of colonial Virginia was most profoundly shaped by high mortality rates. Far more people died than came into the colony, and few children were born to offset the losses. In Middlesex County, for instance, of 239 children born between 1655 and 1724, only 44 reached either marriage or age 21 with both parents alive. In some cases the parents had died, and in others the children had died. Grandparents rarely survived long enough to know their grandchildren. Men and women married several times as spouses died, leaving them with young children. As a result, Virginia's population grew relatively slowly. In 1625 the total population was 1,300, and by 1699 it had reached only 62,800. These figures included Africans, but their number is hard to determine. One estimate suggests that by 1699 there were between 6,000 and 10,000 Africans living in Virginia. The number increased more than tenfold during the eighteenth century, to 116,000 in 1754—only about 50,000 fewer than the 168,000 whites.

Maryland

As the Jamestown settlers struggled to survive, English nobleman George Calvert (1580–1632) was making plans for his own colony. Calvert was a favorite of James I, who had knighted him and appointed him secretary of state. He had bought stock in the Virginia Company in 1609, and in 1620 he invested in a venture group planning to settle Newfoundland (an island off the coast of Canada). Calvert changed his mind when he made a trip to the island and found the climate too harsh, so in 1629 he petitioned the king for a land grant in Virginia. Five years earlier Calvert had converted to Roman Catholicism, a move that had cost him his royal positions and prevented him from being given any other official duty. But as a gesture of friendship, James I had granted Calvert the Irish title of Lord Baltimore. Against the protests of many in England and Virginia, the king also approved Calvert's request for land in the region that was called northern Virginia (later named Mary's Land, after Queen Henrietta Maria, the wife of Charles II).

Calvert did not live long enough to see his new project materialize. The charter was signed a month after his death. The grant was transferred to his son and heir, Cecilius, second Baron of Baltimore. The Lords Baltimore thus received the first proprietary grant (a contract giving an individual or group the right to organize and govern a colony) issued by England for lands in North America. They undoubtedly hoped to make money from their new estate. They also hoped to provide a place where Roman Catholics could freely practice their religion and enjoy other political and legal freedoms (see "Roman Catholicism" in Chapter 11).

Colony joins tobacco trade In 1634, 150 settlers embarked from England on the *Ark* and the *Dove,* the first ships headed to the new colony of Maryland. A few women, "mades which wee brought along," were among them. Unlike immigrants to the other English colonies, however, the passengers included a few Catholic laymen and two Jesuit priests (members of a Catholic religious order, the Society of Jesus). They arrived at Saint Clement's Island in the Potomac River on March 25 and celebrated Mass (the Catholic Eucharist, or holy communion service). They built their first settlement at Saint Marys, on the northern bank of the Potomac. They found that the land was suitable for growing tobacco, and Maryland soon joined the neighboring Virginia colony in the tobacco trade. (The economies of

Maryland and Virginia were so closely related that the colonies are often referred to as the Chesapeake region.) Investors with money or connections acquired large landholdings, usually along one of the many rivers that flow into Chesapeake Bay. Like Virginia planters, Maryland tobacco growers used indentured servants, most of them young men, as laborers. Yet by 1648 the population of Maryland was only three hundred. The English Civil War had reduced migration, and many settlers had died from diseases. The population eventually increased, reaching 162,000 by 1760. Most people lived in scattered settlements or villages, and the only town of any size was Annapolis (which became the capital in 1694). By 1760 a port was developing at the site of present-day Baltimore, now the largest city in Maryland.

Diversity encouraged Maryland's earliest settlers were English, but by the 1730s Irish, German, and Welsh colonists were granted lands along the southern border of Pennsylvania, which the Lords Baltimore claimed over protests from the Penn family. (The formation of the Mason-Dixon line in 1767 settled the dispute, establishing an official boundary between Maryland and Pennsylvania.) Scottish merchants lived along the coast, and they began to dominate the tobacco trade in the 1750s. Prior to the American Revolution, Maryland was attracting the majority of immigrants to the colonies. The most significant change in Maryland's population patterns

Claiborne Rebellion

From 1645 to 1647 Protestants staged Ingle's Rebellion, a protest against the Catholic government of Maryland. Around the same time Maryland colonists also endured the Claiborne Rebellion. This uprising was led by William Claiborne, who had emigrated to Virginia from England in 1621. Claiborne was a Protestant, and he did not want his settlement to come under the rule of the Roman Catholic Calvert family, the founders of Maryland. He established a settlement with a fort on Kent Island in Chesapeake Bay. Problems arose when he opposed the granting of Maryland to Cecilius Calvert, second Baron of Baltimore. Claiborne was arrested and sent to England in 1637, where he argued his case, but the issue was eventually decided in favor of Calvert. Nevertheless Claiborne returned to Virginia, and in 1642 he was elected treasurer of the colony. For several years he continued to invade Maryland. After driving out Governor Leonard Calvert, Claiborne briefly gained control of Maryland. Although Calvert returned in 1646 and put down the uprising, he died the following year. Claiborne controlled Maryland for several years and served on the governing commission of the colony.

took place around 1700, when African American laborers began replacing white indentured servants, especially on the larger tobacco plantations. By 1760 46 percent of planters owned slaves. By the 1750s approximately forty-five thousand black slaves were living in Maryland.

Maryland's proprietors also welcomed various religious groups. The Calverts had founded the colony as a haven for Catholics, but Catholics were never a majority, even on the *Ark* and the *Dove*. Cecilius Calvert had tried to protect his fellow Catholics with a tolerance act (1649), which stated that no Christian would be "troubled [or] molested." (Jews and other non-Christians were excluded.) Catholic immigration to Maryland was meager, but other religious groups took advantage of the colony's tolerance. In the 1650s the Quakers settled in Maryland, and Presbyterians, Baptists, and the Church of England were all represented by the 1670s. The tolerance act was repealed, however, when the Puritans gained control of the government in 1655 and Catholics lost the right to vote. After Protestant monarchs William III and Mary II took the English throne in 1688, Maryland became a royal colony (directly ruled by the English Crown). The Calverts regained control in 1715, but by this time they had converted to Anglicanism (see "Church of England" in Chapter 11).

The Carolinas

The Spanish and French made the earliest attempts to settle the region that became the English colony of Carolina. Although Spaniards had reached the area between 1520 and 1521, they did not actually settle there, content instead to attack local Native Americans. They captured seventy people, taking them back to Hispaniola (now Haiti and the Dominican Republic; see "Christopher Columbus," Chapter 2), where they were freed. In 1540 the explorer Hernando de Soto (see Chapter 2) landed in Florida and proceeded on foot into the interior. He reached the Native American town of Cofitachequi (modern-day Camden, South Carolina), moving into territory that is now North Carolina. He was searching unsuccessfully for an emergency haven on the Carolina coast for Spanish treasure ships, which sailed from Mexico to Spain through the Bahama Channel—a narrow, fast-flowing passage east of Florida that was plagued by hurricanes and European raiders.

In 1562 French commander Jean Ribault and a small group of Huguenots (French Protestants) arrived in Port Royal Sound. They built Charlesfort, a small fort, on what is now the Parris Island Marine Station golf course (see Chapter 3), but they eventually deserted the site. In 1566 Pedro Menéndez de Avilés, the founder of Saint Augustine (see Chapter 2), built a fort called San Felipe on the ruins of Charlesfort. Supporting the fort was the town of Santa Elena, which included a mission, farming community, and such industries as a pottery kiln (oven used for baking clay pottery). But the Spanish were extremely vulnerable to hostile Native Americans and raiders such as English privateer (a pirate licensed by the government) Francis Drake (c. 1543–1596). They abandoned Santa Elena in 1587, retreating to Saint Augustine, the only surviving Spanish settlement on the East Coast.

English pursue colonization English attempts at colonization in the Carolinas began in 1585 when Walter Raleigh organized failed expeditions to Roanoke Island, off the coast of North Carolina, which ended with the "lost colony" of Roanoke. In 1629 King Charles I granted Robert Heath a tract of land located between Virginia and Florida that extended west to the Pacific Ocean. Heath named the tract Carolina in honor of the king, but he was unable to find settlers or financial backing for a colony. A few years later he assigned his grant to Henry, Lord Maltravers, who also ran into problems; eventually the grant expired. In 1642 the English Civil War broke out, and no efforts were made to settle the area for the next eighteen years. The monarchy was overthrown in 1648, and Puritan leader Oliver Cromwell ruled until the monarchy was restored in 1660. The new king, Charles II, was indebted to supporters who had stood by him during that time. One way he showed his gratitude was by granting them land in America. He gave New York and New Jersey to his brother the Duke of York, and he gave Pennsylvania to William Penn Sr.

In 1665 Charles II granted Carolina to eight friends called Lords Proprietors. They were mainly politicians, so they were not seeking religious freedom or trying to help people build new lives. Like the Virginia Company

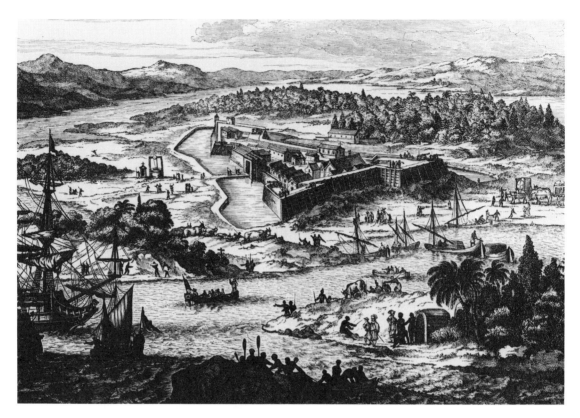

An illustration of one of the settlements in the Carolinas.
Reproduced by permission of Mary Evans Picture Library.

investors or Thomas Weston, they hoped to make money from their new venture. A group of settlers landed on the banks of the Cape Fear River in what is now North Carolina in 1665. They were mostly Barbadians (people from the island of Barbados in the West Indies) and a few New Englanders. They immediately started quarreling and then abandoned the site when they heard about easier ocean access farther south in Port Royal Sound.

Successful venture organized The first permanent settlement in Carolina was organized in 1669 by Anthony Ashley Cooper (1621–1683; later Earl of Shaftesbury), one of the Lords Proprietors. He was assisted by his secretary, the great political theorist John Locke (1632–1704). They proposed the "Fundamental Constitutions," a unique document meant to lure settlers by proposing a hereditary nobility (upper-class status through birth), religious tolerance, and the right to own private property, including slaves. Cooper also persuaded the other proprietors to contribute money. In August 1669 three ships left England to sail via Barbados to the new colony of

Carolina. The ninety-three passengers included four gentlemen and nineteen women as well as servants, surveyors, carpenters, blacksmiths, masons, and surgeons. An "ignorant preacher" was also onboard. The ships first stopped in Ireland, vainly hoping to attract more colonists, then sailed across the Atlantic to Barbados. Rough weather scattered the ships and destroyed one of them. After stopping in Bermuda to pick up more settlers, the remaining two ships finally reached Carolina in April 1670.

Charles Town founded Friendly Native Americans urged the colonists to consider a site up a river that the English named Ashley. On a high hill with the river on one side and marshes on the other, the settlers chose a site for the capital, Charles Town (later Charleston). The first buildings were crude and haphazard—the average house measured fifteen feet by twenty feet, or the size of a modern American living room. The colonists used their energies building a palisade (a fence of stakes for defense), not growing crops. Therefore early Charles Town, like Jamestown, relied on imported foodstuffs for survival. In 1670 and 1671 more settlers arrived, and in 1672 the Charles Town inhabitants included 268 men, 69 women, and 59 children from a variety of ethnic groups—English, Barbadian, Irish, Dutch, and African.

By the 1670s the Carolina colony had yet to make money. They had failed to remain friendly with local Native Americans and to monopolize the fur trade, as the colonists provoked war and encouraged Native American slave trade. Conflicts with the Spanish and the French were also a continuing problem. The proprietors' interests often clashed with those of the most aggressive settlers, making Carolina hard to govern. Moreover, many colonists were unwilling to pay even minimal rents. In 1680 Charles Town was moved to the peninsula formed by the junction of the Ashley and Cooper Rivers. In surveying the new town, the settlers used a grid pattern, following the "grand model" sent from England. They also made rules concerning house size and height. Thirty wooden houses and guns from the old settlement made the new one comfortable and seemingly safe. Within a few years French Huguenots, Presbyterians, and Baptists were drawn to Charles Town by the promise of religious tolerance. While many left for the countryside, some stayed in the city, making Charles Town the largest urban settlement south of Philadelphia in the 1700s.

Conflicts with Native Americans in the early part of the eighteenth century created security problems and debts that the proprietors were unable to pay. For instance, from 1715 to 1716 the Yamasee tribe attacked the colonists; the natives resented their exploitation by Carolina fur traders. The bloody conflict resulted in many deaths and much property destruction. Protesting their lack of protection from the proprietors, the colonists rebelled, and in 1719 the English government appointed a provisional (temporary) governor. In 1729 England bought out the remaining proprietors. Nevertheless Charles Town continued to grow, and by the mid-eighteenth century, highly skilled artisans (craftspeople) and artists could find patrons of taste and discernment. At the end of the colonial period Charles Town was a city of elegance and culture, with theater, music, libraries, and a social season that allowed the elite to view and be viewed by one another. It might well have been the wealthiest city in British North America.

Charles Town was also home to at least two hundred Jews. When Carolina was founded it became the first of the English colonies to provide religious tolerance for Jews. Four Jewish shopkeepers were granted citizenship between 1697 and 1698. Sephardic Jews from London, England, and the West Indies arrived in the city during the late 1730s. They were joined in 1740 by Jews fleeing Savannah, Georgia, who had heard rumors of a Spanish invasion. In 1749 the Jewish community organized a Sephardic-rite synagogue (Jewish house of worship), Beth Elohim.

South Carolina   By the 1680s large plantations were developing in the lower, tidewater region of Carolina—which became South Carolina in 1713—where land was better suited for growing tobacco, rice, and other crops. In the 1740s indigo (a plant used for making dye) became a staple crop and bolstered a thriving economy (see "Eliza Pinckney" in Chapter 7). This area also had better access to water routes for ocean trade. Plantation owners used white indentured servants and Native American and African slaves. The first recorded slave in South Carolina, a "lusty negro man," arrived from Virginia within months of the first settlement on the Ashley River in 1670. The first slave family arrived from Bermuda a month later. Trade with the Caribbean Islands included slaves. In March 1671 John Yeamans arrived from Barbados with eight blacks. These bound laborers worked on his wooded lands, defending against Native American and Spanish raiders when the whites were called back to defend Charles Town. When Yeamans died in 1674, he owned at least twenty-six slaves. By 1708 more than half of the non-Native American population were slaves, making Carolina the only colony with a black majority. In some low-country areas the ratio of blacks to whites was as high as four to one—much like the West Indies. In 1769 South Carolina lieutenant governor William Bull estimated that South Carolina had some forty-five thousand whites and eighty thousand blacks.

North Carolina   In 1713 Carolina was divided into the two colonies of North Carolina and South Carolina; they became royal colonies in 1729. Geography inhibited North Carolina's growth: the colony had no large port, and the long coastline was marked by barrier islands, shifting sandbars, and treacherous currents. In an age when any major travel and all commercial trade relied on ships, the lack of harbors was an almost insurmountable liability (see "Commercial and private transportation" in Chapter 7). In the 1650s, before the Charles Town settlement was established, the first settlers moved into northern Carolina from Virginia. At that time boundaries were indistinct, and the Virginia-Carolina border was not officially determined until 1728. The population of North Carolina grew slowly. Isolated by the lack of harbors and major waterways, the settlers lived on small farms, raising corn, tobacco, and livestock. They conducted trade mainly with Virginia. In 1672 Quakers arrived and became a powerful political force. A few French Huguenot families from Virginia settled near the Pamlico River between 1690 and 1691 and were followed in 1707 by a much larger group. In 1710 German settlers founded New Bern, but they abandoned the town when they were attacked by Tuscarora warriors the next year; it was rebuilt in 1723. By the 1720s problems with Native Americans had decreased, and more immigrants found their way to North Carolina. Among them were Germans, Scots-Irish, Welsh, and Swiss. In the 1750s the Great Wagon Road from Philadelphia opened up the Shenandoah Valley of Virginia as well as North and South Carolina. Slavery also flourished in North Carolina, although not in nearly the same numbers as the plantations of South Carolina. Estimates of the population of North Carolina in the 1760s suggest some eighty thousand whites and around twenty-six thousand Africans were living in the colony.

Barbadians Settle Carolina

Most of the earliest American settlements drew their populations from England. The Carolina colony was unique in that it attracted colonists from the English-held West Indian islands, mainly Barbados. Many congregated on Goose Creek, above Charleston, earning themselves the designation "Goose Creek men." Of some 680 settlers who came to the Carolinas between 1670 and 1680 and whose origins can be identified, more than half were from the West Indies. By 1680 Barbados was a small but wealthy sugar island whose rich families had no land to give their younger sons. Therefore they turned to the Carolinas, where the semitropical climate was ideal for agriculture and slavery. They did well: seven of the Carolinas' twenty-three governors between 1669 and 1737 had Barbadian backgrounds. Less wealthy Barbadians also looked to the Carolinas for economic opportunity. Among the early settlers were small planters, artisans, and indentured servants. Barbados and other West Indian islands also provided a market for the beef, corn, and lumber produced in the Carolinas.

Georgia

Georgia was founded by English social reformer James Edward Oglethorpe (1696–1785) in 1732. As a member of Parliament, Oglethorpe was chair-

Blackbeard the Pirate

Blackbeard was an English pirate whose real name was probably Edward Teach. He was hired as a privateer during the War of Spanish Succession (1701–14); after the war he turned pirate and became notoriously cruel. He had headquarters in the Bahamas and the Carolinas. Between 1716 and 1718 Blackbeard plundered ships and coastal settlements in the West Indies and along the eastern coast of North America. He acquired some protection by sharing his treasure with the governor of North Carolina. However, in 1718 he was killed by a British force from Virginia.

man of a committee that was investigating debtors' prisons. Oglethorpe and his committee discovered extensive corruption among prison officials, who also committed horrible brutalities against inmates. These revelations led Oglethorpe to promote reforms of the treatment of paupers (poor people). At the time the traditional remedy was to send social misfits to a colony. Oglethorpe therefore gathered twenty like-minded partners and applied for a charter to settle Georgia (named in honor of King George II [1683–1760]), a debtors' colony in America. In 1732 they were granted a tract of land located between the Savannah and Alatamaha Rivers along the south Atlantic seaboard.

At the same time Oglethorpe anonymously published an essay in which he solicited funds for the Georgia project. His primary purpose was to justify transporting many of England's poor, who had been imprisoned, to form their own community in a strange land. Oglethorpe carefully explained that he had anticipated the serious problems that could arise among this group. His first step, he wrote, would be to place all of the settlers under his personal supervision. Oglethorpe was a seasoned army officer, so there was little question that he would be able to maintain discipline. He also pointed out that poverty would not be the sole requirement for participation in the venture, and that he would control the selection of settlers.

Buffer zone needed The colony had another purpose: in addition to serving as a refuge for paupers, Georgia would provide a barrier against Spain, which had been mounting raids on British settlements along the Atlantic coast. At the time the southernmost English colony was South Carolina. To the south was the heavily fortified Spanish seaport settlement of Saint Augustine (see Chapter 2). Lying between the British and the Spanish was a wild frontier. The British proposed to establish Georgia on the frontier and build forts that would protect the northern colonies from the Spanish.

Oglethorpe and his trustees received generous funding for the Georgia colony—sizable private contributions were supplemented by 10,000

A depiction of the founding of Savannah, which was to act as a buffer zone between the English and Spanish colonies. *Reproduced by permission of The Ganger Collection.*

pounds (British currency) from Parliament. In November 1732, Oglethorpe and 120 settlers sailed for America aboard the ship *Anne*. Oglethorpe immediately located a site for the settlement and started building the town of Savannah. (Savannah is now considered one of the most beautiful historic American cities.) His next act was to establish friendly relations with the Yamacraws, the local Native American tribe, from whom he acquired more land. The colonists and the Yamacraws maintained a spirit of goodwill throughout Oglethorpe's stay in Georgia. Within two years Oglethorpe had opened the colony to settlers who weren't convicts, the two main groups being Germans and Scots. Georgia settlements had expanded westward, and about 60 miles south of Savannah the town of Frederica was built on an island at the mouth of the Alatamaha River.

Georgia experiment fails In 1734 Oglethorpe went back to England, accompanied by several Native American chiefs. Before he left he appointed a prominent shopkeeper as a temporary supervisor of the colony. The choice was a disaster, revealing Oglethorpe's poor judgment and exposing the settlers' lack of motivation and inability to think for themselves. Some historians have observed that Georgia, a small colony, was organized on a community plan that functioned only if all of the inhabitants did their jobs and followed the rules. Moreover, Oglethorpe was a firm ruler who attended to even the smallest details. The shopkeeper turned out to be dishonest and brutal, and he was unable to keep order. When Oglethorpe returned from England he found chaos.

Most of the problems resulted from Oglethorpe's vision for Georgia. He and the trustees wanted a community of sober, industrious, small landholders. To this end they prohibited strong liquors, landholdings of more than 500 acres, and slavery. These restrictions not only angered many settlers but also made Georgia unappealing to potential investors. South Carolinians especially eyed the rivers and marshes along the Georgia coast, and a few even went so far as to establish illegal slave-based plantations. The rum trade was never completely suppressed because colonists Robert and Mary Musgrove sold liquor less than a mile from Savannah.

Religious leaders add to problems
Unrest was also caused by the English founders of Methodism (a Protestant religious group), John Wesley (1703–1791) and Charles Wesley (1707–1788), whom Oglethorpe had invited to Georgia. The Wesleys had arrived in 1736, Charles as Oglethorpe's private secretary and John as head of missionary activities. Charles and Oglethorpe soon had a disagreement, and Charles returned to England after only a brief stay. John Wesley remained in the colony, but his presence was a source of turmoil and discontent. While Oglethorpe was preparing a defense against Spain, Wesley quarreled with other officials. Then Oglethorpe decided to replace Wesley with the wildly popular English preacher George Whitefield (1714–1770), who arrived in 1739. Whitefield improved the situation somewhat by starting an orphanage, which he called Bethesda, on 500 acres of land granted to him by the Georgia trustees. He was so oppressive and overbearing, however, that he alienated the guardians of the orphans. Finally, after a five-month stay, Whitefield left to continue his preaching tour, which sparked the religious revival called the Great Awakening (see "Great Awakening" in Chapter 11).

Oglethorpe a military hero Although Oglethorpe was losing control of his colony, he took command on the military front. War between Spain and Britain was ready to break out at any time, and Oglethorpe knew that Georgia would become the field of battle. He received word that Saint Augustine residents were being evacuated to accommodate a Spanish troop buildup. In September 1738, Ogle-thorpe raised a volunteer army of six hundred men, among them troops from South Carolina. In the summer of 1739 he led his regiment through the wilderness toward

Saint Augustine. Along the way he formed an alliance with several Native American groups, accumulating a force of two thousand. By fall Britain had declared war on Spain, and the following spring Oglethorpe mounted an attack on Saint Augustine. Although he succeeded in capturing three smaller Spanish forts, he was not able to seize Saint Augustine itself. In the heat of battle many Native American warriors withdrew because Oglethorpe had restrained them from using their usual battle techniques. Sickness also broke out, and the Carolina soldiers deserted. In June 1740 Oglethorpe withdrew his troops. Nevertheless his efforts had been effective—the Spanish did not venture into Georgia for two more years.

In 1742 the Spanish bombarded British defenses around Georgia. During his defense of the colony, Oglethorpe achieved the victory for which he is remembered. Although his troops were unprepared for the attack, Oglethorpe led them into battle and brilliantly fought off the Spanish invaders. At one point he even captured two Spanish soldiers single-handedly. Soon English ships sailed to the colonists' rescue, and Georgia remained intact. Yet Oglethorpe's difficulties were not over. The British government would not give him enough funds for military defense, so over the next year he had to rely on Native American allies to conduct raids into Spanish territory. Finally, Oglethorpe began using his own money to buy supplies and other necessities for the militia. Internal conflict was still brewing, however, and colonists complained about his rigid policies. Oglethorpe was recalled to England and charged with mismanagement.

Georgia now a royal colony In an attempt to sort out his financial situation, Oglethorpe submitted a bill for expenses to the British government. Although the charges against him were eventually dropped, officials did not refund his money, saying the expenses had not been authorized. Oglethorpe intended to return to Georgia, but he never saw his colony again.

In 1750 the Georgia trustees legalized the slave trade and removed the 500-acre landholding restriction. Four years later they turned the colony over to the English government.

Social and Political Issues

5

By the mid-1600s, less than half a century after the English had opened the way for full-scale European settlement, serious crises were brewing in the American colonies. At first tensions were caused by a steadily increasing population: massive numbers of settlers required more land, additional dwellings and other accommodations, greater food supplies, and expanded trade and transportation networks. The immediate victims were Native Americans, who suffered mistreatment at the hands of colonists scrambling to grab land and natural resources. A demand for more laborers also created the institution of slavery, as millions of Africans were transported into the colonies during the seventeenth and eighteenth centuries. Among the colonists themselves, religious differences were escalating into confrontations, land squabbles were causing rebellions, and class divisions were breeding unrest.

A major issue was the way the colonies were governed. This problem had emerged in the first few years of the settlement period and quickly gained momentum in the seventeenth century. By the late 1600s all thirteen colonies had come under English control. Governing bodies therefore consisted either of proprietors (individuals granted ownership of a colony and full authority to establish a government and distribute land) hired by wealthy investors, or councils, controlled by the monarchy (king or queen) and the aristocracy (elite social class) in England. Many of the investors and aristocrats, who came from the upper classes, remained in England, while others took positions of power in colonial governments. Trade, treaties, and taxation were legislated for the benefit of England. The colonial population, however, was highly diverse, consisting of a complex mixture of ethnic, religious, and social groups. During the eighteenth century a unique "American spirit" began to take shape. Colonists were not only questioning English rule but also rebelling against various forms of local authority. Demanding the rights and freedoms—religious, political, economic, and individual—symbolized by the New World (a European term for North and South America), Americans were setting the stage for revolution.

The Pequot War

The first American rebels were the Native Americans. They initially welcomed the European settlers, with whom they willingly shared their land and resources. However, they slowly came to realize that the foreign settlers, by clearing vast territories for towns and farms, were violating native traditions. Native Americans believed that a Great Spirit had created a plentiful and harmonious world in which human beings are no more important than other creatures. Therefore they placed great emphasis on paying proper respect to nature. Native Americans managed their land so that it would accommodate all living creatures, changing it little and taking only what they needed to survive. They thanked a tree for dying and providing them with wood for a fire. They thanked an animal they had killed for giving up its flesh to feed them and its skin to clothe them. Native Americans were shocked to discover that the Europeans viewed humans as the dominant creatures in nature and thus felt free to change the world for their own advantage.

Native Americans were equally troubled by being forced to convert to Christianity and accept European customs. During the early colonial period they regarded the Christian God as simply another name for the Great Spirit. They saw no real need to change their own religious practices. Yet after being nearly annihilated (wiped out) by smallpox (a highly contagious viral disease) and other European diseases, they accepted the European view that believing in the Christian God was the only way they could save themselves. Moreover, they had become dependent on the European-made goods—weapons, cooking utensils, and tools—they received in exchange for jewelry, furs, and other trade items. Consequently they had no choice but to cooperate with the Europeans. After several decades of European domination, however, Native Americans throughout North America began rais-

An illustration of the defeat of the Pequot tribe during the 1637 Pequot War.
Reproduced by permission of The Library of Congress.

ing concerns about the disappearance of their land and traditional culture.

During the seventeenth century trouble began brewing along the frontiers of most colonies, as European settlers expanded onto Native American land. In New England tensions between settlers and Native Americans resulted in the Pequot War (1637). As a result of the "great migration," the

"Thus the Lord was pleased"

John Mason, one of the leaders of the war against the Pequots, gave the following account of the Puritan victory:

Thus were they now at their wits end, who not many hours before exalted themselves in their great pride, threatening and resolving the utter ruin of all the English, exulting and rejoicing with songs and dances. But God was above them, who laughed his enemies and the enemies of his people to scorn, making them as a fiery oven. Thus were the stout-hearted spoiled, having slept their last sleep . . . Thus did the Lord judge among the heathen, filling the place with dead bodies.

And here we may see the just judgment of God, in sending (even the very night before this assault) 150 men from their other fort, to join with them of that place; who were designed—as some of themselves reported—to go forth against the English at that very instant when this heavy stroke came upon them, where they perished *with their fellows. So that the mischief they intended came upon their own pate [head]. They were taken in their own snare, and we through mercy escaped. And thus in little more than an hour's space was their impregnable [impossible to capture] fort with themselves utterly destroyed, to the number of six or seven hundred, as some of themselves confessed. There were only seven taken captive and about seven escaped.*

Thus the Lord was pleased to smite [destroy] our enemies in the hinder parts and to give us their land for an inheritance; who remembered us in our low estate, and redeemed us out of our enemies' hands. Let us therefore praise the Lord for his goodness and his wonderful works to the Children of men!

Source: Mason, John. A Brief History of the Pequot War. Boston, Mass.: S. Kneeland & T. Green, 1736, pp. 9–10, 21.

New England population was rising rapidly (it was four thousand in 1634 and would reach eleven thousand in 1638). The Puritans had begun moving west onto land that was controlled by the Pequots. For instance, the Hartford settlement (in present-day Connecticut) was established by Baptist minister Thomas Hooker (1586?–1647), and nearby Fort Saybrook was built by the English Saybrook Company near the Pequot village of Mystic. The Pequots were not friendly toward the English, who were allies of their enemies, the Narraganset.

The Puritans' real goal was to rid the area of all Native Americans. Even though the colonists had signed a treaty with the Pequots, they hoped to provoke the Native Americans into breaking the agreement. The desired provocation came when Native Americans from an unknown tribe killed two English colonists, John Stone and John Oldham. The Puritans accused the Pequots of committing the murders, but the Pequots denied any involvement and even offered to negotiate with the colonists. The Puritans responded by demanding that the Pequots turn over the killers to prove they were not doing the work of the devil. (The Puritans believed that any disaster or misfortune was caused by the devil, or Satan, against whom they were constantly waging war.) The Pequots could not produce the killers, so in September 1636, John Endecott (1588–1665), the military commander in Massachusetts (see Chapter 4), led an attack on the Pequots and their allies on Block Island (off the coast of Rhode Island), thus beginning the Pequot War. After the Pequots retaliated by laying siege to Fort Saybrook, the conflict remained low-key for some time. When western settlers became worried that the Pequots would be victorious, however, the fighting soon escalated. The war finally ended at Mystic in 1637, after the settlers burned the village and exterminated nearly all the Pequots. The few survivors were either killed later by Puritans or fled to other parts of the country. (In 1638 the Treaty of Hartford declared the Pequot nation to be dissolved.)

King Philip's War

One of the most famous conflicts in New England took place between the Puritans and the Wampanoag, who resented efforts to Europeanize them. They came to believe that they were offending the Great Spirit by converting to Christian-

Metacom, also known as King Philip, began King Philip's War after a dispute with the colonists over land.
Reproduced by permission of Archive Photos, Inc.

ity and by needlessly slaughtering animals for the fur trade. The heavy emphasis on furs in particular disrupted their traditional culture and economy by fostering wars with neighboring tribes over trapping grounds. By 1675 Wampanoag leaders were ready to push the Puritans off their land and reclaim their own religion and culture.

At the forefront was Metacom (also Metacomet; c. 1639–1676), a sachem (chief) the colonists knew as King Philip. Metacom was one of five children of Chief Massasoit (1580–

1661), who had helped the Plymouth colonists (see Chapter 4). Massasoit died in 1661, and a year later Metacom, then in his mid-twenties, assumed leadership of the Wampanoag. He dedicated himself to maintaining the Wampanoag Confederacy, which consisted of many villages and families. As the English population and power continued to grow, the confederacy began to splinter. This was due in part to the influence of colonial authorities and missionaries (people who do religious work in foreign countries). Metacom's land formed a border zone between Plymouth Colony, Rhode Island, and the Massachusetts Bay Colony capital in Boston, each of which wanted to claim the territory. In order to hold on to his political influence, the sachem sold tracts of land to various colonists. Resulting conflicts over the borders of these lands, however, were rarely settled to his satisfaction. Colonial courts seemed biased and insensitive to the Native Americans' concerns. The tribes were also angered by colonists' efforts to shape native politics.

Puritans violate treaty

The conflict over land reached its crisis point in 1667. In violation of an agreement with Metacom, the Plymouth Colony authorized the purchase of land inside Wampanoag borders for the town of Swansea. Tribal war parties, possibly led by Metacom, began to gather around Swansea to intimidate the colonists. In 1671 Plymouth officials demanded a meeting with the chief. When he arrived they forced him at gunpoint to surrender his warriors' firearms and challenged Metacom's previous land sales to other colonies. When Metacom complained to the Massachusetts Bay Colony he was summoned to Boston, but received no support. Instead, both Plymouth and Massachusetts Bay, which had formed the United Colonies several years earlier (see "New England Confederation" in Chapter 6), forced him to sign a new treaty placing the Wampanoag under the colonists' rule.

Metacom wages war

Around this time Metacom started planning the uprising that came to be known as King Philip's War. Although he had the backing of Wampanoag leaders, Metacom knew his tribe was too small to fight the English alone. Therefore, he sought support from other Native American groups. He managed to win over the Nipmuck, who were also bitter toward the colonists. He had difficulty, however, in forming an alliance with the Narraganset, the most powerful tribe in the region and enemies of the Wampanoag. Metacom was now in a difficult position: he had not gained enough support to launch a full-scale uprising, so he had to prevent his angry warriors from raiding colonial villages while keeping their loyalty. Rumors of Metacom's efforts reached colonial authorities in 1674. Soon afterward the body of John Sassamon, a Christianized Native American, was found in a pond. It turned out that Sassamon had told the English about Metacom's plan. The colonists tried and hanged three Wampanoag for committing the murder. On the scaffold (platform where criminals are hanged) one of the three men supposedly confessed that Metacom had ordered Sassamon's murder.

Metacom now had no choice except to declare war on the Puritans. Colonial officials commanded him to disarm his warriors, but he remained defiant. In July 1675 Metacom's men again assembled outside Swansea, triggering King Philip's War. The uprising was apparently touched off more by the rage of Metacom's people than by any organized plan. When a colonial army tried to besiege the sachem near his home on Mount Hope, he escaped with his warriors and their families. Then, joining forces with his Nipmuck allies, he attacked and burned villages west and south of Boston. Native American groups in the Connecticut River valley also rose in revolt when anxious colonists overreacted to the violence. Finally, in late December, the Narraganset joined the uprising after English forces attacked their village. During the ensuing winter, joint tribal raiding parties burned several colonial towns, sending English refugees streaming into Boston.

Native culture destroyed

While Metacom was seeking new alliances in the Hudson River valley, Mohawk warriors and New York colonists attacked his party. All but forty of his men were killed, and his

A depiction of Native Americans attacking a colonial settlement during King Philip's War. *Reproduced by permission of Archive Photos, Inc.*

prestige was shattered. The Mohawk continued their attacks from the west and, joined by other Native Americans and colonists, finally defeated Metacom. As the uprising dissolved, some of

"land is everlasting"

Conflicts occurred between Native Americans and settlers throughout the colonial period. In 1742 Cannassatego, an Iroquois chief, made the following speech to Pennsylvania colonists while negotiating a new land and trade treaty. Note that he apologized for not bringing a bigger gift, pointing out that colonists had reduced his people to poverty and thus he could not afford any more skins.

We know our lands are now become more valuable: the white people think we do not know their value; but we are sensible that the land is everlasting, and the few goods we receive for it are soon worn out and gone. For the future we will sell no lands but when Brother Onas [one of the Pennsylvania proprietors] is in the country; and we will know beforehand the quantity of the goods we are to receive.

Besides, we are not well used with respect to the lands still unsold by us. Your people daily settle on these lands, and spoil our hunting. . . .

It is customary with us to make a present of skins whenever we renew our treaties. We are ashamed to offer our brethren [brothers (the colonists)] so few; but your horses and cows have eaten the grass our deer used to feed on. This has made them scarce, and will, we hope, plead in excuse for our not bringing a larger quantity: if we could have spared more we would have given more; but we are really poor; and desire you'll not consider the quantity, but, few as they are, accept them in testimony of our regard.

Reprinted in: Gunn, Giles, ed. Early American Writing. New York: Penguin Books, 1994, pp. 407–08.

the sachem's former supporters organized a squad and began to track him down. The chief's wife and son were captured and apparently sold in the West Indies as slaves. Finally, on August 12, Metacom's dwindling band was surrounded, and a Native American serving with the colonial forces shot him. Metacom's head was cut off and hacked into quarters. The pieces were sent to the colonial capitals, where they were placed on public display for more than twenty years.

Metacom's defeat had disastrous consequences for the New England native groups. The Wampanoag and their allies were helpless against the colonists, who numbered seventy thousand and had large supplies of food and ammunition. The war had destroyed the Wampanoag's habitat, so they were not prepared for the upcoming winter. Colonial authorities pursued surviving tribes and either killed them or sold them into slavery. Any remaining native peoples were forced into isolated settlements. Within a brief period the Native American way of life had completely disappeared from New England.

King Philip's War not only broke the power of New England native peoples but also had a devastating impact on the English colonies. Before the yearlong conflict was over, twelve towns were destroyed and half of the remaining seventy-eight were seriously damaged. The colonies accumulated huge debts, which produced lasting economic hardship. About 10 percent of the adult males in New England were killed—making it the costliest war in American history (measured by the proportion of casualties to total population).

Bacon's Rebellion

Similar conflicts between colonists and Native Americans had been taking place in Virginia since the 1640s, but the situation there was complicated by internal problems among the colonists. These problems could be traced back to the founding of Jamestown in 1607 (see Chapter 4). The original leaders at Jamestown were English gentlemen (members of the nobility) of high social, economic, and educational standing. Within twenty years, however, this group had either gone back to England or died without leaving descendants to take their place. By the 1630s more rugged, self-made families had risen to positions of authority in Virginia. But, like the earlier leaders, they failed to pass their power on to the next generation. In the latter half of the seventeenth century, a third aristocracy began to emerge in Virginia: around 1650 sons

of influential English merchants and government officials began to settle in the colony.

This new wave of settlers was sent by the king of England, who wanted to gain more control of the colony. They were aristocrats whose families owned property or had made investments in the colony. Virginia had originally been owned by the Virginia Company (a group of investors based in London, England), but the colony had been controlled by the British government since 1624, when the Virginia Company declared bankruptcy (went out of business because of lack of funds). Although Virginia was not yet under a royal charter (direct rule of the English king), various monarchs had been trying to take advantage of the huge profits that could be made in Virginia, which was in the midst of a tobacco boom. (Tobacco was the principal crop in Virginia. A broadleaf plant grown in warm climates, tobacco was processed and then sold in Europe, where it was in great demand for smoking in pipes.) Tobacco planters had become quite prosperous and owned large tracts of land that produced high tax revenues for England. Within ten years the king's plan had succeeded, and a new elite that was favorable to the monarchy now dominated Virginia politics.

Berkeley causes crisis

But a crisis began building in 1670 when William Berkeley (1606–1677), the royal governor (the highest colonial official, appointed by the king), initiated the Franchise Act. This law gave voting rights only to landowners and people who owned houses. It also enabled Berkeley to appoint a royal council that would move to place the colony's wealth in the hands of a few well-to-do property owners. (The royal council was a committee appointed by the governor, with the approval of the king, that helped administer the colony.) He named this group the Green Spring faction, after his Virginia plantation. Before Berkeley had taken office ten years earlier, the Virginia assembly (House of Burgesses; the first representative government in America) and the royal council had formed a unified government. Now there was a deep division between social classes. Council members, who came from ruling families, were the governor's inner circle and exercised central authority. On the other side of the divide stood the majority of colonists, who were not part of the elite class. In an effort to maintain local representation, leaders from settlements throughout Virginia began to take seats in the House of Burgesses. This alarmed the Green Spring faction, who protested that the socially inferior assemblymen were unfit for governing.

Freed servants challenge social order

In the meantime, unrest had been developing on another level. By the mid-1600s a high percentage of Virginia's population was composed of male indentured servants (immigrants who signed a contract to work for a specific length of time) or former servants (see "Wage laborers" in Chapter 7). Most of them had no families—male servants outnumbered female servants by four or six to one. In addition, they were worked extremely hard by masters who were driven by the quest for wealth in a thriving tobacco industry (the death rate among servants was reportedly higher than 40 percent). Servants' lives generally did not change for the better if they survived long enough to gain freedom from their indenture contracts. They could rarely afford to buy farms, even though land was inexpensive, because they did not have enough money for surveyor's fees (payment for measuring and dividing the land), livestock, and equipment. As a result, only 6 percent of ex-servants became successful planters who employed their own workers. The majority were tenant farmers (farmers who rented land), overseers (supervisors), or laborers. Many lived on the frontier, and they had no role in Virginia society because they did not have the right to vote. They lived an aimless existence, spending their time drinking and having wild parties. Most colonists looked down on these people as socially inferior and a source of trouble, even danger, in the colony.

Conflicts arise on frontier

Despite these problems, the colony continued to grow (the population reached thirty thousand in 1670), and soon the borders of the settlement were encroaching on Native American territory. The rough, unruly frontier settlers did not get along with the native peoples, whom they often accused of stealing from their farms. One of the first serious incidents occurred in 1675, when members of the Doeg group killed an overseer. Afterward, Native American raids become more intense and frequent, often resulting in the death of colonists. The Virginia government responded by forming a militia (citizens' army) led by Colonel George Mason and Captain John Brent. When the militia attacked two Native American cabins, they did not realize that Susquehannock were inside, not Doegs. After killing fourteen Susquehannock, the militia continued their advance. Five Susquehannock chiefs immediately protested that the colonists had been killed by a Seneca war party, not by Susquehannock. The Virginians refused to believe them, claiming Susquehannock had recently been seen in the area, wearing the clothes of the white victims. The Virginians then executed the chiefs. In retaliation, the Native Americans launched more attacks. To avoid an outright war, Berkeley told Virginians not to cross the borders of the colony.

However, this measure was completely ineffective because colonists had already begun moving west onto native land. The fighting simply escalated, and raiding warrior parties killed many frontier colonists, including women and children. At this point Berkeley tried to end the conflict by declining to retaliate. But many Virginians protested, accusing him of trying to protect the fur trade with Native

Nathaniel Bacon confronts Virginia governor William Berkeley. Bacon accused Berkeley of not protecting colonists from Native American raids. *Reproduced by permission of The Granger Collection.*

Americans. They contended that the fur trade was more important to Berkeley because it ensured his support among

Nathaniel Bacon

Nathaniel Bacon was an unusual figure on the Virginia frontier. He was born into the English aristocracy and attended Cambridge University and Gray's Inn, a law school in London. After graduating he traveled throughout Europe. In 1673 he married Elizabeth Duke, daughter of nobleman Edward Duke. They emigrated to Virginia and settled at Curl's Neck in Henrico County, on the James River near the border of Native American territory. Because of Bacon's abilities and connections, he quickly gained influence in the colony. His uncle was a member of the royal council, which made it easy for the younger Bacon to gain a seat on the council as well. Being of a rebellious nature, Bacon set out to change the system as soon as he took office.

ley, they turned to Nathaniel Bacon (1647–1676).

Bacon becomes opposition leader

Bacon was one of the new settlers who belonged to the English upper class. Through his uncle, who was a member of the royal council, he had gained a council seat. He lived on the frontier, however, and he allied himself with the common people. He charged Berkeley with taking the side of Native Americans against Virginia farmers in the conflicts that were increasing at an alarming rate in outlying regions. Bacon then organized a group of frontiersmen, with reinforcements from the Ocaneechee tribe, to go against the Susquehannock in defiance of Berkeley. The newly formed militia immediately tracked down a group of Susquehannock and defeated them. Berkeley was furious with Bacon and declared him a traitor (one who betrays his government).

By now Berkeley had realized his government was in trouble. Therefore, in May 1676 he ordered new elections and issued a declaration defending his actions as governor and suggesting several measures to resolve the crisis. The assembly met in Jamestown on June 5 to act on Berkeley's proposals, which included three important features. First, he planned to pardon Bacon and give him a commission to raise a militia against Native Americans (see "The militia" in Chapter 6). Next, Berkeley wanted to draft a measure that permitted Virginians to

local wealthy merchants. Berkeley actually had another motive for keeping peace with Native Americans: English authorities wanted to Christianize them so that they could eventually obtain land in an orderly manner. The complicated situation only served to distance Berkeley even further from settlers, especially in Charles and Henrico counties. Frontiersmen in these outlying areas wanted to continue fighting to protect their property. Since they could get no support from Berke-

trade only with "friendly Indians." Finally, he planned to abolish the Franchise Act of 1670, thus restoring the vote to all freemen (former indentured servants who had gained their freedom), not just landowners.

Bacon organizes militia

The Virginia legislators approved all of Berkeley's proposals. Nevertheless, Bacon was dissatisfied because they planned to draw militia members from the entire colony, whereas Bacon wanted to use only men from the border territories. He felt they had a greater stake in the conflict and would be more willing to fight because they had farms in the area. Bacon also demanded that the militia be formed immediately, instead of waiting for three months until enough taxes had been collected to fund the operation. On June 23, 1676, Bacon led four hundred armed men up the steps of the Jamestown assembly hall. Bacon's Rebellion had begun. There was an immediate confrontation between the legislators and the militia, and Bacon threatened violence. After forcing the assembly to exempt (free or release from liability) him and his men from arrest for causing a disturbance, Bacon and the demonstrators eventually left the assembly hall. Berkeley was humiliated because the legislature had given in to Bacon's demands, so he once again declared Bacon a traitor. Berkeley also called up the colonial militia to oppose Bacon's men.

When Bacon and his men returned on July 30, they easily overcame the colonial militia and drove Berkeley out of Jamestown to his plantation on the eastern coast. This time Bacon carried with him a manifesto (statement) titled "In the Name of the People of Virginia," which accused Berkeley of committing numerous injustices. With Berkeley absent, Bacon controlled Jamestown. The governor sneaked back into town, however, while Bacon was leading his men out into the country to attack the Pamunkeys, another troublesome Native American tribe. On September 18, Bacon launched a final assault on Jamestown, burning the settlement to the ground. By now lawlessness reigned, and Berkeley fled once again as looters (robbers) ransacked his plantation at Green Spring.

Virginians hold divided opinions

Although Bacon claimed he had unanimous support for his actions, many Virginians denounced him. Among the most vocal critics of Bacon were colonists who lived on plantations along the coast, away from the frontier regions. They accused Bacon and his men of being troublemakers who were deliberately violating the law and provoking Native Americans so they could seize more land. And while Bacon did have widespread support, many Virginians continued to ally themselves with Berkeley. In 1676 the citizens of Gloucester County sent a letter to Berkeley pledging their continued support. They praised the governor "for securing our neighbors the frontiers of this country from the incursions of the barbarous Indians." Even though Bacon had also raised a militia to fight Native Americans, these citizens cited his lawlessness in requesting more resources from the county with orders "grounded, as he pretends, upon a commission from your Honor to be general of all the forces in Virginia against the Indians." They were most disturbed by the behavior of Bacon and his men, who "did in many places behave themselves very rudely both in words and actions." The crisis threatened to shake the foundations of Virginia government, as colonists were not only trying to fend off the Native Americans but were also pitted against one another in a struggle for power.

Bacon's Rebellion might have lasted longer if Bacon had not become ill and died the following October. After his death, Berkeley put down the insurrection, executing twenty-three of Bacon's men—in spite of a royal order pardoning all participants except Bacon. Berkeley finally gave up his position as governor to Colonel Herbert Jeffreys, who appointed a commission to investigate the uprising. The commission members mostly blamed Bacon and his ability to influence the leaderless frontiersmen.

Historians have long debated the impact of Bacon's Rebellion on colonial American life. In the nineteenth century many thought the insurrection was a bid for American independence from England and that Bacon was nearly equal in importance to George Washington, a revered leader in the American Revolution (1775–83; a conflict in which American colonists gained independence from British rule). Other scholars point out, however, that Bacon had no clear philosophy of liberation and was not fighting the English. They also suggest that the rebellion was mainly fueled by Bacon's desire for personal revenge against Berkeley. Therefore, because Bacon considered his own motives a priority over the interests of the colony, he is considered less of a hero. Some historians have even linked Bacon's Rebellion to the full-scale use of slavery in America. They note that after the insurrection, many plantation owners decided African slaves were easier to control than indentured servants.

Slavery

Slavery in North America began simply as a way to fill a labor shortage. In the early seventeenth century, African slaves were working on European plantations in the Caribbean, but slavery had existed in Africa long before Europeans started an international slave trade off the west coast of the continent in the fifteenth century. For hundreds of years Africans had taken members of other groups into slavery during wars or used slavery as punishment for crimes within their own groups. There were also enslaved craftsmen, warriors, and advisers to tribal chiefs and kings. While a small slave trade was conducted between Africa

An illustration of the first slaves arriving at Jamestown in 1619. The issue of slavery would later divide the country. *Reproduced by permission of A/P Wide World Photos.*

and Europe prior to the discovery of the Americas, it increased significantly when the Spaniards discovered that marketable products such as sugar could be grown on the Caribbean islands. Initially the Europeans used Native Americans as workers on sugar plantations, but they quickly died from European diseases. As a result, plantation owners turned to Africa for slaves. Even at its height, the slave trade was not well organized, nor was it controlled by Europeans, who found the African coast too unhealthy to settle. Instead, African traders sold other Africans. They took their captives from an area that stretched 3,000 miles south along the Senegambia River to the Congo River—a distance greater than that between present-day New York and California.

The first slaves in North America arrived at Jamestown in 1619 when a Dutch trader exchanged twenty slaves for provisions (a stock of food). Soon Africans were essential to the American plantation economy, and the slave trade became a booming business (see Chapter 7). After the mid-1600s slavery was legalized through a series of laws called slave codes (see

"Slave codes" in Chapter 6). Soon slaves were worth large sums of money, so even harsher laws gave owners the right to demand the return of runaways, who were considered "property." By 1720 a majority of slaves in the Chesapeake region (Virginia and Maryland) were American-born. Some slaves had even gained their freedom. In 1760, for instance, there were two thousand freed slaves (2 to 3 percent of the African American population) in Virginia, and in the northern colonies about 10 percent of the total African American population were freedmen.

All colonies use slaves

Although most slaves worked on southern tobacco and rice plantations, all of the colonies used slave laborers. Whether slavery caused racism (prejudice because of race) or racism caused slavery may never be fully determined, but Africans were generally considered inferior to white people. At first owners made an effort to keep slave families together. Gradually Africans lost these rights and, as slaves were routinely bought and sold, families were torn apart (see Chapter 9). Husbands and wives tended not to live together, and children were often sold at a young age since they decreased the amount of time their mothers could spend working. By the 1740s the majority of African slaves remained in bondage throughout their lives. The number of slaves in a colony depended on economic factors. In areas where slavery was most profitable, there were more Africans—for instance, they made up the majority of the population of South Carolina as early as 1708. Slaves had their own cabins in the South, whereas in the northern colonies they lived in cellars, attics, and sheds. Africans were frequently mistreated by white masters and overseers, who beat them for such infractions (violations) as not working hard enough or trying to run away.

Growing opposition to slavery

By the late 1600s European colonists were interacting with Africans on a daily basis, and many masters even regarded their slaves as part of their own families. Historians have noted some improvements in the quality of life for slaves during this period. The Society for the Propagation of the Gospel, a religious organization in New England, advocated the education of blacks (see "Church of England" in Chapter 11). Colonial leaders such as Massachusetts preacher Cotton Mather (1663–1728) taught Africans to read (see "Education of Africans" in Chapter 12). There were also a few isolated protests against slavery. The first was voiced in 1688 by Francis Pastorius (1651–c. 1720), a German-born Quaker (a member of a Christian Protestant group that advocated direct communication with God through an "inner light") who founded Germantown, Pennsylvania. In 1700 Samuel Sewall (1652–1730), a Massachusetts merchant and judge, published a pamphlet titled *The Selling of Joseph* in which he attacked slavery as being un-Christian. Yet racism and mistreatment of blacks was still prevalent throughout the colonies, and whites rarely questioned the morality of slavery—it was too essential to the economy.

Woolman starts abolitionist campaign

The movement against slavery did not gain momentum until nearly half a century later, when Quaker pastor John Woolman (1720–1772) set out on the first of thirty annual excursions to attend Quaker meetings (religious services). From his home in Mount Holly, New Jersey, he journeyed around New England and down to the Carolinas. Wherever he went—in both the South and the North—he encountered slavery, and he was deeply troubled by the sight of people being owned as property. Woolman therefore resolved to mount a vigorous abolitionist (antislavery) campaign as he made his annual trips. When he traveled in the South, he carried his message to slaveholders. In Rhode Island he tried to persuade shipowners not to transport slaves from Africa to North America. He refused to buy any products connected with the slave trade, and he would not accept hospitality from slave owners. Frequently he made payment for lodging directly to slaves rather than to their masters.

Especially disturbing to Woolman was the fact that Christians, and even Quakers, held Africans as slaves. In fact, in the 1720s, the Society of Friends (the official name of the Quaker group) had expelled at least one member who opposed the keeping of slaves. Finally

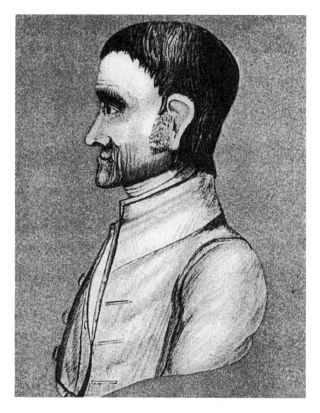

A drawing of Quaker pastor John Woolman, one of the earliest abolitionists in colonial America. *Reproduced by permission of The Granger Collection. Drawing by Robert Smith.*

he decided to limit his abolitionist efforts to the Quaker community, writing essays on social injustices for Quaker publications. One of those essays was *Some Considerations on the Keeping of Negroes,* which was published in 1754. It is considered the first published abolitionist statement in America.

Anti-Puritanism: The maypole of Merry Mount

The Puritans dominated all aspects of life in the New England

From *New English Caanan*

The following is an excerpt from Thomas Morton's *New English Caanan* describing a May Day celebration in Merry Mount. (May Day was a celebration held in England on May 1, in the tradition of the spring fertility rites of Egypt and India.)

> *They prepared to set up a Maypole upon the festival day of Philip and Jacob [saints in the Roman Catholic Church]; and brewed a barrel of excellent beer, and provided a case of bottles to be spent [drunk], with other good cheer, for all comers of that day. And because they would have it in a complete form, they had prepared a song fitting to the time and present occasion. And upon Mayday they brought the Maypole to the place appointed, with drums, guns, pistols, and other fitting instruments, for that purpose; and there erected it with the help of Savages [Native Americans], that came there to see the manner of our revels [festivities]. A goodly pine tree, eighty feet long, was reared up, with a pair of buck's horns nailed on, somewhat near unto the top of it: where it stood as a fair sea mark for directions; how to find out the way to my host of Merry-Mount [Morton was referring to himself].*
>
> *The setting up of this Maypole was a lamentable [regrettable] spectacle to the precise separatists that lived at new Plymouth. . . .*

Reprinted in: Colbert, David, ed. Eyewitness to America. New York: Pantheon Books, 1997, pp. 25–26.

instance, Puritans did not observe the holy days traditionally celebrated by the Catholic Church and the Church of England—not even Christmas (the celebration of the birth of Jesus of Nazareth) and Easter (the commemoration of Jesus's resurrection, or rising from the dead). They thought the Catholic Church had simply made up religious holidays to fit the dates of pagan (non-Christian) rituals so it would be easier to convert nonbelievers to Christianity. They also considered popular holidays such as May Day to be mere superstitions. (May Day was a celebration held in England on May 1, in the tradition of the spring fertility rites of Egypt and India.)

Morton enrages Puritans

Plymouth and Massachusetts Bay officials passed laws that prohibited any special observances of Christmas, Easter, and other holidays. They strictly enforced these laws by imposing stiff fines and other punishments on violators. As a result there were frequent conflicts between the Puritans and colonists who did not share their beliefs. The most famous was an incident at the town of Merry Mount in Massachusetts Bay. In 1627 Plymouth governor William Bradford (1590–1657; see Chapter 4) led a small party of Puritans into Merry Mount and disrupted a May Day celebration. The festivities had been organized by Thomas Morton (c. 1590–c. 1647), the leader of the town. Morton had long been a nuisance to the Puritans because he not only ridiculed their

colonies. Religious leaders controlled the government, establishing laws that all citizens had to observe. For

way of life but also encouraged rowdy behavior at a trading post he operated in Merry Mount.

Morton was an Englishman who arrived in New England in 1625 with a company headed by a Captain Wollaston. Wollaston founded a settlement called Mount Wollaston (now the city of Quincy, Massachusetts), and Morton set up a trading post, which he named Merry Mount. After Wollaston moved to Virginia, Morton took control of Mount Wollaston and renamed the town Merry Mount. He immediately had problems with the Puritans, particularly the Plymouth settlers, who lived nearby. Morton and his companions were Anglicans (members of the Church of England opposed by the Puritans) who engaged in all of the "sinful" activities prohibited by the Puritans. Plymouth citizens objected to Morton's trading post, where he sold whiskey, weapons, and ammunition to Native Americans in exchange for furs. Moreover, in violation of the law, he showed Native Americans how to use firearms. But the Puritans were especially troubled because he had interfered with their own fur trading. For instance, when the Plymouth settlers opened their first trade route in Maine in 1625, Morton followed them and established his own contacts with Native American traders.

Plymouth authorities claimed that Merry Mount undermined morality in New England. Bradford later wrote in his history of Plymouth, *Of Plymouth Plantation* (first published in 1857), that Merry Mount was a "den of iniquity [sin]." Morton's establishment attracted drunken carousers (people who drink liquor and engage in rowdy behavior) and men of questionable character—historians say it was a favorite meeting place for pirates (bandits who robbed ships at sea). Even worse, upright Christians came there to drink rum and often socialized with Native Americans.

Morton sets up maypole

Morton's troubles reached a peak on May Day 1627 when he built an eighty-foot maypole (a flower-wreathed pole that is the center of dancing and games) at Merry Mount and hosted a noisy celebration. Colonists and Native Americans enjoyed a day of drinking and dancing. The Puritans were furious because Morton was violating their law against the celebration of holidays.

Resolving to shut down Merry Mount, Puritan officials tried unsuccessfully to reason with Morton over the next several months. In 1628 a company of men led by Plymouth colonist Myles Standish (c. 1584–1656) arrested Morton, who managed to escape. He was soon recaptured and charged with selling guns to Native Americans. He was then deported (forced to leave a country) to England for trial. After Morton's departure John Endecott (1588–1665), the extremely stern governor of Massachusetts Bay (see Chapter 4), took over Merry Mount, chopped down the maypole, and changed the name of the town to Mount Dagon.

A depiction of the raising of the maypole during a May Day celebration at Thomas Morton's Merry Mount settlement. *Reproduced by permission of Corbis-Bettmann.*

Morton was finally acquitted (found innocent) of the charges in England, so he returned to Massachusetts. He resumed trading with the Native Americans and stirred up opposition to Endecott. In 1630 Morton was again arrested, more or less for being a public nuisance. Historians speculate that he may also have been a spy for Ferdinando Gorges (c. 1566–1647), head of the Council of New England (a private organization that promoted trade and settlement in New England), who wanted to make Massachusetts a royal colony. (A royal colony would be under the direct control of the English king. The Plymouth Colony and the Massachusetts Bay Company had been given private charters, or grants of land. They were permitted to form their own governments without interference from the king.)

New English Canaan becomes a classic

Before deporting Morton to England for the second time, Massachusetts authorities placed him in stocks (a device used for public punishment; see Chapter 6), took all of his property, and burned down his house. Morton was acquitted once again and remained in England for more than a decade. He worked as a legal counsel for Gorges, who was trying to revoke the charter of the Massachusetts Bay Company. In the mid-1630s Morton wrote *New English Canaan,* in which he encouraged others to seek their fortune in New England. ("Canaan" in the title refers to the Promised Land, or destined home, of the Israelites in the Christian Bible. Likewise, New England was the promised land of the Puritans, who sought religious and political freedom.) Yet he also ridiculed Puritan manners and narrow-mindedness, depicting the Native Americans as being more Christian than the Puritans. Morton was unknown at the time of his death in 1647, but *New English*

Canaan became a classic work of literature that influenced several American writers. Among them was Nathaniel Hawthorne (1804–1864), an author who was harshly critical of the Puritans. In addition to such tales as *The Scarlet Letter,* Hawthorne wrote "The Maypole of Merrymount," which was based on Morton's celebration.

The Salem witch trials

During the colonial period most people had little understanding of the natural environment, so they looked to supernatural forces (spirits) for explanations. To Native Americans, Africans, and some Europeans, magic and religion were inseparable. They believed that people with special powers (called priests, shamans, and witches by various groups) could control good and evil spirits with prayer and rituals. Shamans, priests, and witches used special objects called charms—bags of herbs, magical stones, crucifixes—to ward off evil spirits. One of their rituals was fortune-telling, predicting future events by "reading" the pattern of tea leaves in a cup, the shape of a raw egg dropped into a bowl, or the arrangement of special pebbles thrown onto the ground.

Shamans, priests, and witches also used their powers to ward off diseases. Before the introduction of modern medicine, people understandably dreaded sickness and injury. Native Americans, Africans, and Europeans alike believed illness and death came from spiritual as well as natural causes.

Thus they called upon healers, or "white" (good) witches, who combined charms with medicinal roots, barks, and herbs to produce cures. Yet other rituals were also called into play. If a cow was going dry (producing less milk), for instance, a European might pour milk over a red-hot iron poker while repeating the names of the Trinity (a Christian concept of God as the Father, Son, and Holy Spirit). Freckles might be removed by washing one's face with cobwebs.

Witchcraft practices feared

Good spirits were relied upon to influence events. Native American priests were believed to instill the spirits of animals into young warriors to protect them in battle. Africans conjured up the spirits of gods who guided them in their religious ceremonies. On the other hand, evil spirits were greatly feared. Europeans believed that a "black" witch could control the thoughts and actions of others for evil purposes. In fact, to most believers in magic the word "witch" usually meant an evil sorcerer (a person who uses power gained from the assistance or control of evil spirits) or sorceress. Native Americans were more apt to blame evil spirits in general or an enemy in particular for their problems. Africans believed that the spirits of evil witches left them while they were asleep and entered the bodies of animals. The bewitched animals then fled to a meeting with other witches and consumed a human soul, thus killing the soul's owner.

Europeans tended to single out a particular person, usually an old woman, and accused her of making a covenant with the devil to cause all manner of trouble among good people. They believed that witches flew through the air to engage in orgies (sexual encounters involving many people) with the devil. American colonists believed that a witch (again, usually a woman) signed a pact with the devil in order to seek revenge on a neighbor or an enemy. For example, a witch could cause the death of a child, produce crop failures, or prevent cream from being turned into butter. It was also believed that witches could enter the bodies of animals and prowl around undetected.

Hysteria reaches peak in Salem

People were convinced that witches could be detected. One way was to make a "witch's cake" from grain mixed with a substance from a bewitched victim's body, such as urine, and bake it in ashes. The cake could then be fed to a familiar, which would reveal the name of the witch who had cast the spell. Another way to identify a witch was to find out whether the suspect poked pins into a rag doll or a clay model of a victim to work her magic. People suspected of practicing witchcraft would be given the chance to confess their sins and renounce (give up) their covenant with the Devil. By thus opening themselves to God, they could rejoin the community.

The glaring exception was the witchcraft hysteria that erupted in

"A Brand Pluck'd out of the Burning"

In 1692 Cotton Mather wrote an essay titled "A Brand Pluck'd out of the Burning," in which he described the possession of a young woman named Mercy Short. After taking her into his home, Mather observed one of her fits and conversations with evil spirits:

> Her Discourses [conversations] to Them [evil spirits] were some of the most Surprising Things imaginable, and incredibly beyond what might have been expected, from one of her small Education or Experience. In the Times of her Tortures, Little came from her, besides direful [desperate] Shrieks, which were indeed so frightful, as to make many people Quitt [leave] the Room. Only now and then any Expressions of marvellous Constancy [steadiness] would bee heard from her; [for instance] "Tho' you kill mee, I'll never do what you would have mee.—Do what you will, yett with the Help of Christ, I'll never touch your Book.—Do, Burn mee then, if you will; Better Burn here, than Burn in Hell." But when her Torturer went off, Then t'was that her senses being still detained in a Captivity to the Spectres [spirits], as the only object of them. Wee were Ear-witnesses to Disputacions [disputations; arguments] that amazed us. Indeed Wee could not hear what They said unto her; nor could shee herself hear them ordinarily without causing them to say over again: But Wee could Hear Her Answers, and from her Answers Wee could usually gather the Tenour [tenor; meaning] of Their Assaults.

Reprinted in: Burr, George Lincoln, ed. Narratives of the Witchcraft Cases: 1648–1706. New York: Barnes & Noble, 1946.

Salem Village in the Massachusetts Bay Colony. During the winter of 1691 to 1692, a group of young girls got together to read their fortunes. Most of them worked as servants, but one was Elizabeth Parris, the daughter of the local Puritan minister. She knew that Puritans strictly forbade trying to predict God's will through magic. Nevertheless she participated in the ritual, which involved dropping a raw egg white into a bowl and then "reading" the future from its shape. As the girls watched in horror, the egg white took the form of a coffin (a sign of death). Elizabeth instantly felt as if someone was pinching and suffocating her; she then began to hallucinate (see things or people that do not exist). The other girls were seized by the same sensations, so doctors were called to examine them. Finding nothing physically wrong, the doctors suggested the symptoms had been caused by witchcraft.

Puritans seek culprits

In an effort to track down the witch who had cast a spell on the girls, a concerned neighbor asked the Parris' Caribbean slave, Tituba, to bake a witch cake. Yet the cake did not reveal the culprit. Finally the girls "con-

A man helps an alleged witchcraft victim during the infamous Salem witch trials in Massachusetts. *Reproduced by permission of The Library of Congress.*

fessed" that they had been bewitched by Tituba and two old women in the village. By April the girls were identifying others as witches, including a former minister, and soon accusations were flying around the colony. By the time the hysteria finally died down, 156 suspected witches were in prison. Thus began one of the most infamous events in American history: the Salem witch trials. The trials violated many proper legal procedures. For instance, the judges were not trained lawyers, and suspects were not allowed to have attorneys. The court also accepted "spectral evidence"—that is, an accuser's claim that a specter (spirit) resembling the "witch" had committed evil deeds. Since the Puritans believed such a specter could be seen only by the victim, other witnesses could not prove whether the accusations were true or false.

Leaders hold trials

In June 1692 Puritan leaders decided to appoint a special court to try the suspected witches. By this time witch hysteria had been sweeping Europe for more than 250 years, and fear of witches had been mounting in

New England for several decades. In 1684 Increase Mather (1639–1723), a Puritan clergyman and well-known intellectual, had published *Remarkable Providences.* The book was a collection of "proofs of witchcraft," which Mather had found in works by other writers. Mather and his son Cotton actively promoted the Salem witch trials. In 1689 Cotton Mather published *Memorable Providences Relating to Witchcraft and Possession,* which stirred up antiwitch mania. Four years later he wrote *Wonders of the Invisible World,* in which he defended the trials as the only way to rid the colony of the devil's influence.

Judges plagued by doubts

The Salem witch trials resulted in hundreds of accusations, more than one hundred guilty verdicts, and the executions of twenty persons, mostly women. Nineteen people were hanged for refusing to give confessions, four died in prison, and, as judge Samuel Sewall noted, one man was crushed to death with stones during questioning. Within a year Puritan ministers were expressing grave doubts about the trials. Foremost among them was Increase Mather, who wrote *Cases of Conscience Concerning Evil Spirits* (1693), in which he attacked the use of spectral evidence. Cotton Mather also changed his mind, eventually supporting his father's view that the witch hunts had been unjustified. By 1697 Massachusetts officials concluded that the trials had been a terrible mistake. The governor pardoned all condemned prisoners, and the legislature designated January 14 as a special day of atonement (expression of regret and request for forgiveness). Sewall had also begun to regret the role he played in the tragedy, so he wrote an admission of error and guilt. On January 14, 1697, he stood in front of the congregation in the Old South Church in Boston as the Reverend Samuel Willard read the statement aloud.

Why did it happen?

Historians suggest that the Salem witch furor was unleashed because the Puritans were afraid their way of life was coming to an end. In 1684 the Massachusetts Bay Colony lost its charter (see Chapter 4), which had allowed the Puritans to wield absolute power through self-government. The new charter of 1691 brought the colony under the control of the English monarchy. It required Puritans to share votes and public offices with Anglicans (members of the Church of England), whom they hated and feared. Since Puritans genuinely believed that good and evil spirits fought for human souls, they thought witches were moving among them and causing evil events, such as the loss of the charter.

Scholars have analyzed the Salem community for patterns of witchcraft accusations. They found that the majority of accusers were social outsiders. Many came from rural Salem Village, and a third of the accusations originated from members of a single family, named Putnam. Suspected witches were generally prosperous older women who were unmarried

"the blame and shame of it"

Samuel Sewall regretted his participation as a judge in the Salem witch trials of 1692 and 1693. On January 14, 1697—a special day of atonement set aside by the Massachusetts legislature—Sewall stood and faced the congregation in the Old South Church in Boston. The Reverend Samuel Willard then read aloud this statement Sewall had written:

> Samuel Sewall, sensible of the reiterated [repeated] strokes of God upon himself and his family; and being sensible, that as to the guilt contracted, upon the opening of the late Commission of Oyer and Terminator [the court that conducted the witchcraft trials] at Salem (to which the order for this day relates), he is, upon many accounts, more concerned than any that he knows of, desires to take the blame and shame of it, asking pardon of men, and especially desiring prayers that God, who has an unlimited authority, would pardon that sin and all his other sins; personal and relative: And according to his infinite benignity [kindness], and sovereignty [supreme power], not visit the sin of him, or of any other, upon himself or any of his, nor upon the land: But that He [God] would powerfully defend him against all temptations to sin, for the future; and vouchsafe him the efficacious [having the power to produce a desired effect], saving conduct of his word and spirit.

Reprinted in: Gunn, Giles, ed. *Early American Writing*. New York: Penguin Books, 1994, pp. 246–47.

and childless and who lived in Salem Town, the commercial center of the area. Many of the young girls who made accusations had lost a parent in Native American raids and worked as servants around Salem. Superstitions about evil spirits did not disappear in the American colonies after the miscarriage of justice at Salem. Accusations of witchcraft continued to surface until the early eighteenth century.

Religious dissent: The Anne Hutchinson trial

Massachusetts Bay was founded as an ideal Puritan community, yet the colony was soon torn apart by religious dissension (opposition to the church). Although religion and government were supposedly separate, only men who were members of the church could vote or hold office. The Puritans expected some debate, but they would not tolerate views that threatened the religious harmony of the colony. A few years after the initial settlement of Massachusetts Bay, several dissidents (those who oppose established authority) engaged in activities that undermined Puritan society. One of the most prominent was Puritan minister Roger Williams (1603?–1683), who advocated the complete separation of church and state. He argued that religion was corrupted by any government interference in spiritual affairs. In his view, magistrates (officials who administer laws) should have no power to enforce church doctrine (system of belief).

Williams went even further by challenging the legal basis of the colony itself. He claimed that the English king, Charles I (1600–1649), had had no right to grant a charter for the founding of Salem in 1629 because the land belonged to the Native Americans who lived there. After a prolonged struggle with Puritan officials, Williams was banished from (forced to leave) Massachusetts Bay. He then founded and governed Rhode Island, the first American colony to be based on the separation of church and state. Williams also left the Puritan church and started the first Baptist church in the American colonies. (Baptist is a shortened form of Anabaptists, a Christian group that believed infants should not be baptized, or inducted into the Christian faith through immersion in water; see "Baptists" in Chapter 11.)

Hutchinson accepts covenant of grace

Another famous dissident was Anne Marbury Hutchinson (1591–1643), who moved to Massachusetts Bay in 1636. Before emigrating to America she attended St. Botolph's Church, where John Cotton (1585–1652) was the minister. Cotton was attempting to modify Puritan teachings, mainly the belief that salvation (being saved from sin) could be earned only through good works (moral behavior). This was known to many as the covenant of works, one of many covenants that Puritans used as the basis of their society (see "Puritanism" in Chapter 11). Hutchinson was especially inspired by Cotton's emphasis on the covenant of grace rather than the covenant of works. According to the covenant of grace, a Christian believer could gain salvation through revelation (direct communication with God). This doctrine became popular because it freed people from having to conduct good works in order to be saved from sin. Cotton insisted, however, that his followers continue doing good works whether or not they had received revelations from God. Hutchinson took the idea much further.

Hutchinson believed that Christians who had achieved grace actually became the spirit of God. Therefore, according to Hutchinson, the covenant of grace made the covenant of works unnecessary. That is, if people had this special connection with God, they did not have to do good works to show that they had been saved. Hutchinson embraced the covenant of grace after the deaths of two of her daughters in 1630 and the later death of her father. She claimed to have received revelations from God during these experiences. Therefore, according to the covenant of grace, she was still saved despite the tragedies in her life. (Puritans believed that if they suffered misfortune they had done something to offend God and had to gain his forgiveness by doing good works. Hutchinson believed that if they had already been saved, however,

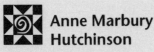

Anne Marbury Hutchinson

Anne Marbury Hutchinson was born in Alford, England, the oldest of thirteen children of Anglican clergyman Francis Marbury and his second wife, Bridget Dryden Marbury. Before Anne's birth Francis Marbury was imprisoned twice for rejecting church doctrine. Anne was baptized in the Anglican faith and received an education far superior to that provided to most young women in the seventeenth century. From an early age she was exposed to religious discussions in her home, and she became familiar with church doctrine and Scripture (passages from the Bible). She was also influenced by her father's rebellious spirit and his contempt for authority. In 1605 the family moved from Alford to London. Anne lived in London until 1612, when she married William Hutchinson, an affluent businessman.

they could not be held responsible for misfortunes that befell them.)

Holds religious meetings

In 1633 Cotton was forced out of his ministry because of his views. He then fled to the Massachusetts Bay Colony and took a position at the Puritan church in Boston. Soon afterward Hutchinson announced to her family that God had instructed her to follow Cotton to Massachusetts. Her husband

had always supported her religious beliefs, so a year later the Hutchinsons left England onboard the ship *Griffin*. In September 1634 they arrived in Boston, where William Hutchinson entered into the textile (fabric) trade. He eventually became quite successful, and the family occupied a prominent position in the community. Anne Hutchinson's kind manner and her skills as a midwife (a person who assists women in childbirth) made her popular with affluent Boston women. During this time she became aware of the Massachusetts Puritans' belief in the covenant of works.

Determined to promote the covenant of grace, Hutchinson held private meetings for both men and women in her home. These gatherings usually began with a calm discussion of Cotton's sermons. Then, because Hutchinson possessed an intense intellect, people asked her to explain some of the more confusing aspects of Puritan doctrine. Finally, her religious fervor would take over, and she often became careless in advancing her own ideas and labeling them as Cotton's. Before long, Hutchinson had many followers who believed in her version of the covenant of grace.

Opposes Puritan ministers

Hutchinson conducted her meetings without interruption until 1635, when the prominent Puritan clergyman John Wilson returned to Boston from England. Hutchinson became increasingly troubled by Wilson's sermons, so she informed her followers that he was simply preaching another version of the covenant of works. Then she announced that most Massachusetts clergymen were promoting this doctrine. The only exceptions, she said, were Cotton and her brother-in-law, John Wheelwright (1592?–1679), who both preached the covenant of grace. Soon Hutchinson had created a division between her followers and traditional Puritans, who charged that she was committing a form of heresy (a religious opinion contrary to church teachings) called antinomianism. Antinomianism was the belief that God had predetermined who would be saved from sin, so all people—including ministers—were powerless to change the situation by doing good works. Puritan leaders were especially angry because Hutchinson was challenging their authority to decide who was worthy of salvation. The rift rapidly spread throughout the entire colony, becoming a serious threat in 1637, when her male followers refused to fight in the Pequot War.

Put on trial

Although Hutchinson was the principal agitator (one who stirs up public feeling) in the Puritan conflict, she was not the first to be punished. In March 1637 Wheelwright was brought before the Massachusetts General Court and charged with sedition (resistance to lawful authority). It was not until September 1637 that a church synod (advisory council) finally condemned Hutchinson for her religious beliefs. By this time, she had lost much

An illustration of Anne Hutchinson preaching at her house in Boston, Massachusetts. Hutchinson was later brought to trial on charges of heresy because her teachings challenged the authority of Puritan leaders.
Reproduced by permission of The Library of Congress.

From the Heresy Trial of Anne Hutchinson

Court: . . . what say you to your weekly public meetings? Can you show a warrant for them?

Hutchinson: I will show you how I took it up, there were such meetings in use before I came, and because I went to none of them, this was the special reason of my taking up this course, we began it but with five or six, and though it grew to more in future time, yet being tolerated at the first, I knew not why it might not continue.

Court: There were private meetings indeed, and are still in many places, of some few neighbours, but not so public and frequent as yours, and are of use for increase of love, and mutual edification [learning], but yours are of another nature, if they had been such as yours they had been evil, and therefore no good warrant to justify yours; but answer by what authority, or rule, you uphold them.

Hutchinson: . . . where the elder women are to teach the younger.

Court: So we allow you to do . . . privately, and upon occasion, but that gives no warrant of such set meetings for that purpose; and besides, you take upon you to teach many that are elder than yourself, neither do you teach them that which the Apostle commands [namely] to keep at home.

Hutchinson: Will you please to give me a rule against it, and I will yield?

Court: You must have a rule for it, or else you cannot do it in faith, yet you have a plain rule against it; I permit not a woman to teach.

Hutchinson: That is meant of teaching men.

Court: If a man in distress of conscience or other temptation . . . should come and ask your counsel in private, might you not teach him?

Hutchinson: Yes.

Court: Then it is clear, that it is not meant of teaching men, but of teaching in public.

Hutchinson: It is said, I will pour my Spirit upon your Daughters, and they shall prophesie . . . If God give me a gift of Prophecy, I may use it.

Reprinted in: Kupperman, Karen Ordahl, ed. Major Problems in American Colonial History. *Lexington, Mass.: D.C. Heath and Company, 1993, pp. 159–61.*

of her support. After John Winthrop (1588–1649), an especially stern Puritan, was reelected governor, several of Hutchinson's followers were removed from public office. Cotton even sided with church officials after making sure he would not be in trouble himself for teaching the covenant of grace. Wheelwright, Hutchinson's only remaining ally, was banished from the colony in November 1637.

Soon after Wheelwright was banished, Hutchinson was brought before the General Court and accused of defying the teachings of Puritan ministers. She was also charged with violating laws that forbade her, as a woman, to speak in public and to teach men or people older than herself. At one point during the trial, Hutchinson was nearly cleared of all charges. Then she announced that she had received a direct revelation from God. This was clearly a heretical claim because Puritan leaders believed that God spoke to humans only through the Bible. The frightened judges immediately ruled that Hutchinson was to be banished from the colony. She would be allowed to remain through the winter, but she was to be placed in the custody of deputy Joseph Weld of Roxbury. Despite Weld's attempts to persuade her to repent (express regret for her behavior), Hutchinson continued to speak out against the church.

Banished from colony

When Hutchinson was brought to trial again in March 1638, she failed to convince the judges that she had genuinely repented. She was therefore formally excommunicated (banished) from the church. Hutchinson left Massachusetts with her family and joined her husband at a settlement on the island of Aquidneck in Narragansett Bay, off the coast of Roger Williams's Rhode Island colony. She was followed by more than eighty families of supporters who had also been excommunicated. After William Hutchinson died in 1642, Anne Hutchinson moved with her six youngest children to the Dutch colony of New Netherland (now New York). They settled in Pelham Bay Park (now the Bronx section of New York City, near the Hutchinson River, which was named for Anne Hutchinson). The following year Hutchinson and five of her children were attacked and killed by Native Americans.

Nathaniel Hawthorne, the great nineteenth-century American writer—and a harsh critic of Puritan society—used Hutchinson as the model for the character Hester Prynne in *The Scarlet Letter* (1850). Now a classic in American literature, *The Scarlet Letter* tells the story of Prynne, a woman who has a child without being married and is forced to wear the red letter "A" at all times as a sign of her sin.

Government and Law

6

uropeans brought Old World government and legal tradi- tions with them when they settled in North America. There they were confronted with the challenge of transplanting European systems to a strange environment populated by native peoples who did not share European cultural experi- ences. In the early 1600s, France, the Netherlands (Holland), and England were all governing colonies in North America. By the turn of the eighteenth century, however, England domi- nated the territory that would become the United States.

French, Spanish, and Dutch colonies

The presence of the French and the English, along with the resistance of Native Americans, had prevented the Spanish from moving beyond the "borderlands"—the Southeast (pre- sent-day Florida and Alabama) and the Southwest (present-day New Mexico, Arizona, and Texas). France was operating a thriving colony in New France (present-day Canada), and French missionaries (people who do religious work in foreign countries) had founded settlements around the lower Great

No Separation of Church and State

The modern idea of the separation of church and state was nowhere to be found in any of the early European colonies. Churches were actively involved in colonizing North America. French and Spanish settlements were based on missions established by Catholic religious orders, and the Dutch Reformed Church was the official religion in New Netherland. Nearly all of the early English colonies had an official church. For instance, the Church of England (also known as Anglicanism) was instituted in all royal colonies. The New England colonies, however, were heavily influenced by Puritans and usually established the Puritan church. After the English took over New Netherland in 1664, the colony had two established churches, the Dutch Reformed and Anglican.

Some colonists rejected official churches. For instance, the founders of Rhode Island had left Massachusetts because they disliked the Puritans' intolerant attitude toward religious dissenters (those who opposed the church). Therefore, Rhode Island had no official church. Pennsylvania was created in part as a refuge for Quakers, who had been persecuted by both Anglicans and Puritans in England, so Pennsylvania also did not have an official church. Some Anglican colonies, such as Georgia and North Carolina, had so few Anglicans that they tolerated other religious groups.

Lakes and along the Mississippi River valley to the Gulf of Mexico. Yet the English had kept the French confined to areas outside the borders of English colonies. The Dutch founded the New Netherland colony in 1624, but the English took it over and renamed it New York forty years later. At the end of the colonial period, England governed the thirteen American colonies: Virginia, Massachusetts, Maryland, Connecticut, Rhode Island, New York, Delaware, New Hampshire, Pennsylvania, New Jersey, North Carolina, South Carolina, and Georgia.

The Spanish

After conquering rich Native American empires in South America and Mexico (then called New Spain), the Spanish expanded their search for gold and silver farther north (see Chapter 2). They founded the first permanent European settlement in what would become the United States, at Saint Augustine, Florida, in 1565, and Franciscan friars (priests belonging to the order of Saint Francis of Assisi) began a large-scale missionary effort. By 1655 the Franciscans had created a chain of missions (churches surrounded by settlements and often towns) in the region the Spanish called La Florida, from south of Saint Augustine northward to South Carolina and westward to present-day Alabama. In the 1630s Spanish colonies of the Southwest were inhabited by 250 Spaniards, 750 Native Americans, and about 24 Franciscan friars who served 25 missions.

Military government Spanish colonies were governed by the viceroy (representative of the king) of New Spain, whose headquarters were in Mexico City. The other two parts of the government were the *audiencias* (appeals court) and the Catholic Church (a Christian faith based in Rome, Italy, and headed by a pope). The viceroy supervised all military and governmental functions, including appointing governors of provinces (local regions) such as New Mexico, Texas, and Saint Augustine. New Mexico was headed by a military governor based in Santa Fe, who appointed *alcaldes* (administrators) to govern the larger towns. Although Texas was sparsely settled, it also had a governor and administrators. Saint Augustine was organized along more traditional Spanish lines. When Pedro Menéndez de Avilés founded the city, he assembled a *cabildo* (council), which collected taxes and distributed lots for houses. Other offices included the treasurer, an accountant, and garrison supervisors.

Pedro Menéndez de Avilés, founder of Saint Augustine, Florida. *Reproduced by permission of The Library of Congress.*

In theory the three levels of government—the viceroy, the courts, and the church—were supposed to work together, but they were frequently involved in disputes over authority. Conflicts most often occurred between the viceroy and the church. This confusion was partly intentional; government officials in Spain believed that if responsibilities overlapped, no single agency would become too powerful. But another reason was that the system reflected the Spanish monarchy itself: the monarch was seen as both a ruler and a vicar (representative) of Christ, so government and religion were nearly inseparable.

New Mexico was a typical example. Franciscan friars first moved into New Mexico in 1581. Their positive reports prompted the king to award a *capitulacion* (charter) to military leader Don Juan de Oñate in 1595 to conquer the region for Spanish settlement, which he did in 1598. In the years that followed, the Franciscans had the upper hand and the military served largely to enforce their influence with settlers and Native Americans. The result was a nearly theocratic state (government ruled by the church), until the Spanish were temporarily driven out of New Mexico during the Pueblo Revolt of 1680 (see Chapter 2).

Laws not enforced A distinctive feature of Spanish colonization in the Southwest was a land grant called an *encomienda,* which was used to establish ranches (large farms). Oñate awarded these grants to the conquistadors (conquerors) who invaded New Mexico. *Encomiendas* could be inherited for up to two generations, but the ranches could be inherited indefinitely and became the basis of many large estates. An *encomienda* entitled the recipient not only to use the land but also to receive tribute (payment) from people who lived on the land. The first *encomiendas* were unregulated, and as a result many *encomenderos* (landowners) enslaved Native Americans and forced them to pay large tributes. Although this practice was against the law, governors and *alcaldes* often had little incentive to enforce it because the *encomenderos* were very powerful men. Consequently, after more than eighty years of mistreatment, the Pueblo tribe drove the Spanish out of the Southwest.

Spanish plans for acquiring more territory in North America were eventually weakened by ineffective government. The Spanish monarchy was primarily interested in Spain's holdings in the Caribbean, where plantation owners were making huge profits from rum and sugar and slave traders were doing a booming business. Therefore governors in North America had virtually no contact with Spain, and their link with the viceroy's office in Mexico City was not much better. Settlements in La Florida and the Southwest were in constant danger of being attacked by Native Americans, and they could not count on support from Mexico. In the case of Saint Augustine, soldiers and settlers were not even supplied with enough food.

French colonies

The French were attracted to the New World (a European term for North and South America) by the prospect of a profitable fur trade in the Saint Lawrence River valley and the Great Lakes region, along the borders of Canada and New York (see Chapter 3). Like Spain, France also sought to spread Roman Catholicism among the Native Americans. In the early 1600s French interests in North America were chiefly in the hands of explorers like Samuel de Champlain (c. 1567–1635) and the Company of New France, which possessed a royal monopoly on the fur trade (see Chapter 3). However, in the 1660s New France became a royal colony (under direct rule of the king), with an appointed governor, an army, and an order to increase profits from the fur trade.

Leaders share power Power in New France was shared among the governor, a judge called an "intendant," and a bishop. The governor was responsible for military and Native American affairs, and the judge presided over the legal system. The bishop was the representative of the Catholic Church. The governor, intendant, bishop, and several other officials formed the Sovereign Council. The council was based in Quebec (the capital of New France) and served as the highest court in New France. The local courts handled most legal matters, while appeals (requests for new trials) were heard by royal courts at Montreal, Quebec, and Trois-Rivières. Royal court decisions could be appealed to the Sovereign Council. Some wealthy colonists appealed all the way to the Counseil de Parties, France's highest court, in Paris. Consequently, the upper classes had a significant legal advantage over less-prosperous citizens.

Courts and punishments Lawyers were not highly regarded in France, and New France outlawed them altogether. The intendant was trained in law, but notaries (officials who process legal documents) handled most routine legal matters at the local level. In court people represented themselves, and witnesses were paid for their appearances, the fee varying according to their social rank. Though their testimony could be challenged, they could not be cross-examined. French law allowed the accused to be interrogated and under some circumstances even tortured.

Punishments for convicted criminals varied widely. Executions were rare but could be inflicted through hanging, beheading (for

Torture Boots

French law allowed an accused criminal to be interrogated and under some circumstances even tortured. In France torture usually involved pouring water into the mouth of the accused. In New France "torture boots" (wooden slats) were tied to the prisoner's legs and then wedges were driven between the wood and the flesh. Three physicians were required to be in attendance when this method was used, but the rule was not rigorously obeyed. Any confession obtained under torture became invalid if the prisoner did not confirm it after he or she had recovered. The practice could be used only under strict circumstances, and only eight men are known to have been tortured in New France.

nobles), or being broken on the rack (a device that stretched the body). From 1665 until 1763 only eighty-five persons were executed in New France. Hangings were not popular among colonists, and they were not nearly the public spectacles they were in England and its colonies. Indeed, workers tried to avoid constructing the gallows (a structure used for hanging) or removing the corpse afterward. The stocks (a wooden frame with holes for the hands, feet, and head) and lashing with a whip were infrequently used. Theft or breaking and entering might be punished by banishment (forced removal) or service on a king's galley (ship). Branding with a fleur-de-lis (lily; the official symbol of France) was another punishment that was not only painful but also served to permanently identify a convicted criminal.

Illinois village governments In the late 1600s the French explored the Mississippi River valley and established villages in what came to be known as *le pays des Illinois* (Illinois country) and Louisiana. The villages of Kaskaskia, Cahokia, Fort de Chartres, Saint Philippe, Prairie de Rocher, and Sainte Genevieve never had large populations, and until 1718 they were controlled by the government in New France. After that they were technically under the jurisdiction of Louisiana. The government of the province of Illinois then consisted of a council made up of the commander of the fort, military officers, and officials of the Company of the Indies. (The company had been given a monopoly over land in Illinois and Louisiana.) In 1721 the territory became a military district. Villagers elected a syndic (representative) who represented the village in lawsuits and took on such responsibilities as fencing the commons (a grassy area in the middle of the village). Local decisions were discussed in a public outdoor meeting of all males over the age of fourteen. Widows also frequently attended the meetings. This group decided when to plant and harvest crops, build and mark roads, and repair fences.

Dual leadership in Louisiana Louisiana had a slower start than Illinois. In 1710 the king appointed military leader Antoine de la Mothe, sieur de Cadillac (1658–1730) as governor. A second official, called a *commissaire ordonnateur,* was in charge of financial and commercial affairs and the administration of justice. The king also appointed a judicial council called the Superior Council, which handled court cases. The division of responsibility between the governor and the *commissaire* caused problems because the two men were often jealous of each other. In 1719 the Company of the Indies embarked on a failed effort to make a profit by attracting thousands of immigrants to the Louisiana territory (see "Mississippi Bubble" box in Chapter 3). In 1731 the company turned Louisiana over to the French government.

French efforts to acquire more territory were halted by the English. Like the Spanish, the French played no active role in the development of the thirteen American colonies. Nevertheless they posed a continuing obstacle to the English's westward expansion, sparking decades of conflicts called the French and Indian War (1689–1763). At the end of this war, the Treaty of Paris (1763) gave control of New France and all territory east of the Mississippi River to the British, thus ending the French presence in North America. In the Treaty of Fontainebleau (1762), however, France had secretly given the area west of the Mississippi and the "Isle of Orleans" to Spain to prevent the British from gaining control of the entire Louisiana territory.

Dutch New Netherland

The Dutch were also attracted to North America by the fur trade. In 1624 the Dutch West India Company founded the New Netherland colony at the mouth of the Hudson River and on Manhattan Island. The privately owned company controlled New Netherland, so the government (headed by the company director) was loosely structured and plagued by weakness from the outset. Investors were mainly concerned with maintaining some order and concentrated most of their energies on profiting from the fur trade. Within five years the colony had two directors who showed little talent for governing. In 1629 the Dutch West India Company attempted to form a central government and increase settlement by opening the colony to wealthy investors, known as patroons. The patroons were granted lands, required to bring in tenants, and permitted to enter the fur trade. The only successful patroonship (estate) was Rensselaerswyck, near present-day Albany, New York. Rensselaerswyck had its own government, with commissioners, a director, and a court.

In 1640, under pressure from the Dutch government, the company allowed New Netherland villages to nominate magistrates (justices of the peace) from which the company director would choose one to appoint. English settlers from New England took advantage of this freedom and petitioned the Dutch for town sites. The Dutch, however, had to be encouraged to come together as villagers. Eventually they nominated two types of town

A portrait of Peter Stuyvesant, governor of New Netherland. *Reproduced by permission of The Library of Congress.*

officials, the *schouts* (magistrates) and a *schepen* (sheriff). In the meantime the Dutch West India Company still had problems finding a capable director. Finally, in 1647, they appointed Peter Stuyvesant (1610–1672) as director general (see Chapter 4). Faced with financial problems and the difficult task of controlling numerous ethnic groups, Stuyvesant gave himself and his council absolute power. Although he managed to conquer the neighboring colony of New Sweden (settled in 1638 by Swedes and Finns), his seventeen-year tenure as governor ended in

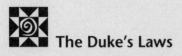

The Duke's Laws

The English were confronted with a delicate situation when they took over New Netherland and established the colony of New York in 1664. Specifically, they had to govern their new subjects without alienating them. The English also had to become accustomed to Dutch laws. Prior to 1664 the Dutch had developed burgomaster (mayor's) courts, which were awkward for the English because they had a country system headed by appointed officials. To ease the transition, in 1665 the new governor, Richard Nicholls, initiated the Duke's Laws (named for the English proprietor James, the Duke of York; later King James II). Under the laws Nicholls agreed to preserve the authority of the Dutch courts, and in return Dutch citizens swore allegiance to the English king. In areas settled by English Puritans, Nicholls created county courts like those in Massachusetts. Prominent Dutch and English politicians received enormous land grants on both sides of the Hudson River, and they were allowed to administer their own courts. For several decades two different legal systems operated in New York, but tensions did not ease between Dutch and English colonists. The Dutch who gained economically from the new government allied with the English, but less well-off Dutch residents felt left out.

disaster. In 1664 the English defeated the Netherlands in the Second Anglo-Dutch War. As part of the peace treaty, England claimed rights to the land occupied by New Netherland. New Netherland was renamed New York, and former New Sweden holdings eventually became the colonies of Delaware and New Jersey.

English colonies take diverse forms of government

While Spain, France, and the Netherlands were settling in North America, England was establishing colonies along the Atlantic coast. By the early 1700s the English controlled all thirteen colonies in three main regions: New England (Massachusetts, Connecticut, Rhode Island, and New Hampshire), the mid-Atlantic (New York, Delaware, Pennsylvania, and New Jersey), and the South (Virginia, Maryland, North Carolina, South Carolina, and Georgia). Governments were based on charters (land grants and governing contracts) that England had granted to organizers of colonizing ventures. There were three types of charters: joint-stock company, proprietary, and royal.

Joint-stock company charter

Most of the early English colonies were issued joint-stock company charters by the king of England. These charters were initially given to a group of investors, usually no more than twenty, to form a joint-stock company, which enabled them to pool their money to finance their venture. In addition, the charter organized the company, gave specific economic advantages to investors, and granted land and governing powers. Typical examples of colonies founded by joint-stock companies were Virginia and Massachusetts. For seventeen years, the Virginia Company of London owned and administered the colony at Jamestown, which was founded in 1607 (see Chapter 4). After the Virginia Company declared bankruptcy, the charter was revoked in 1624 and Virginia became a royal colony. Although the Massachusetts Bay Colony (founded 1629) was owned by a joint-stock company, its charter failed to specify where the company should hold its annual meetings. The early stockholders used this loophole to hold meetings in Boston, thus distancing themselves from supervision by the English government (see Chapter 4). In 1631 Massachusetts Bay officers who lived in the colony decided to add 116 members to the company. Later expansions had the effect of turning the charter into a constitution (document that establishes an independent government). The Massachusetts Bay colonists had formed a government virtually independent from Britain, making their own decisions and even printing their own money, which violated the British policy of tight control on the colonies. Massachusetts operated under this charter until 1683. In 1691 the colony was placed under a royal charter. In the interim, the status of the charter remained in dispute as Massachusetts officials tried to regain their original company charter.

Proprietary charter

A proprietary charter was issued by the monarch to one or more individuals who received large tracts of land and the power to govern a colony in place of the king. In 1632 Maryland was founded upon a proprietary charter issued to Cecilius Calvert, Lord Baltimore, giving him and his heirs extensive powers to organize and govern the colony (see Chapter 4). During the second wave of colonization, between 1660 and 1685, the Carolinas, the Jerseys, New York, and Pennsylvania were also founded on proprietary charters (see Chapters 4 and 5). These colonies were practicing a limited form of representative government (government officials are elected by the people) by 1700.

Other early colonies had no charters. Since settlers had no clear legal authority from the king, they drew up agreements called compacts. For instance, Plymouth was governed by the Mayflower Compact from 1620 until 1691, when the colony merged with Massachusetts Bay (see Chapter 4). The colonies of Rhode Island, New Haven, and Connecticut followed with their own compacts in the 1630s. Compacts had their drawbacks, however, because the English government often did not recognize them as legally valid.

Royal charter

By the mid-1700s eight of the thirteen colonies had been placed under royal charters, which mandated direct control by the king of England. (Pennsylvania, Maryland, North Carolina, South Carolina, and Georgia were still under proprietary charters.) Since the king, not Parliament (England's lawmaking body), held supreme power over royal colonies, their foremost function was to benefit the monarchy. The royal takeover of some colonies was a gradual process that began when it became clear that the colonies could become a source of huge profits for England. This was especially true of Virginia, which had a booming tobacco trade. The first permanent English colonies, Jamestown and Plymouth, were founded during the reign of King James I (1566–1625), who considered them "dependent local jurisdictions." Although he supervised both ventures through a committee called "Our Council of Virginia," he granted some independence to the leaders of the colonies. James was followed by a succession of monarchs who tightened English control. During the 1600s numerous royal boards and commissions worked with Parliament to regulate land acquisition, government, and trade in the colonies. By the early 1700s each royal colony was ruled by a governor and a council who took up residence in America and reported directly to the king. The governor and council presided over an assembly of elected representatives from the various settlements, which proposed legislation.

Problems for royal governors The royal governor was an English aristocrat (a member of the nobility, or ruling class), usually chosen because of his social connections, who acted as the king's representative in a colony. He recommended members of the royal council, who were then chosen by the Board of Trade and approved by the king. Councillors usually had a lifetime appointment, and the average number of council members was twelve. The governor and his council controlled the finances of the colony. Historians have differing opinions about the degree of freedom given to governors and councils, but most conclude that they ruled somewhat independently. Although the governor was given a salary, councillors received no pay. Nevertheless, like the governor, they were wealthy men, and they often found lucrative positions within the government. Sometimes several members of a family served on one council. The governor and council also acted as the highest court in a colony, and any appeals of their decisions were referred to England. The governor had veto power (authority to prohibit) over the colonial assembly, and the Crown expected him to use it to advance English interests. However, a governor who ignored colonists' concerns, particularly those expressed in the assembly, placed himself at considerable political risk. For this reason, royal governors encountered numerous problems and were frequently replaced or recalled to England to answer charges brought against them.

One of the greatest challenges for a colonial governor was keeping a council quorum (a minimum number of members required to approve legislation). Although only three out of twelve councillors was considered a quorum in an emergency, governors still had difficulty calling even that small number of members together. Councillors were so often absent from the colonies that in 1720 the Crown authorized all governors to suspend a council member if he was absent for twelve months without permission. Few governors acted on this, however, even as absenteeism became more frequent in the mid-1700s. Although governments remained fairly stable during the colonial period, some colonists became uncomfortable with the fact that, aside from the governor, three men could determine the fate of legislation passed by an entire assembly of representatives from the settlement. In a few colonies voters began supporting the elected assembly over the governor and council.

Rise of the colonial assembly Royal charters were not designed with the idea that elected assemblies would become the central governing force in the American colonies. But this is precisely what happened. In 1619 the first local representative body in America was assembled in Virginia. It was called the House of Burgesses after the English system, in which a burgess represented a borough (an area under the jurisdiction of a local government) or town. Members of local assemblies, from the first in Virginia to the last in Georgia, considered their duties to be based on English common law (the body of law determined by custom and precedent). In fact, by the end of the seventeenth

A meeting of the Virginia House of Burgesses.
Courtesy of the National Archives and Records Administration. Illustration by P. H. Rothemel

century many assemblies began to see themselves as similar to the English Parliament—that is, the supreme law-making body. They obtained what has been called "negotiated authorities," which later strengthened their resolve to bypass Parliament and appeal directly to the king.

Navigation Acts

Royal control of the colonies increased from 1651 onward, when the English Parliament passed a series of

New England Confederation

In 1643 the New England colonies formed the first federation in America. Called "The United Colonies of New England" (usually referred to as the New England Confederation), it was intended to give "mutual safety and welfare" for Massachusetts Bay, Plymouth, Connecticut, and New Haven. Representatives from the colonies met in Boston, Massachusetts, and drafted a constitution that provided for coordinated military defense and settlement of boundary disputes. Each colony was free to manage its own internal affairs. The confederation was based on compromise, which was its main weakness. Almost immediately the colonies began to squabble. For instance, Massachusetts Bay had a larger population, so the colony had to pay more taxes and furnish more men for the militia—but without having a greater say in decisions. In 1653 Massachusetts Bay refused to participate in a war against the Dutch. Maine and the Narragansett Bay settlements (later Rhode Island) wanted to join the group but were denied admission for political and religious reasons. (Some settlers in Maine supported royal control of Massachusetts, and Narragansett Bay settlers were critical of Puritanism.) The commission that was set up to administer the league had no real power; commissioners could only give advice on resolving conflicts. By 1665 the commission was meeting only once every three years, and the league went into decline. It was revived from 1675 to 1676 to defeat the Native Americans in King Philip's War (see Chapter 5). The Confederation of New England was dissolved when the Massachusetts Bay charter was revoked in 1684.

laws called the Acts of Trade, or Navigation Acts, to regulate American trade (see Chapter 7). These acts were based on a theory called mercantilism, which held that the colonies existed for the economic benefit of England. The Navigation Acts established a system of regulations that worked both for and against the colonies. Under these laws, any commodities (trade items) transported to and from the colonies had to be carried on British ships commanded by British captains, and three-quarters of a ship's crew had to be British. (In this case, "British" meant anyone from the British Isles—England, Scotland, Ireland, and Wales—and the American colonies.) This provision greatly aided American sailors and shipbuilders. Other provisions required that certain items, called enumerated articles, be taken to England before they could be transported to other European ports, while other goods could not be sold anywhere but in England. Among them were tobacco, rice, furs, indigo (a blue dye), and naval stores (masts, hemp, pitch, tar, and turpentine). The acts also included bonuses to be paid to Americans for producing things that England needed, such as hemp for rope, iron, dyes, silk, and lumber. However, the colonies could not ship these items to other countries without paying high tariffs (trade fees).

In the mid-1700s the British created still more regulations. The Iron Act of 1750 outlawed the building of colonial forges for turning pig iron (crude iron that has been made in a blast furnace) into steel. However, this law also dropped duties (taxes) that had previously been applied to pig iron, so in theory the statute both helped and hindered the colonies. The Currency Act of 1751 seriously restricted the use of paper money in New England. Eventually many colonists would come to see such measures as unnecessary and unlawful interferences with their freedom.

Edmund Andros was appointed royal governor of the Dominion of New England in order to prevent the colonies from gaining too much independence.
Reproduced by permission of Archive Photos, Inc.

Dominion of New England In 1686 James II dealt another blow to New England. The Catholic king was in danger of being removed from the throne by his Protestant opponents, and he wanted to elevate England to a major world power. The Navigation Acts, which created an English trade monopoly on goods from the colonies, had been part of this plan, but James realized he had to go a step further and centralize his government. In addition, he had to prevent Massachusetts, the main New England colony, from gaining too much independence (Massachusetts was virtually a self-governing colony). Therefore he forced royal rule on Massachusetts, the other New England colonies, New York, and New Jersey. He united them under the title of Dominion of New England and appointed Edmund Andros (1637–1714) as royal governor. James initiated many changes that affected the lives of the colonists. For example, the Massachusetts general court was replaced by a council. Andros and the council (which he appointed) had the power to make all laws and raise taxes, and the Privy Council (king's council) was the final court of appeal. Colonists were required to obtain deeds (legal contracts) for land they purchased from Native Americans, and quitrents (a fixed tax) were then levied on the land. Only five ports were open for customs clearance (taxing of trade items coming into and going out of the colonies). Worst of all, Andros was an Anglican in a Puritan region (populated by those who believed in strictness in matters of religion and conduct), and he had brought British troops with him to enforce the law.

In 1687 citizens in Ipswich and other Massachusetts towns protested that taxes were not only too high but also illegal. Andros arrested the demonstrators and crushed all opposition. The following year he imposed a rule that public meetings could be held only once a year, to elect public officials. Furthermore, representatives could serve only two years, thus preventing local politicians from gaining power. Events turned in the colonists' favor between 1688 and 1689, however, when James II was removed from the throne in the Glorious Revolution (the name given to the ascension of Protestant monarchs William III and Mary II). Now that Andros had no backing in England, the colonists sent him and other officials to England as prisoners. The Dominion of New England was soon disbanded, but all of the colonies remained under royal charter. In 1691 Massachusetts Bay was combined with

Plymouth and Maine to form the single colony of Massachusetts.

Leisler's Rebellion

The fall of the dominion also resulted in Leisler's Rebellion, one of the most significant political events of the colonial period. While Andros was serving as governor, there was great fear among Puritans and Dutch Reformed Church members that Catholics or Anglicans would seize control in New England. (Both the Puritan and Reformed Churches followed the teachings of Protestant reformer John Calvin [1509–1564], who advocated rejecting Roman Catholicism. The Puritans also rejected Anglicanism, the established church of England, as being equally corrupt.) After Andros and other English officials were removed from office, Dutch colonists in New York immediately chose Jacob Leisler (1640–1691), a German-born merchant and a member of the Reformed Church, to head the colony. Leisler had held political positions in the past, so he managed to establish control. Yet he was not widely supported by other colonists. For instance, prominent Dutch families resented the fact that the colony was now governed by a group of socially inferior traders. As a result, Leisler was backed mainly by poor merchants and farmers. He attempted to gain wider support in 1690, when he launched a military expedition to protect northern New York from French soldiers and Native Americans. The militia (citizens's army) arrived too late, however, and sixty colonists were killed. By now Leisler had also alienated powerful English merchant families, since his followers were mainly tradesmen and farmers, who were considered socially inferior by the wealthy elite.

When the newly appointed governor, Henry Sloughter, arrived in March 1691, Leisler refused to surrender the fort at New York. There was a brief skirmish, in which several English soldiers were killed. After Leisler surrendered the fort the next morning, he and nine others—including his English son-in-law, Jacob Milborne—were arrested for treason (betrayal of one's country). The resulting trials demonstrated the difficulties Dutch colonists had with the English legal system. The accused men did not understand the charges against them. Two were acquitted and six others were convicted, although they were later pardoned. But Leisler and Milborne were not so lucky. They had refused to answer the charges, which they claimed had no legal foundation. Leisler's domineering ways had also weakened his support over the past several months. The jury was packed with his enemies, so he and Milborne were found guilty. In spite of popular protests, they were drawn and quartered, a particularly gruesome method of execution reserved for traitors and rebels. (Being drawn and quartered meant that a person's internal organs were removed and then the body was dismembered.)

Unfortunately, the executions did not end the political turmoil in New York. The anti-Leisler faction proceeded to seize land belonging to Leisler supporters. In 1695 Parliament

Jacob Leisler was the leader of Leisler's Rebellion, one of the most significant political events of the colonial period. *Reproduced by permission of The Library of Congress.*

halted this practice and reversed the convictions of Leisler and Milborne. But the passionate hatred between the leaders of the two factions lingered and would have an impact on New York politics for the next twenty-five years.

The militia

During the colonial period there was no permanent, national army. Instead each colony followed the Eng-

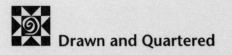

Drawn and Quartered

The order of execution for Jacob Leisler and Jacob Milborne called for them to be drawn and quartered, an ancient punishment reserved for rebels and traitors. Accordingly, they were to be hanged by their necks and "being alive their bodys Cutt downe to the Earth and Their Bowells be taken out and they being Alive, burnt before their faces; that their heads shall be struck off and their Bodys Cutt in four parts." Both men met their fates in 1691, but their bodies did not receive proper burial until 1710.

Source: Hoffer, Peter Charles. Law and People in Colonial America. *Baltimore, Md.: Johns Hopkins University Press, 1992.*

lish practice of forming a militia in the event of a conflict or war. For instance, Leisler commanded the New York militia in the skirmish with Sloughter's English troops, who were themselves members of a militia. According to Anglo-Saxon tradition, every able-bodied adult male was obligated to render military service if called upon. An important feature of colonial militias was short-term utilization of the militia. This was based on an English law that forbade the king to maintain a professional standing army because he might use it to oppress his people.

Militias differed from colony to colony according to particular circum-stances and defense needs. In 1622 the Virginia House of Burgesses passed an act requiring all men to "go under Arms." Likewise, in 1628 the Massachusetts Bay charter allowed for the formation of a colonial militia "to incounter, expulse, repell and resist by force of arms, as well by sea as by lands." Massachusetts drew upon its large supply of manpower and close-knit communities to maintain a strong defense of its shores and borders. In New York, on the other hand, a diverse ethnic population and lack of cohesive communities made the colony more dependent on an alliance with the Iroquois Confederacy (see Chapter 1) than on a militia. Pennsylvania, which was predominantly populated with Quakers (members of the Society of Friends), did not have a militia because the Quakers were pacifists—that is, they did not believe in bearing arms. As late as the 1730s South Carolina had such a scattered population that the militia could not provide adequate protection. Also, the increasing ratio of black slaves to white colonists in South Carolina kept the militia there on the alert against possible slave rebellions.

Eventually militias tended to attract less qualified recruits. In the early colonial days, men who were sent from England to provide military protection—such as John Smith in Jamestown and Myles Standish in Plymouth—were often veterans of English wars. By the mid-eighteenth century, however, militias were often composed of wanderers who had no permanent address or lacked social standing within a colony. Virginia and Massachusetts lawmakers called them "strollers." In 1755, when Virginia needed a stronger militia, officials called for "such able bodied men, as do not follow or exercise any lawful calling or employment, or have not some other lawful and sufficient maintenance. . . ." At the same time, qualified men—anyone "who hath any vote in the election of a Burgess or Burgesses"—were excused from service. During the Seven Years' War (1756–63) British officers expressed contempt for the strollers who made up the majority of troops in the American army, which had by then become semiprofessional. The officers' attitude would later come back to haunt them when colonists rallied this capable army against England in the Revolutionary War (1775–83; a conflict in which American colonists gained independence from British rule).

Slave codes

The militia was frequently called out along the frontier and in southern colonies where plantation owners and tenant farmers lived in fear of slave rebellions. Slavery was introduced in the Chesapeake colonies of Virginia and Maryland in the early 1600s and soon spread into South Carolina. Slaves were also present in smaller numbers in the northern colonies. The first Africans in Virginia were probably indentured servants (laborers who worked for a specific number of years) who worked on plantations. Gradually the accepted view

became that whites should be indentured servants while blacks should be slaves (permanent servants regarded as property), a status that their children would inherit. English common law, which was the basis of laws in the colonies, did not mention slavery, though it did describe varieties of relations between masters and servants and parents and children. Therefore there were no specific English legal traditions for slavery in the colonies. After the mid-1600s colonial legislatures passed slave codes. In Virginia a 1662 statute made the child of a slave woman a slave, even if the father was free or white. A 1669 law declared that if a slave died while resisting his master, the master could not be charged with a felony (a serious crime). The assumption was that no master would deliberately choose to kill his own slave, and therefore the death must have been unintentional. A 1680 law inflicted twenty lashes with a whip on any "negro or other slave" who chose to carry a weapon or to "depart from his master's ground without a certificate from his master, mistress or overseer."

In South Carolina a comprehensive slave code was passed in 1740 after the Stono Rebellion, an uprising that resulted in the deaths of far more blacks than whites. The code stated that Negroes, mulattos (those of mixed white and black ancestry), Native Americans, and mestizos (mixed Native American and white parentage) were assumed to be slaves "unless the contrary can be made to appear." Slaves could travel only with the written permission of their masters, and

"If I purchase a Man"

During the colonial period, many religious leaders voiced opposition to the holding of African slaves as property. Foremost among them was John Woolman, a Quaker preacher who initiated the Quaker abolitionist (antislavery) movement of the 1760s. As he traveled to meetings (religious services) from his home in New Jersey, he carried his message to slaveholders in the North and South. In Rhode Island he tried to persuade shipowners not to transport slaves from Africa. He refused to buy any products connected with the slave trade, and he would not accept hospitality from slave owners. In 1754 he published *Some Considerations on the Keeping of Negroes,* in which he argued that slaves' rights were being violated:

> If I purchase a Man who hath never forfeited his Liberty, the natural Right of Freedom is in him; and shall I keep him and his Posterity [children] in Servitude and Ignorance? How should I approve of this Conduct, were I in his Circumstances, and he in mine? It may be thought, that to treat them as we would willingly be treated, our Gain by them would be inconsiderable: And it were, in divers [various] Respects, better that there were [no slaves] in our Country.

rewards were paid to whites or free Native Americans for the return of a runaway slave. Attempting "to raise an insurrection [rebellion]" could bring the death penalty for slaves. They could suffer death for lesser crimes as well, such as maliciously destroying "any stack of rice, corn or other grain" or setting fire to "any tar kiln, barrels of pitch, tar, turpentine or rosin." If accused of such a crime, slaves were entitled to a trial before two justices, but they had fewer legal protections than white colonists.

The "Negro Plot"

Slave rebellions were feared by whites in the North as well as those in the South. One example was the "Negro Plot" case, which took place in New York City in 1740 and 1741. At that time the New York colony had the highest number of African slaves north of the Chesapeake. In fact, one-sixth of New York City residents were slaves. A strict slave code had been adopted in the 1730s, but it was only partially successful in controlling slaves. By 1740 fear of Africans was intense and widespread among whites. Anxieties were heightened by rumors of a plot by African and their white co-conspirators to poison the city's water supply. Then in 1741 a rash of arsons (deliberately set fires) and thefts were committed in the city. A reward of 100 pounds (British currency) was posted for information leading to the arrest of the criminals. Mary Burton, a teenage indentured servant, claimed the reward after telling about a ring of African and white thieves that included her white master. However Burton's charges went even further: she said there was a slave plot to burn the city, kill all white males, and put her owner in charge as mayor.

Despite inconsistencies in Burton's story, many New Yorkers believed her. One hundred and fifty blacks and twenty-five whites were jailed. Court trials lasted for almost a year, coming to an end only when Burton's accusations became even wilder and began to implicate prominent citizens. After verdicts were reached, eighteen slaves and four whites were hanged and thirteen slaves were burned to death. Another seventy slaves were deported (forcibly sent) to other colonies after "confessing" under threats of torture and death. Burton left New York soon afterward. In the years that followed, rumors of other plots periodically surfaced, and New Yorkers came to prefer free white laborers to slaves.

Lawyers in the colonies

For most people in the early colonial period, going to court meant representing oneself. There were few lawyers because their skills were rarely required. In colonies such as Massachusetts Bay, where the level of education was generally high, some men may have had knowledge of the law. But there were no professional, full-time lawyers, and in colonies like Virginia practically no one had any familiarity with English law. By 1700 the major towns—New York, Philadelphia, Boston, and Charleston—boasted several successful lawyers, but they had very few clients. Consequently one wealthy client could retain all the local lawyers. In 1695 New

York had to impose restrictions on the number of lawyers available to any one litigant. Between 1675 and 1769 only forty-nine lawyers practiced in New York City. Virginia was slower in developing qualified legal professionals. A major reason was that the plantation owners who dominated Virginia politics in the late 1600s did not want lawyers getting in their way. But after Virginia regularized its court system in 1705, lawyers were in greater demand.

John Peter Zenger trial

One of the most famous court cases of the colonial era was the trial of John Peter Zenger (1697–1746), a German-born printer and journalist who published the *New-York Weekly Journal* in New York City. The newspaper was a political forum for colonists who opposed the policies of New York's royal governor, William Cosby, whom they accused of misusing his power. Although Zenger did not write the articles he published, he was held responsible for their content. In 1734 Cosby had Zenger jailed for seditious libel (making a false statement that exposes another person to public contempt), then ordered copies of the newspaper to be burned. James Alexander, a lawyer and one of the backers of the *New-York Weekly Journal,* planned to defend Zenger along with one of his colleagues. But when the attorney general, a supporter of Cosby, had them disbarred (disqualified from practicing law), they turned to Philadelphia attorney Andrew Hamilton (c. 1676– 1741). Hamilton was one of the best-known

A scene from the John Peter Zenger trial, which established the idea of freedom of the press in the colonies. Alexander Hamilton is standing to the right, while Zenger is in the witness box.

lawyers in the colonies and speaker of the house (legislative body) of Pennsylvania.

In the trial Hamilton readily admitted to the jury that Zenger had published the articles. Nevertheless he argued that Zenger had also printed the truth, and this should excuse his actions. The chief justice—also a supporter of Cosby—ruled that Hamilton could not use truth as a defense because sedition (undermining the government) was a crime, regardless of whether it was true. Hamilton then appealed directly to the jury, noting that "the facts which were offered to prove [Cosby's misuse of his office] were not committed in a corner; they are notoriously known to be true: and therefore in your justice [just verdict] lies our safety." The jurors shared Hamilton and Zenger's opinion of Cosby, so they were only too happy to find Zenger not guilty. Although the verdict in the Zenger case did not change the law, it established the first victory for freedom of the press (the right of newspapers to print truthful information) in America. Hamilton wrote and published a narrative account of the trial, and thus the story was handed down to a later generation of colonial leaders, who wrote freedom of the press into the First Amendment of the United States Constitution (1789).

Legal status of women

When a colonial woman got married she ceased to exist, legally speaking, as an individual. A single woman maintained much greater control over her property than did a married woman. Under the English common-law doctrine of coverture, upon marriage the wife became "covered" by the husband—that is, she could not act without her husband in legal matters. While the law allowed a married couple to act together, the husband controlled all legal affairs and was under no legal obligation to consult his wife. A husband could even be found liable for his wife's wrongdoing, on the assumption that it must have occurred with his encouragement or knowledge. In some instances a husband could be whipped for his wife's crimes, including adultery.

Coverture was part of colonial law, but with some modifications, as in the case of dower rights. Under English law one-third of a deceased husband's estate, called a dower, had to be preserved for the support of his widow. In Britain this law was frequently ignored, but in the colonies it was protected and strengthened. Often, especially in New England, the court would

Freedom of the Press

The John Peter Zenger trial had a far-reaching impact on opposition to English control of the colonies. Historians note that although the case did not change the law, it influenced the writing of the United States Constitution (1787). In 1789 the framers added ten amendments, called the Bill of Rights, that guaranteed individual liberties under the federal government. Freedom of the press is one of the rights protected by the First Amendment, which states: "Congress shall make no law respecting an establishment of religion, or prohibiting the free exercise thereof; or abridging the freedom of speech or of the press; or the right of people peaceably to assemble; and to petition the government for redress of grievances."

enlarge the dower to more than one-third of the estate in order to give better protection for widows. Unlike Englishwomen, Dutch women could sign joint wills with their husbands. The joint will option meant that, until 1695, Dutch women in New York often had greater say in matters of inheritance than did Englishwomen.

Crime lower among women During the 1600s it was not uncommon for women

An Exceptional Woman

Margaret Brent (c. 1600–c. 1671) was a unique figure in seventeenth-century colonial America. As an independent, wealthy woman, she was actively involved in the legal and political affairs of the Maryland colony at a time when women had little or no power. Brent is remembered today as a feminist because she demanded the right to vote in Maryland, even though she knew she would be denied the privilege on the basis of her gender. She is also considered the first practicing female attorney in America. Some historians point out that Brent was not actually advocating equality for women in general, and she was never licensed as a lawyer. Nonetheless, she was an exceptional woman for her day: she owned and managed a large estate, she was the executor of the estate of Leonard Calvert, the governor of Maryland, and at one point she was in sole charge of supplying and paying an army.

to appear in English colonial courts in place of their husbands, and some even acted as their husband's attorney. After 1700 the economic life of the colonies became more complex, and knowledge of English common law proved useful. At the same time, however, there was more bias against women, and the acceptance of women in the courtroom lessened. On the other hand, divorce,

though rare and difficult, was easier to obtain in America than it was in England. It is possible that crimes committed by women were underreported, but from available data it appears that women were less likely than men to commit crimes in any category except witchcraft in the colonies. In New England the only women accused of murder before 1660 had killed children. And women were particularly susceptible as victims of crime. Although there were strict laws against the exploitation of women, female servants were frequently subject to sexual harassment.

The law commonly treated women differently from men. Connecticut and Massachusetts laws against homosexuality, perjury (lying), and idolatry (idol worship) applied only to men on the theory that women could not commit these crimes. Since fornication (sex outside of marriage) was most likely to be discovered by the pregnancy of the woman, women were at much greater risk of being charged. Unless she revealed the name of the father, he would probably remain undetected and not receive punishment. It became common to question mothers during childbirth to ascertain the father's name, both to ensure his punishment and to guarantee his support of the child.

Crime and punishment

Surviving court records from New England offer a glimpse of the crimes that were being committed and punished during the colonial period. From 1630 to 1644 in Massachusetts,

An illustration of a woman being dunked in front of fellow colonists as a punishment for an unknown crime. *Reproduced by permission of Corbis-Bettmann.*

ninety-nine people were charged with drunkenness, and seventy-three of them were fined. For the fifty charged with theft, the most common punishment was whipping. About half of the twenty-two charged with fornication were whipped, while whippings were given to nineteen of the twenty-two servants charged with running away. The twenty-four people accused of cursing (to call upon God to injure someone) or swearing (to use obscene language) received a fine or whipping. There were only nine assaults, three attempted rapes, one rape, and one murder. Of the four people executed,

one cause was unspecified, two were for adultery (having sex with someone other than one's spouse), and one was for murder.

Punishment most often was a public affair because it also served, at least in theory, to deter others from committing the same crimes. In New England sermons were often preached before executions, and prisoners were known to offer moral advice to the crowd before meeting their deaths. Colonial laws often appeared harsher on paper than in real life. Adultery could be punished by death, but it seldom was. A Plymouth law of 1671 cre-

Public Humiliation

Crimes like drunkenness, fornication, and theft dominated most New England courts throughout the seventeenth century. Fines were common, but for more serious or repeated offenses, bodily punishment like whipping was inflicted. It was also common to humiliate the offender. Such was the purpose of bilboes, a bar and shackles used to raise an offender's legs off the ground in a position both uncomfortable and embarrassing. Over time these methods were replaced by the less expensive wooden stocks, a device with holes in which the offender's feet or hands, and often head, could be locked. The stocks were put in a public place such as the commons or village green to increase the humiliation of the punishment. The stocks did no physical harm unless the offender was locked in for an extended period of time. Colonies limited the number of hours in the stocks—usually no more than three or four, though Rhode Island allowed six. The first man placed in the stocks in Boston was carpenter Edward Palmer. His offense was overcharging the town for building the stocks.

ated twenty-one capital offenses (crimes requiring the death penalty), including cursing one's natural parent and "profaning the Sabbath provocatively." From 1641 onward, Massachusetts allowed the death penalty not only for crimes such as murder and manslaughter but also for idolatry, blasphemy (irreverently speaking of God), and witchcraft.

Exceptions to the violence of colonial punishments were found in Pennsylvania and East and West Jersey due to Quaker influence. The Quakers had experienced much persecution—in England their ears were cropped (the upper part of the ear was cut off), and in Massachusetts in the 1650s they were executed (usually for returning repeatedly after being banished). Therefore they believed in reform rather than punishment of criminals.

Local government in the New England colonies

The New England colonies were organized around towns, which were in turn based on the English manor (private estate) and parish (church community). Thus the town was the center of government and religion (in this case Puritanism for the surrounding villages and rural area.) The New England colonies, which tended to resist royal control, governed primarily through town meetings that were held at least once a year in a church or tavern. All white adult male property owners of good character were eligible to vote in yearly elections at a town meeting. Elected offices included selectmen (chief executives), constables (policemen or watchmen), a town clerk (record keeper), tax officers, highway surveyors, fence viewers (those who ensured fences were properly placed), tithingmen (officials who made sure colonists observed the Sabbath and behaved morally), and cattle catchers.

Local government in the middle colonies

Colonies in the mid-Atlantic region (New York, New Jersey, Pennsylvania, and Delaware) had a more diverse system of local government. Pennsylvania, for example, was organized into townships, cities, counties, and boroughs. All cities except Philadelphia came under county authority. Each county was sectioned off into townships. The highest official in a township was the constable, and in a county, the sheriff. Unlike New England towns, Pennsylvania townships did not hold town meetings. The constable was appointed by the Court of Quarter Sessions, while other officers were elected. Boroughs, on the other hand, held meetings conducted by burgesses and councillors. A borough was comparable to a village, but it functioned much like a city.

After the English took over New Netherland from the Dutch and established the colony as New York in 1664, the county emerged as the basic unit of government. Counties were subdivided into municipalities (which had local self-government), manors, and towns. The sheriff was the most powerful figure in a New York county. He made court decisions, supervised elections, performed police duties, and collected taxes. The county was administered by the Board of Supervisors, and judges

presided over court trials. The governor appointed the sheriff and judges, whereas members of the Board of Supervisors were elected yearly by freedmen.

Local government in the southern colonies

Local government in the colonies of the upper South (Virginia and Maryland; also called the Chesapeake) operated primarily under a county system. The governor appointed six to eight magistrates in each county. The magistrates had specific duties in their respective neighborhoods, where they often held hearings in their homes. Together they made up a county court, which could appeal decisions made by individual magistrates and pass and enforce local regulations. The primary law-enforcement official was the sheriff, who served under the magistrates. Court-appointed constables also served with the sheriff. Other officers appointed by the governor were the coroner, clerk, and road supervisors.

In the lower South (the Carolinas and Georgia), the dominant form of local government was a county subdivided into parishes. Although the governor appointed magistrates, the most powerful officers were parish vestrymen (a member elected to make decisions regarding the church). Each parish appointed seven men to a one-year position, which involved supervising parish schools, caring for the poor, and enforcing moral codes. Vestrymen acted as judges, enforced laws, and collected taxes. The parish in Carolina was similar

Low Tax Burden

The American Revolution resulted, in part, from the Sugar Act (1764), the Stamp Act (1765), the Townshend Acts (1767), and other repressive taxes levied on colonists by the English government. This fact has led to the modern misconception that American colonists always bore a heavy tax burden. Actually, the average colonist paid at most a moderate amount in taxes because governments had small budgets. For instance, Massachusetts employed only six full-time government officials, and the largest expenditure in any colony was the governor's salary—around $100,000 in today's dollars. The absence of a standing army also meant minimal defense costs except in time of war. Taxation therefore did not cause widespread discontent until the end of the eighteenth century.

to the New England town, in that it was the center of the established church, in this case the Church of England (Anglicanism). Unlike the Puritans, however, Anglicans often worked harmoniously with dissenters. Dissenters were therefore a more integral part of the community and were able to receive public services.

Taxes

Colonial governments levied taxes for a variety of purposes. For

instance, taxes paid for officials' salaries, schools, churches, charities, road construction and maintenance, and the militia. Unlike today, there were no income or sales taxes. Revenue was acquired mainly through trade duties and excise (internal) taxes, thus allowing for lower taxation on individuals.

Land taxes

On both the local and provincial (colony) levels, land was the primary source of tax revenue. The only way colonists could avoid paying taxes was to demonstrate that their property was dormant (not producing crops). Most owned a considerable amount of property that produced income, which was therefore taxable. Proprietary and royal colonies also used quitrents to generate revenue. Colonial authorities regarded this as a convenient way to fund government operations and to gain personal profit. The system was introduced in Virginia and later adopted in the Carolinas and Pennsylvania. Although some northern colonies collected quitrents, the method never attained widespread use as it did in the South.

Poll tax

The poll tax was a flat labor tax imposed on anyone, most commonly white adult males, who earned an income. If a son worked for his father on the family farm, the father was taxed as long as he drew a profit from his son's labor. In England the poll tax was first used during the fourteenth century and applied to laborers over the age of fourteen. Near the end of the seventeenth century the poll tax was abolished in England because it was considered unfair. Around that time, in 1693, Pennsylvania enacted a poll tax on sixteen-year-old white males who had been free from indentured servitude for at least six months and whose net worth did not exceed a certain amount. For many colonies the poll tax covered at least half of the expenditures involved in supporting the colonial-level government.

Excise taxes

The excise tax was another considerable source of income for colonial governments. Slaves and liquor in particular produced substantial revenues from excise taxes. Since slaves existed for their owners' profit, they were a form of production and subject to taxation. The most common excise tax in all the colonies was paid by tavern owners on liquor, a cost that was passed on to the consumer. Provincial leaders were following the lead of the English Parliament, which had established an excise tax on intoxicating drinks in 1643. In a period of growing Puritan influence, both in England and in the colonies, the tax reflected Puritan disapproval of alcoholic beverages.

The vote

Voting procedures in most American colonies were based on English practices. Among them was the "forty-shilling [an early American

 Women Denied Vote

Regardless of whether women had a high social status or owned property, they were not allowed to vote. Future U.S. President John Adams (1735–1826) expressed the thinking of the time: "[Women's] delicacy renders them unfit for practice and experience in the great businesses of life, and . . . the arduous cares of state. Besides, . . . nature has made them fittest for domestic cares."

coin] freehold," which stated that only a landowner had the right to vote. The reasoning was that a landowner would have a stake in the outcome of an election and would benefit from the political well-being of the colony. Officials assumed that people who did not own land had no interest in the outcome of elections. Although each colony had different voting requirements, the general criteria were citizenship, residence, and age. Yet other limitations deprived many colonists of the right to vote—the most common being gender. Regardless of whether women had a high social status or owned property, they were not allowed to vote.

Voting restrictions

Religious affiliation also played a significant role in voting eligibility. Until the late seventeenth century, a voter was required to belong to the established church in the colony where he lived. Protestant dissenters such as Quakers, Presbyterians, and Baptists were usually barred from casting ballots (Rhode Island was an exception). After the Glorious Revolution of 1688 to 1689, when the Protestant monarchs William III and Mary II took the English throne, many dissenters were permitted to vote. But even as restrictions on Protestants were being lifted, Roman Catholics were prevented from going to the polls. In Maryland, which had the largest Catholic population in the colonies, Protestant officials announced that Catholics "would tend to the Discouragement and Disturbance of his Lordship's Protestant government" and therefore should not be allowed to vote. Virginia, New York, Rhode Island, and South Carolina enacted similar policies toward Catholics. Many Jews also lost voting rights in at least seven colonies during this time. Rhode Island, the colony best known for permitting religious freedom, had the harshest restrictions against Jews.

Africans were not allowed to vote while they were enslaved, but they were given the privilege once they were free. Although there is no record of free blacks voting in northern colonies, there were no official statutes prohibiting them. In the southern colonies, however, free blacks did vote. In early eighteenth-century South Carolina, for instance, Berkeley County records stated that "free Negroes were received and taken as good Electors as the best Freeholders in the Province." Similar participation was recorded in Virginia and North Carolina, and free blacks could vote in Georgia prior to 1761.

Economy and Communications

7

Native Americans had an extensive economic and trading system for at least 2,500 years before Europeans reached North America in the mid-1500s (see Chapter 1). Native peoples in the Southwest (present-day New Mexico, Arizona, and Texas) irrigated (watered) their land to grow maize (corn), beans, and squash. Native Americans who lived in the eastern part of the continent (the Eastern Woodlands) burned forests and prairies to stimulate crop production and wild berry growth. They grew maize, potatoes, beans, squash, sunflowers, and tobacco. Archaeologists (scientists who study ancient cultures) have found pottery fragments, baskets, stone weapons, and shells, which reveal that a vast trade network flourished among the 7,000,000 to 10,000,000 Native Americans who inhabited North America. But Europeans disrupted these productive enterprises when they seized native lands, introduced deadly diseases, and gained dominance with their sophisticated weapons. During the seventeenth and eighteenth centuries, 90 percent of the Native American population north of the Rio Grande (the river that forms part of the border between Mexico and Texas) was wiped out. The continent was now open for European settlement and trade. Yet European economic development in North America would have been impossible without the contributions of the surviving Native Americans. They offered food to starving settlers, provided pelts (animal skins) for the profitable European fur trade, and taught struggling colonists how to grow crops.

Spanish and French retreat to borders

The first Europeans to cross the Atlantic to the New World (the European term for North and South America) were the Spanish, who conquered fabulously rich Native American empires in South America and Mexico and took the treasures back to Spain. In the 1560s they moved into the Southwest and present-day Florida, Alabama, and South Carolina, hoping to find more gold and other precious metals. During the early seventeenth century the French occupied the upper northeastern part of the continent, founding fur-trading posts in present-day Canada around the Great Lakes. Then they sent explorers south through the Mississippi River valley to the Gulf of Mexico in search of more trade routes. Ultimately, however, the Spanish and French failed to gain a permanent foothold in the territory that became the United States. Colonizing attempts by both nations were defeated by poor planning, natural disasters, long distances between settlements, and fierce competition from the English. Although the Spanish and French did not have a direct impact on the colonial economy, Spanish involvement in the Caribbean slave trade and French efforts to expand their fur-trading networks helped shape colonial American history.

English use natural resources

A major factor in France and Spain's failure were the English, who were founding or taking over successful colonies along the Atlantic coast (see Chapter 4). The English far outnumbered other immigrants in the New World: during the seventeenth and eighteenth centuries, more than 155,000 English men and women made the journey across the Atlantic to settle in North America. Many were seeking social, political, and religious freedom, but nearly all—rich and poor alike—were drawn by promises of prosperity in a fertile and abundant land. Advertisements promoted the continent as "one of the goodlyst [goodliest], best and frutfullest cultures that ever was sene, and where nothing lacketh." Members of the gentry (upper or ruling class) were lured by the prospect of quick wealth. Farmers, tradesmen, and servants were often forced onto the Atlantic shores by overpopulation and lack of jobs in England.

The English government actively encouraged settlement ventures in North America as a way to expand its empire. Rather than searching for gold and silver as Spain did, England sought natural resources for

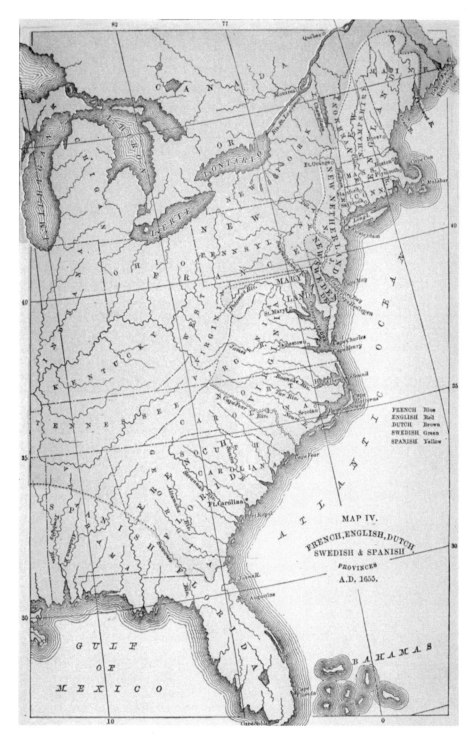

A map of the Eastern half of colonial America. *Reproduced by permission of Archive Photos, Inc.*

Settlers Seize Land

From the earliest years of colonial settlement, land was an important and relatively inexpensive commodity. European colonists acquired land primarily by driving out Native Americans. Initially the two groups engaged in trade, and in many cases native leaders helped the immigrants in their feeble attempts at settlement. Soon, however, Native Americans realized that the colonists were more interested in claiming land than in establishing commercial relations. Native resistance to European expansion resulted in more than a century of violence throughout the colonial period. Pennsylvania was the only colony that maintained peaceful relations with Native Americans because of a treaty written by William Penn in 1682, requiring colonists to purchase land. Yet even that agreement broke down in 1729 when settlers made false claims and then sold the land to speculators. Eventually many native groups moved farther west. Those who stayed behind became economically dependent on the European settlers.

severed, and within a few decades they had created a thriving economy. As the English were putting down roots in the New World, they were joined by other Europeans motivated by the same desires for freedom, wealth, and economic security. Soon America had a highly diverse population that included the Dutch, Germans, Jews, Africans, Swiss, Swedes, Finns, French Huguenots (members of a Protestant religious group), Italians, Welsh, and Scots-Irish.

Land is basis of economy

From the earliest years of colonial settlement, land was an important and relatively inexpensive commodity. By offering land at reasonable rates and under flexible terms, colonial governments hoped to stimulate settlement and economic development. Wealthy investors bought huge tracts of land, often in parcels of 10,000 acres, to develop farms, estates, and plantations. Low land prices and high wages meant that even people who were less well-off could become landowners. In some colonies the first step in acquiring land was a head right, a grant from the colony to a settler who paid his own way to North America. For instance, Virginia awarded a head right of 50 acres, and Carolina granted 50 to 100 acres. An enterprising settler could increase his head right by paying the travel costs of other people, such as family members, indentured servants, and slaves. After receiving a head right, a colonist could purchase additional

its factories. Another incentive was an American market for English-manufactured goods, which England could then tax to increase revenues. Like the Spanish and French, the English at first encountered serious obstacles and made several false starts. Yet they per-land. Indentured servants (laborers who worked for a specific number of years) could also buy land at the end of their contract. Other settlers, called squatters, simply claimed land for their own, claims that were often honored once an area had been cleared and developed. In New England communities the colonists divided land among themselves.

Agriculture is first industry

European settlers from a wide array of social backgrounds became prosperous in the New World. Some immigrants had enough money to finance their own ventures, while others needed assistance. At first they relied on investors, who provided capital (money used for business purposes) for developing North America's abundant resources. Eventually the settlers established local credit markets so they could borrow money from neighbors. During the early colonial period, most capital was invested in small farms in the northern colonies and plantations in the Chesapeake region (Maryland and Virginia). Regardless of their occupations in England and Europe, the majority of American settlers turned to farming for a livelihood. This situation continued throughout the colonial era, with 90 percent of the economy being agricultural. Crops varied from one geographic region to another. Fertile riverbanks, rocky terrain, grassy pastures, sandy hills, and fruitful forests determined what could best grow in a particular area. Agricultural experimentation led to an aggressive program of cultivating profitable crops in colonies that needed an economic base. Other colonists were satisfied with a subsistence culture that sustained their families.

Tenant farmers Settlers who could not afford to buy land became tenant farmers—that is, they paid rent for farmland with cash or with a share of the crops they produced. This arrangement was common in Maryland, Pennsylvania, New Jersey, and New York, where market crops (crops sold to others) were the basis of the economy. Tenant farming suited both immigrants who needed work and colonial leaders who needed settlers. Frequently landowners provided food, supplies, farming equipment, and livestock. In addition to paying rent, some tenant farmers were required to build a house, plant an orchard, or put up a fence. This was a particularly efficient way for landowners to improve their property. Tenant farmers knew their rents could go up or they could be forced off the farm at the whim of the owner. Therefore tenant farming could become simply another form of servitude (servant status) or poverty. Because tenants remained poor, they often had little cash to pay rent and could not improve their economic status by entering nonagricultural occupations or resettling on distant frontiers. By the end of the colonial period tenants in long-settled areas like Maryland and Pennsylvania made up nearly half of the men who did not own land.

A depiction of a colonial farmer plowing his fields. The majority of English settlers turned to farming to make a living. *Reproduced by permission of The Granger Collection.*

Farmers form community network
Contrary to popular myth, colonial American farmers were not totally self-sufficient. Settlers placed a high value on independence, but they also developed close-knit communities. Even farmers living in remote areas needed the support of distant neighbors. The household was the fundamental unit of production in American agriculture. Farmers produced crops for consumption and sale, and their families provided most of the labor. Although servants, hired hands, and slaves performed some tasks, this workforce

was generally not sufficient to sustain a colonial family. Neighbors depended on one another to build homes and churches, harvest crops, break sod, cut timber, raise barns, build fences, establish herds of livestock, and deliver babies. Neighbors exchanged soap, candles, butchered meat, spun thread, or woven fabric on a daily basis. One family could not consume an entire butchered sow (an adult female swine) before the meat spoiled, so they preserved some and traded the rest for such items as clothing or shoes. A family might also trade the meat for a service, such as help in weaving a blanket or harvesting a crop. This barter (trade) economy allowed families to specialize in particular crafts or to maintain a minimum of tools. The ways in which settlers relied on one another also determined the nature of the economies in the four colonial regions: New England, the mid-Atlantic, the upper South, and the lower South.

New England The New England colonies were founded by Puritans who wanted to create a community where they could pray and practice their beliefs without interference. They envisioned family farms that would support these self-contained communities. Condemning excessive profits, which they felt promoted greed, Puritan farmers planted wheat, oats, and barley on just enough land to sustain their families. For example, officials in Dedham, Massachusetts, allotted each family 65 acres outside of town and a 1-acre house lot in town. Cattle, sheep, and hogs ranged freely in community fields and woodlands. After disease destroyed the wheat crop in 1660, New England farmers relied on maize to sustain their families. Relatively short growing seasons and rocky soil prevented the development of a staple crop for export. Farmers had not yet copied the Native American practice of rotating crops (planting different crops to replenish the soil), so New Englanders found that their soil was depleted after five or six years. While some families moved away, many turned to raising cattle for meat and dairy products. Several others became fishermen, eventually producing the first large-scale commodity to be exported from New England.

Mid-Atlantic With a combination of industrious families and rich soil, Pennsylvania and New Jersey thrived in the early days of settlement. English, Dutch, and German farmers used European agricultural practices on farms from 100 to 300 acres in size. In the 1720s Pennsylvania began exporting wheat, flour, and bread, which were in high demand in Ireland and southern Europe. In *American Eras: The Colonial Era*, a merchant described the numerous exports flowing from the region two decades later:

> We make our Remittances [payment for trade items] a great many ways, sometimes to the West Indies in Bread, flour, Pork, Indian Corn, and hogshead Staves, sometimes to Carrolina and New-foundland in Bread and Flour sometimes to Portugall in Wheat, Flour and Pipe Staves [tubs] sometimes to Ireland in Flax seed Flour, Oak and Walnut Planks and Barrel Staves and to England in Skinns, Tobacco, Beeswax, staves of all Kinds, Oak and Walnut Planks, Boat Boards, Pigg Iron, Tarr, Pitch, Turpentine, Ships, and Bills of Exchange.

In New York, which was the Dutch colony of New Netherland until 1664, Dutch and Swedish settlers had developed a thriving fur trade with various Native American tribes. By the early eighteenth century wheat exports were replacing the fur trade. One reason for the slow agricultural development in New York was the preference of Dutch patroons (proprietors of large estates) for holding on to their land rather than developing it for the commercial market. They were more inclined to lease the land to tenants who raised only enough to feed their families and pay their rent.

Upper South Virginia Company investors financed the founding of the Virginia colony. They were primarily interested in making money when Jamestown was settled in 1607. Therefore they pressured the settlers to find a profitable crop or other commodity that could be traded in Europe. By 1612 John Rolfe (1585–1622) had developed a marketable strain of tobacco, and Virginia and neighboring Maryland soon became the first colonies to rely on a single export crop. In 1619 planters exported 20,000 pounds of tobacco, and by 1700 they were exporting 38,000,000 pounds. Because tobacco initially fetched such a high price, Chesapeake planters mainly grew tobacco and imported all necessities except food and timber. The tobacco boom ended a mere ten years later, in 1629. During the 1630s the price of tobacco fell from sixteen to five pennies per pound as a result of overproduction, and by 1670 it brought only a penny per pound. Although tobacco remained profitable, it would never again command the high prices of the first quarter-century. During the eighteenth century exports of tobacco fluctuated between 25,000,000 and 160,000,000 pounds per year. To maintain a profitable venture, planters needed to continually grow and export more tobacco, but the crop was hard on the soil. The yield declined after only three or four years, so planters moved farther inland or switched to growing wheat.

Lower South Carolina was settled by Englishmen who needed land to grow food for their sugar plantations in the West Indies. They were joined by cavaliers (gentlemen trained as cavalry soldiers) who had been given land by King Charles II (1630–1685). Before finding a marketable crop, English settlers relied on trading deerskins with neighboring Native Americans. Between 1699 and 1715, two hundred traders sent an average of fifty-three thousand skins a year to England. In addition to the flourishing deerskin trade, Carolina produced bowsprits (a large pole projecting from the front of a ship), masts, pitch, resin (a natural substance used in varnishes and medicine), tar, and turpentine. Although these commodities supported the colony, they did not produce the huge profits envisioned by the proprietors. Therefore planters began experimenting to find a crop that could be traded on the world market. Quickly eliminating silk, sugarcane, ginger, tobacco, and grapes, in the 1720s they found that rice would thrive best in the low-lying Carolina terrain.

In 1698 Carolina exported its first shipment of rice, which weighed 12,000 pounds, an amount dwarfed by the 18,000,000 pounds they sent out in 1730. To accommodate the demand for more rice, planters expanded their plantations and acquired more slaves. Planters in the Caribbean supplied capital to develop the plantations and slaves to work the crop. The production of rice increased with the advanced knowledge of African slaves from Senegambia, who had harvested rice in their homeland. Crop yields were also improved with the development of irrigation, better seed, and an innovative cleaning process. In the 1740s Carolina also began exporting indigo (a blue dye), which became the fifth most valuable commodity exported from the mainland colonies, after grain, tobacco, rice, and fish.

Industries slowly emerge

Manufacturing in the American colonies remained limited during the seventeenth and early eighteenth centuries. Low population, poor roads, and scarce labor discouraged investors from starting full-scale manufacturing enterprises. Colonists preferred instead to invest their energy and money in agricultural endeavors. The most common form of manufacturing were small industries run by craftsmen in workshops attached to their homes. The family was the primary unit of production, with the master craftsman assisted by his wife, children, and an occasional apprentice (one who learns by practical experience under skilled workers). These shops were located primarily in New England and Pennsylvania, where staple crops did not dominate the export economy.

Shipbuilding is major industry

There were exceptions, however, especially in larger cities along the Atlantic coast from New England to the South. In the early 1600s shipbuilding began developing to meet transportation and communication needs. The first European settlers in

Eliza Pinckney

Elizabeth (Eliza) Lucas Pinckney (c. 1722–1793) is credited with perfecting a strain of indigo, a blue dye that became a staple crop in South Carolina in the 1740s. Encouraged by her father, a British military officer, she began her experiments when she was only sixteen years old. During this time Pinckney also ran Wappoo, the family plantation, while her father was in the West Indies. At first she tested a variety of crops, such as ginger, cotton, indigo, and figs, in an attempt to develop a profitable commodity for the colony. After consulting experts, in 1738 she decided to concentrate on indigo. Finally, in 1744, she produced a strain that would grow well in South Carolina soil. That year she married Charles Pinckney, who helped her distribute indigo seeds to local planters. Within a few years, the Carolinas were shipping thousands of pounds of indigo to England for use in the textile (cloth) industry.

America founded towns along navigable rivers and next to deep Atlantic harbors. Out of necessity colonists used boats as their principal means of travel and trade. Soon shipbuilding became a prosperous business. After the Navigation Act of 1651 limited American commerce to English and colonial vessels, Massachusetts grew into a major shipbuilding center. Penn-

Colonists working in a shipyard. Shipbuilding became a major industry in the colonies, especially in Massachusetts and Pennsylvania. *Reproduced by permission of The Granger Collection.*

sylvania also had a thriving industry that made ships known for their speed and beauty.

Colonial shipyards produced five different classes of vessels: the sharop (a single-masted boat without a deck), the bark and the ketch (both of which had decks and two masts), the pinnace (a vessel designed to sail along the coast), and the ship. As the largest of all the vessels, the ship had a cargo capacity of well over 100 tons. During the 1700s the types of vessels changed, and four new classes of boats appeared. The sloop (a single-masted boat) was in

widespread use along the coast but was not as popular as the schooner (a boat with two or more masts), a more maneuverable boat. The brigantine was much larger than the schooner, and the snow larger than the brigantine. Colonial vessels usually had square sails in the fore and main masts (front and center of vessel) and a lateen (triangular) sail on the mizzenmast (at the stern). Shipbuilding involved the work of many craftsmen such as glassblowers, pewter makers, silversmiths, wheelwrights, cobblers, weavers, wainwrights, gunsmiths, tanners, millers, and coopers. They supplied goods for domestic and foreign trade as well as for the use of the captains, mates, and sailors.

Distilleries and tanneries

A range of small industries in Philadelphia, Pennsylvania, and New England produced such goods as alcoholic beverages and leather. With increased access to West Indian molasses in 1717, sixty-three distilleries ran full-time in Massachusetts. Beer was the favorite beverage of colonists until the Scots-Irish introduced whiskey. By 1721 Pennsylvania brewers were shipping beer as far south as Charleston, South Carolina. Eventually the production of rum surpassed that of beer and cider in New England. Nearly every farmer on the frontier operated a still (a shortened term for distillery). Tanning proved to be another profitable venture, providing leather to shoemakers, saddlers, and harness makers in larger towns and villages. Pennsylvania was first among colonies in leather production, supplying most of the tanned leather and shoes for southern trade.

Textile manufacturing

Textile (fabrics) manufacturing was another important part of the colonial economy, especially in Pennsylvania. By 1750 inhabitants of the colony were making nine-tenths of their cloth from materials produced on their own farms. Although wool was the major product, textile makers also worked with flax (a type of plant) to

Colonial Ironworks

Iron-making was another industry that started during the colonial period. America was the perfect place for iron production because bogs contained rich ore deposits and plentiful forests offered resources for making charcoal, which was used to melt the ore. Iron was produced mainly for use in the colonies, and any surplus was exported directly to Britain, where it was processed into steel. Colonial ironworks were small operations, and few were a financial success. One of the most famous was the Saugus Ironworks in Massachusetts. Opened in 1648, it produced about a ton of iron a day. In spite of high production, however, the company went bankrupt in 1652.

weave linen. Their industry affected the larger economy by giving employment to dyers, fullers, card makers, comb makers, spinners, and weavers. On a much smaller scale, artisans produced bricks and tiles, pottery, clocks, silver, pewter, and gold artifacts.

Gristmills (mills for grinding grain) and sawmills (mills for sawing logs) emerged as the first industries that required separate facilities. Mill operators employed a larger workforce, required a more substantial investment in buildings and equipment, and depended in large part on water power.

The mills supplied flour and lumber for local and foreign trade. Other such structures housed ironworks, glassworks, paper mills, and powder mills. Small iron forges and furnaces multiplied in Pennsylvania because of abundant ore (a mineral containing a valuable substance for which it is mined and worked) and water power. By 1750 Pennsylvania had taken the lead in the manufacture of iron.

Fishing and whaling

New England exports consisted almost equally of foodstuffs (the raw material of food before and after processing), fish, and wood products. Yet fishing was considered the backbone of the New England economy. In 1669 citizens in the town of Marblehead, Massachusetts, protested an export tax on fish because it was "the only great stapple which the Country Produceth for forraine [foreign] parts and is so benefitiall [beneficial] for making returns for what wee need." Fishing was indeed a main source of livelihood for New England colonists, who exported their catches south to the West Indies and across the Atlantic to the Mediterranean countries. Codfish from the icy North Atlantic waters were unsurpassed for salting and drying. New Englanders produced three grades of fish for export. The highest grade was dun fish, which was buried and allowed to dry and mellow before being shipped to Spain, Portugal, and France. The middle grade, which was easy to process and transport, was the favorite winter food of colonial farmers. Merchants exported the lowest grade to the West Indies along with pickled mackerel and bass. In fact, the highest profits were made by merchants who distributed dried fish and other New England-manufactured goods rather than selling them at home.

Whales were another valuable New England commodity that provided raw materials—ambergris (a waxy substance found floating in tropical waters, believed to originate in the intestines of the sperm whale) for perfume, whalebone for stays and stiffeners (used in clothing) and oil for lamps—that colonies processed and sold to domestic and overseas markets. Ships sailing out of Cape Cod, Nantucket, and Martha's Vineyard sought whales that swam freely in the northern waters of the Atlantic.

Currency takes many forms

As commerce and trade continued to grow, colonists relied on several kinds of currency (money or other forms of payment). At first wampum (woven belts of seashells) was used for trade with Native Americans. Whenever possible colonists exchanged English currency, such as the sterling pound and the shilling, for European trade. But English money was in short supply because colonists usually sent it back to England when they bought manufactured goods. Some colonies issued paper money (notes) based on the English pound, but exchanging money across borders caused problems because the value of notes differed from colony to colony. Innovative colonists relied on other means of exchange. In the Chesapeake region, for instance, planters used tobacco to pay taxes, court fees, and even clergymen's salaries. Many planters exchanged their tobacco at warehouses that issued receipts, which could be used as money. Other colonists purchased items on credit, with the agreement that they would pay their debts when they harvested their crops.

Capital market brings prosperity

During the first half of the eighteenth century, the American colonies developed a new capital market. The two primary forms of capital were bonds and mortgages. A bond was a legal loan agreement drawn up between a lender and a borrower. The person taking out the loan did not have to provide collateral (a guarantee of his ability to pay, usually in the form of property) and made payments for a specified period of time, usually six months or a year. A mortgage was also a legal loan agreement, but it required collateral worth twice the value of the mortgage. Slaves and personal goods were the most common forms of collateral put up for such loans. Colonists could earn substantial amounts of money by investing in bonds and mortgages.

 Women Invest in Market

According to English common law, when a woman got married all of her property was transferred to her husband. Therefore only unmarried or widowed women were property owners. Colonial American women often took advantage of this status. Many single and widowed women made profits in the booming bond and mortgage market during the first half of the eighteenth century. Wealthy investors were able to live off the interest; even women with limited means could receive a good income by investing in only a few bonds or a single mortgage. One successful investor was Elizabeth Buretel, a French Huguenot widow in Charleston, South Carolina. From 1703 to 1727 she lent money to 110 South Carolina settlers for the purchase of land and slaves. Buretel was the most active female investor in the colony at the beginning of the eighteenth century.

Mercantilism protects England

During the 1600s and 1700s European nations relied on an economic policy called mercantilism (a system that advocated government intervention in the economy to increase the power of the state) to develop trade with colonies and make huge profits. Initially this strategy benefitted both England and the American colonies. The demand for labor to process the abundant natural resources of North America provided opportunities for English workers who could not find employment in England. In turn, laborers in the colonies produced the raw materials England needed to avoid relying on other nations. The growing population in America increased the flow of consumer goods (items sold on the market) from England to the colonies, which in turn stimulated the English economy.

The American colonies exported a variety of foodstuffs and raw materials for English consumption and manufacture. England then traded the finished products, such as tobacco or fur hats, on the international free market. Under the ideal trading situation, a colony would export commodities it did not need and import commodities it could not produce. The southern American colonies came closest to the ideal, since they produced rice and tobacco for export and imported consumer goods from England and the other colonies. Eventually all of the American colonies were involved in a thriving export trade in fish, furs and pelts, grain, indigo, livestock, lumber, naval stores (masts, pitch, tar, turpentine), rice, and rum. At the same time the colonies had become England's primary market. Half of the copperware, ironware, glassware, earthenware, silk goods, printed cotton, and flannel produced in England went to the colonies. Between two-thirds and three-quarters of cordage, iron nails, beaver hats, and linen were also sent to America.

Navigation Acts limit free market

Although American colonial trade was financed by private investors, the English government soon stepped in to protect England's economic interests. Between 1651 and 1733 Parliament (the lawmaking body in England) enacted a series of laws known as the Navigation Acts that controlled shipping and markets. In 1651 Parliament specified that commodities produced in English colonies could be carried only on ships owned by Englishmen. In 1660 it ruled that certain goods such as furs, indigo, naval supplies, rice, sugar, and tobacco could be sold only to England or to other English colonies. A 1663 law stipulated that goods imported into the colonies must first pass through English ports. Finally, Parliament prohibited the colonies from manufacturing goods that would directly compete with English products. The Navigation Acts were supplemented with the Woolen Act of 1699, the Hat Act of 1732, and the Iron Act of 1750, which limited the mass production of those goods for export. This intentional effort to control trade for the benefit of England prevented the development of a competitive free market in the American colonies—ultimately triggering the American Revolution.

Economy expands, workers needed

The emerging economy of the American colonies was directly linked to the labor supply. Reliable, able-bodied workers were needed by farmers, plantation owners, estate managers, housewives, merchants, fishermen, shippers, mill owners, and a host of other settlers who were making their way in the New World. This was certainly not a unique situation, as every society requires a labor force for its economic survival. Yet a colony was different from an established nation; settlers were confronted with physical and organizational challenges—clearing land, laying out towns, building houses, planting crops, operating farms and households, running businesses—that required large numbers of skilled people.

Especially in the early years, colonists had to rely heavily on servants and other laborers to avoid disaster. For instance, the first group of settlers at Jamestown were nearly all gentlemen who had never done any physical labor. They did not know how to plant crops, hunt for food, or even meet their own daily needs. Although the Powhatans, the local Native Americans, assisted them, most of the original settlers died or returned to England. Jamestown leaders soon realized they had to bring over more servants and workers, including women, or the settlement would end in failure (see Chapter 4).

Even more workers were needed as the colonies continued to grow, and employers used various strategies to entice immigrants. Eventually laborers made up the majority of new arrivals in America. Apprentices,

 Shipbuilding: A Complex System of Workers

Shipbuilding was a major industry in colonial America that involved the efforts of various kinds of workers. Master shipwrights drew up the plans and then directed the building of vessels. Noise and activity filled the shipyards. Dozens of craftsmen worked for more than a year to build one vessel on elaborate scaffolding at a site near the water. Workers included journeymen, apprentices, indentured servants, and slaves. The journeyman was a former apprentice who worked for the shipwright, learning the master's craft. Apprenticeship was a widespread colonial program of providing vocational education for boys under the age of twenty-one. Parents bound their sons to a master craftsman in return for room and board, education, and sometimes a small wage. The master shipwright's apprentices did odd jobs and various chores around the shipyard, slowly learning the craft until their contract ended. Servants worked up to seven years for no pay. English convicts transported to the colonies worked up to fourteen years. Southern shipyards also frequently used black slaves for manual labor, although some slaves were skilled workmen. For instance, one Maryland merchant in 1754 used slave shipwrights to design and construct his ship.

indentured servants, redemptioners, wage laborers, and slave laborers all helped establish the American colonies.

Apprentices

During the early colonial period a common way to acquire workers was to train children through an apprentice system (a legal and contractual arrangement for occupational training; also called indenture), which settlers brought from Europe. Both boys and girls received their occupational training at home. Most would remain there, being taught farming or domestic skills as they grew into adulthood. Others lived with relatives or friends and acquired the same instruction. Under the apprentice system, boys, usually between ten and fourteen years of age, were sent by their parents to be trained by a master craftsman or merchant in a particular trade or profession. A boy frequently remained an apprentice until he was twenty-one. A young man who had completed his apprenticeship could then work as a journeyman for wages. After serving for a specific length of time as a journeyman, he could then apply for master-craftsman status. Girls were sometimes apprenticed by their parents to become seamstresses or housemaids, serving until they turned eighteen or got married. The apprentice system was also used to train lawyers and doctors, since there were no professional schools in America during the colonial period. Frequently church or government officials used apprenticing as a way to place orphaned children in decent homes.

Indentured servants

Most workers in the American colonies were indentured servants. An indentured servant (also called a bound laborer) was an immigrant who signed a contract to work for an employer for a specified period of time, usually four to seven years. In return, the servant's passage to the colonies was paid for. Employers also provided shelter, food, clothing, and a Sunday free of hard labor. Upon completion of the contract, a servant typically received a suit of clothing or a dress with some additional "assets" such as land. Often the "freedom dues" (items given to a servant at the end of service) were determined according to gender. For instance, a man received a horse, a gun, or tools, and a woman was awarded a cow or a spinning wheel. High mortality (death) rates in some areas meant that many indentured servants—40 percent in the Chesapeake region—died before they could reap the final benefits of their contracts.

Rural Pennsylvania farmers and Chesapeake plantation owners relied most heavily on indentured laborers to plant and harvest their crops. For instance, three-quarters of English migrants to the Chesapeake arrived as bound laborers. According to some estimates, one-half to two-thirds of all Europeans who traveled to the American colonies were committed to some form of labor contract in exchange for their transatlantic passage. As many as fifty thousand convicts served out sentences of seven to fourteen years as indentured servants. Servants worked for farmers, bakers, blacksmiths, bricklayers, butchers, chair makers, coopers, masons, plasterers, potters, tailors, weavers, and wheelwrights.

In the seventeenth century indentured servants could capitalize on economic opportunities and rise in society. But the road to success was not easy. Abusive conditions and harsh punishments plagued the lives of many servants. Contracts could be sold, thus obligating the servant to a different master for the rest of his or her term. A master could extend the contract if a servant ran away or became pregnant. Opportunities for social and economic advancement had decreased by the eighteenth century. By the end of the colonial period Pennsylvania farmers had turned to day laborers, and Chesapeake planters had shifted to African slaves.

Redemptioners

Redemptioners were similar to indentured servants in that they agreed to work for a specific period in return for transatlantic passage. The difference was that they arranged a contract once they arrived in the colonies rather than agreeing to terms for labor in England or Europe before beginning the trip. These bound laborers could not leave the ships until they found a colonist who was willing to pay for their voyage in return for labor. Whereas most indentured servants were unmarried men and women from England, redemptioners were usually families from Germany. In some cases an entire family would commit to a

 "I have nothing to Comfort me"

In 1623 Richard Frethorne, an indentured servant in Virginia, wrote a letter to his parents in England about his miserable experience. The following excerpt details his lack of proper food and clothing. (The Virginia legislature later passed a law requiring masters to furnish servants with adequate food, clothing, shelter, medical care, and other protections.)

. . . . I have nothing to Comfort me, nor is there nothing to be gotten here but sickness, and death, except that one had money to lay out in some things for profit; But I have nothing at all, no not a shirt to my backe, but two Rags nor no Clothes, but one poor suit, nor but one pair of shoes, but one pair of stockings, but one Cap, but two [collar] bands, my Cloak is stolen by one of my own fellows. . . . I am not half a quarter so strong as I was in England, and all is for want of victuals [food], for I do protest unto you, that I have eaten more in a day at home than I have allowed here for a Week. You have given more than my day's allowance to a beggar at the door. . . .

Reprinted in: Kupperman, Karen Ordahl, ed. Major Problems in American Colonial History. Lexington, Mass.: D. C. Heath, 1993, pp. 93–94.

labor contract, or parents would obligate a child or children to a contract that would pay for the family's passage. These terms were also for four to seven years.

Wage laborers

Wage laborers (also called day laborers) made up the smallest group of workers in the colonies. During the seventeenth century they tended to be young, unmarried men and women who worked for a daily wage. Some wage laborers were former indentured servants who had completed their contract but were not yet self-sufficient. They were rarely available in rural areas, however, because most had purchased land or had moved to urban centers where the demand for labor was higher. For these workers wage labor was a lifelong condition. For example, in 1762 a laborer would have needed fifty pounds (British money) a year for food, rent, fuel, and clothing for his family. That amount would not cover additional outlays for soap, candles, taxes, or medical expenses. Since worker demand depended on the seasons and employers' business needs, a wage laborer could hope to bring home no more than sixty pounds a year. Even if his wife also earned an income, it would be only about half that amount, so the family would constantly live in poverty. Injury or pregnancy could doom them to dependence on the community.

Slave laborers

By 1750 slaves lived in all thirteen colonies, but most were concentrated on southern plantations, which required a large labor force. The first slaves in North America arrived in Virginia in 1619 when a Dutch trader exchanged twenty slaves for provisions (a stock of food). Because slaves were more expensive than indentured servants, who were readily available, planters initially preferred short-term contracts with English servants. In 1670, for instance, a slave cost three times as much as an indentured servant. Twenty years later slaves were less than twice as expensive and could be purchased for a lifetime rather than seven years. By 1703 slaves outnumbered indentured servants in the Chesapeake and in Carolina. This change had taken place primarily because West Indian planters had successfully promoted the benefits of slave labor for producing such staple crops as tobacco in the Chesapeake and rice in Carolina. Soon enslaved blacks and Native Americans made up 47 percent of the population of Carolina. Slaves in the southern colonies typically worked in the fields, although some worked as domestics (household servants) or artisans. Farming in the northern colonies depended on family labor, so the need for large-scale enslaved labor never developed. Slaves in the northern colonies more frequently worked as domestic servants and craftsmen rather than farmhands.

The slave trade

The demand for slave laborers grew into a thriving trade in the American colonies, not only in the South but also at busy ports in the North. By the latter half of the seventeenth century England had taken control of the Atlantic Ocean away from Holland. In

Slaves in Virginia

In 1705 wealthy Virginia planter Robert Beverley described the duties and status of slaves and servants in *The History and Present State of Virginia*. He hoped to encourage immigrants to come to Virginia as indentured servants. Critics in England had accused Southern planters of mistreating servants and slaves, so Beverley made an effort to put the situation—especially the treatment of white women—in a positive light.

Their Servants, they distinguish by the Names of Slaves for Life, and Servants for a time. . . . Slaves are the Negroes, and their Posterity [children], following the condition of the Mother, according to the Maxim [wise saying], partus sequitur ventrem [Latin: status proceeds from the womb; that is, if the mother is a slave the child will be a slave]. They are call'd Slaves, in respect of the time of their Servitude, because it is for Life. . . .

The Male-Servants, and Slaves of both Sexes, are imployed together in Tilling [plowing] and Manuring [fertilizing] the Ground, in Sowing and Planting Tobacco, Corn. . . . Some Distinction indeed is made between them in their Cloaths, and Food; but the Work of both, is no other than what the Overseers, the Freemen [freed servants], and the Planters themselves do.

Sufficient Distinction is also made between the Female-Servants, and Slaves; for a White Woman is rarely or never put to work in the Ground [in the field], if she be good for any thing else: And to Discourage all Planters from using any Women so, their Law imposes the heaviest Taxes upon Female-Servants working in the Ground, while it suffers all other white Women to be absolutely exempted: Whereas on the other hand, it is a common thing to work a Woman Slave out of Doors; nor does the Law make any distinction in her Taxes, whether her Work be Abroad [in other places], or at Home. . . .

Reprinted in: Kupperman, Karen Ordahl, ed. Major Problems in American Colonial History. *Lexington, Mass.: D. C. Heath, 1993, pp. 98–99.*

1672 the English Crown reorganized and rechartered a trading company, calling it the Royal African Company. For the next twenty-six years this group maintained a monopoly (an exclusive ownership through legal privilege, command of supply, or action) over the sale of African slaves. With the termination of the monopoly, New England merchants became active in the colonial slave trade. They sent goods to West Africa, where they traded for slaves, whom they then sold in the West Indies or Carolina. New England slavers sailed primarily from Massachusetts until 1750, when the center of trade shifted to Rhode Island.

Millions of slaves sold

Between the sixteenth and nineteenth centuries, 10,000,000 to

11,000,000 African slaves crossed the Atlantic Ocean. Most (85 percent) went to Brazil and the British, French, Spanish, Danish, or Dutch colonies in the Caribbean. Nine percent of the slaves were sent to the Spanish mainland. Only 6 percent, or 600,000 to 650,000 Africans, went to the American colonies. Most of the slaves were from the coast of West Africa or from the Congo/Angola area farther south. At best a trip between Senegambia and Barbados lasted three weeks. Storms or still waters could delay a ship so that the transatlantic voyage took three months and exhausted food and water supplies. During the seventeenth century, between 5 and 20 percent of the slaves died in transit, but the mortality rate declined in the eighteenth century. Merchants made money only if the slaves arrived alive, so they sought captains who could deliver healthy slaves.

Africans packed into ships

Sailors referred to the shipboard experience of enslaved Africans across the Atlantic Ocean as "the middle passage." During the voyage men were usually chained, while women and children were allowed some freedom of movement on the ship deck. Captains chose one of two methods for transporting slaves: tight packing or loose packing. Tight packing squeezed as many slaves into a space as possible. Male slaves lay in spaces six feet long, sixteen inches wide, and two and one-half feet high. Female slaves lay in spaces five feet long, fourteen inches wide, and two and one-half feet high.

Such tight spaces prevented the slaves from moving about or even sitting up. Captains who chose this style of storage did not want to waste space. They believed their net receipts were higher from the larger cargo even if a higher percentage of slaves died. Other captains chose loose packing. They believed that more room, better food, and a degree of freedom reduced the death rate of slaves. Healthy slaves increased their profit. Some captains insured their stock of slaves against drowning. Because insurance did not cover slaves who died aboard a ship, some captains dumped dying slaves overboard and claimed they drowned in order to collect insurance benefits.

Slaves auctioned in marketplace

Once slave ships had docked, the goal of slave merchants was to make a profit from a quick sale. In some cases an entire cargo might be reserved for a planter or a group of planters, thus closing the sale to anyone else. A more common practice was to sell slaves in an auction where buyers would place bids. Prior to bidding, slaves were exhibited before prospective buyers, who poked and prodded them. After the slaves had been examined, an auctioneer would sell them to the highest bidder. Another method involved merchants setting a price beforehand and then selling the slaves in groups as buyers scrambled into a holding pen to pick out the choicest slaves. Olaudah Equiano, a freed slave, described the chaotic scene of such a sale in his autobiography: "On a signal

British soldiers lead an African family up the ramp of a ship that will take them to the colonies to be sold as slaves. *Reproduced by permission of The Library of Congress.*

given, the buyers rush at once into the yard where the slaves are confined, and make choice of that parcel they like best. The noise and clamor with which this is attended, and the eagerness visible on the countenances of the buyers, serve not a little to increase the apprehensions of terrified Africans."

Commercial and private transportation

During the sixteenth century Spain established regular routes across the Atlantic to North and South Amer-

ica. As travel and trade between Europe and the American colonies steadily increased in the seventeenth century, shipwrights learned how to make their vessels larger, faster, and more seaworthy. By 1740 a traveler embarking for London, England, from Boston, Massachusetts, could expect to reach his or her destination within eight weeks, a good speed by the standards of the day. Yet conditions on the ship were poor. Except for the few who could afford private quarters, passengers had to stay with the crew. Quarters were cramped, unsanitary, poorly ventilated, and hot in summer and cold in winter. Food—usually hard biscuits, salt pork, and peas—was often worm-eaten by journey's end. Drinking water was often scarce and contaminated.

Navigation

Travel from colony to colony was accomplished most quickly and easily by boat. In the early seventeenth century vast tracts of virgin forest separated the small centers of English settlement in New England, New York, and the Chesapeake. Only the hardiest souls could make the trip between them by land. Everywhere in colonial America settlements sprang up first near navigable rivers. As population and commerce grew, a bustling trade was carried on through inlets and along coastal waters in single-masted pinnaces or schooners. Travel up the rivers was more difficult, and colonists built a variety of canoes, barges, and rafts to manage it. In the Southeast two types of river vessel were most common: dugout canoes called pirogues carried small cargoes, while long (up to forty feet), flat-bottomed boats known as bateaux handled larger loads. Farther north in New England the birchbark canoe was most efficient vessel. River travel everywhere in America was slow and fraught with danger. To travel inland a boat crew had to paddle or pole upstream. Floating debris could tip a boat, submerged rocks could sink it, and sandbars could catch and hold it. Ice in northern rivers made travel impossible during the winter.

Travel by land

Land travel between colonies could also be difficult. The number and condition of roads depended on the size of the population and the support provided by colonial legislatures. By the 1700s a system of short roads was developing from New England to the Chesapeake region. The roads extended farther inland each year as more extensive commerce and communication were required by new towns along the frontier. Wealthy colonists traveled the roads in elegant carriages, which they imported from Europe or purchased from colonial craftsmen. A horse could take a traveler to areas a carriage could not, but horses were usually expensive. Farming families often used their plow oxen to pull wagons. Poorer colonists who needed to travel often had to make their journeys on foot.

In many places roads were poor and bridges few. During the rainy seasons shallow fords (part of a body of water that may be crossed by wading) became deep and treacherous, and roads became impassable tracks of mud. Even at other times of the year, the going was rough, and it became rougher the farther inland one traveled. For instance, in the winter of 1738 to 1739 English evangelist George Whitefield took more than a month to journey 660 miles from Philadelphia to Charleston by horseback (an eleven-hour automobile trip today). His route took him through almost trackless forests and treacherous swamps and across flooded rivers.

Some of the most treacherous colonial roads could be traveled by sturdy Conestoga wagons drawn by oxen or horses. These wagons were built by German immigrants living in the Conestoga region of Pennsylvania, near Lancaster. Each year Conestoga wagons made longer trips as roads extended farther into the backcountry. By the 1760s one of the longest roads, the Great Wagon Road, stretched nearly 800 miles along old Native American trails from western Pennsylvania through the Shenandoah Valley in Virginia to Georgia.

Communications

Throughout the colonial period travel and commerce across the Atlantic intensified the need for quick and accurate information on both sides of the ocean. In Europe, investors were anxious to know whether a settlement was turning a profit and people longed for word from family members 3,000 miles across the ocean. In the colonies planters and traders awaited news from European merchants about market prices and shipment schedules. The fate of the colonies depended on the English government maintaining regular communication with colonial officials.

Informal information networks

At first colonists devised informal ways of staying abreast of personal matters and public affairs. Ships arriving from Europe carried business

Sarah Knight's Famous Trip

In 1704 Sarah Kemble Knight (1666–1727), a Boston businesswoman, made a trip through New England. She kept a diary that was later published as *The Journal of Madame Knight* (1825). The trip through the wilderness from Boston to New Haven, Connecticut, was extremely difficult and hazardous. (Knight followed the route now used by the Pennsylvania Central Railroad.) For a woman to undertake such a journey alone—and on horseback—was considered unthinkable at the time. Since there were very few roads or bridges en route, Knight had to seek the help of guides. Despite encountering hardships, she gave a lighthearted and sometimes humorous account of the trip in her diary. She recorded all the "Bugbears to a fearful female travailer," such as "Bridges which were . . . very tottering and of vast Length." When bridges were lacking Knight crossed rivers in canoes or on horseback. After traveling for five days, she arrived at New Haven. Along the way she had recorded a vivid portrait of colonial America, which enlightens and entertains readers even today.

documents and private letters. Special couriers and traveling government officials delivered notices of orders from the king or recent acts of Parliament. Information made its way along the Atlantic coast from dockside

A colonial postman delivering the mail by horseback. A postal route linking New York, Connecticut, and Massachusetts was developed in the 1690s.
Reproduced by permission of Corbis-Bettmann.

taverns, where sailors gathered to exchange news and gossip. For instance, black sailors used this method to help African Americans stay in touch with slave communities in the Caribbean. Information moved inland from the coast in similar ways. Travelers stopped at taverns to leave letters and catch up on local events. People discussed news and delivered letters at church gatherings. From the pulpit ministers read royal proclamations or governor's orders, made announcements of important public matters, and read aloud correspon-

dence from fellow ministers in the British Isles.

Postal service

Postal services began emerging in the colonies during the early seventeenth century. For instance, in 1639 Boston officials designated the tavern kept by Richard Fairbanks as the site for depositing and receiving letters carried by ships from Europe. Other colonies set up similar sites, but postal service to inland towns or even overland between major cities was not established until much later. Finally, in the 1690s, a postal route linked New York, Connecticut, and Massachusetts. Mailmen riding on horseback initially followed a monthly schedule; then they began making weekly deliveries and pickups to handle the increasing volume of mail. Colonies followed England in passing special postal acts that set rates, specified procedures for appointing postmasters, and authorized private postal services. Rates varied widely from colony to colony. Massachusetts, for example, set the charge for an overseas letter at two pence (pennies), while New York set it at nine. A letter from Rhode Island to Boston cost six pence, the equivalent of a half-day's pay for a sailor. Postal routes played an important part in stimulating the colonial economy. For instance, craftsmen and merchants were able to move to smaller ports and market towns, where the cost of living was lower, and still stay in touch with customers and suppliers in larger cities. During the eighteenth century, prominent printers such as Benjamin Franklin of Philadelphia served as postmasters. Printers also published newspapers, and they often expanded postal routes to deliver their newspapers to readers throughout the colonies.

Newspapers

Between 1660 and 1695 newspapers were rare even in England. Publication was tightly controlled by the king through legislation known as the Licensing Act because royal officials feared that newspapers could be used

 Franklin Builds Fortune as Publisher

In 1728 Philadelphia printer Benjamin Franklin purchased a struggling newspaper and renamed it the *Pennsylvania Gazette.* He acquired a fortune through witty writing and shrewd competition with a rival newspaper, the *American Weekly Mercury.* Franklin also printed books, government documents, and the popular *Poor Richard's Almanack.* He built a network of publishers throughout the colonies, extending his influence as far away as Charleston. Franklin's own paper benefitted greatly from this because contacts in other colonies gave him access to even more news.

to spread rebellious ideas. Consequently, when Boston printer Benjamin Harris published *Publick Occurrences,* the first newspaper in America, in 1690, colonial officials quickly suppressed it. Within five years, however, the Licensing Act had expired, and English printers responded with a variety of publications designed to meet the demand for news. Many of these "publick prints," as they were called, made their way to the colonies. In 1704 Boston postmaster and printer John Campbell (1653–1728) borrowed freely from the format and articles of English newspapers to publish one of the first successful newspapers in

America, the *Boston News-Letter*. Over the next three decades eighteen additional papers appeared in the colonies, seventeen in English and one in German. Six were published in Boston, where rival printers competed for readers with interesting essays and news stories. Writers took opposing positions on issues of the day, carrying on fierce debates that increased sales.

Advertising emerges

Early colonial newspapers were published for well-to-do merchants, planters, and government officials who needed to know what was happening in England and Europe. For this reason the papers usually focused on European news, often reprinting articles directly from London newspapers or publishing excerpts about European affairs from private letters. News from Europe was often two to three months old, but in most cases it was still useful for scheduling the next shipment of goods to Europe, keeping up with English fashions, or catching the latest gossip from London. Colonial newspapers also provided a forum for public debate, carrying essays on controversial issues of the day. News from the colonies rarely occupied much space, since business and politics depended more on happenings overseas. Nevertheless newspapers became an important tool for advertising and public notices, or for masters to track down runaway servants or slaves. By 1740 at least two pages of an ordinary four-page newspaper consisted of lost-and-found items and ads for imported British goods, colonial services, local real estate, printed materials, and public notices.

Where to Learn More

The following list focuses on works written for readers of middle school or high school age. Books aimed at adult readers have been included when they are especially important in providing information or analysis that would otherwise be unavailable, or because they have become classics.

Adler, Bill, ed. *The American Indian: The First Victim.* New York: Morrow, 1972.

Armstrong, Joe C. W. *Champlain.* Toronto: Macmillan of Canada, 1987.

Bacon, Margaret Hope. *Mothers of Feminism.* New York: Haper-Collins, 1986.

Bailyn, Bernard. *Voyagers to the West: A Passage in the Peopling of America on the Eve of the Revolution.* New York: Vintage, 1986.

Barbour, Philip L., ed. *The Complete Works of Captain John Smith* *(1580–1631).* 3 Vols. Chapel Hill, N.C.: University of North Carolina Press, 1986.

Barbour, Philip L. *Pocahontas and Her World.* Boston: Houghton Mifflin, 1969.

Barbour, Philip L. *The Worlds of Captain John Smith.* Boston: Houghton Mifflin, 1964.

Bataiile, Gretchen M., ed. *Native American Women.* New York: Garland Publishing, 1993.

Bergman, Peter M. *The Chronological History of the Negro in America,* New York: Harper & Row, 1969.

Berkeley, Edmund and Dorothy Smith Berkeley. *The Life and Travels of John Bartram from Lake Ontario to the River St. John.* Tallahassee: University Presses of Florida, 1982.

Berkin, Carol. *First Generations: Women in Colonial America.* New York: Hill & Wang, 1996.

Biographical Dictionary of Indians of the Americas, Vol. 1. Newport Beach, Calif.: American Indian Publishers, 1991.

Blackburn, Joyce. *James Edward Oglethorpe.* New York: Dodd, Mead, 1970.

Blodgett, Harold. *Samson Occom.* Hanover, N.H.: Dartmouth College Publications, 1935.

Bolton, Herbert Eugene. *Coronado: Knight of the Pueblos and Plains.* Albuquerque: University of New Mexico Press, 1964.

Bolton, Herbert Eugene. *Kino's Historical Memoir of Primería Alta,* Vol. 1. Cleveland: Arthur H. Clark, 1919.

Bourne, Russell. *The Red King's Rebellion: Racial Politics in New England, 1675–1678.* New York: Atheneum, 1990.

Bradford, William. "Governor William Bradford on the Plymouth Colonists' Relations with the Indians, Early 1620s." In *Major Problems in American Colonial History,* Edited by Karen Ordahl Kupperman. Lexington, Mass.: D. C. Heath, 1993.

Breen, T. H. and Stephen Innes. *"Myne Owne Ground": Race and Freedom on Virginia's Eastern Shore, 1640–1676.* New York: Oxford University Press, 1980.

Brill, Marlene Targ. *Encyclopedia of Presidents: John Adams.* Chicago: Children's Press, 1986.

Burrows, Edwin G., and Mike Wallace. *Gotham: A History of New York City to 1898.* New York: Oxford University Press, 1999.

Cady, Edwin Harrison. *John Woolman.* New York: Washington Square Press, 1965.

Calloway, Colin G., ed. *After King Philip's War: Presence and Persistence in Indian New England.* Hanover, N.H.: Dartmouth College, 1978.

Cameron, Ann. *The Kidnaped Prince: The Life of Olaudah Equiano.* New York: Knopf, 1995.

Campbell, Elizabeth A. *The Carving in the Tree.* New York: Little, Brown and Company, 1968.

Champlain, Samuel de. *Voyages of Samuel de Champlain.* Edited by W. L. Grant. New York: Barnes and Noble, 1952.

Colbert, David, ed. *Eyewitness to America.* New York: Pantheon Books, 1997.

Columbus, Christopher. *The Voyage of Christopher Columbus: Columbus's Own Journal of Discovery.* Translated by John Cummins. New York: St. Martin's Press, 1992.

Connors, Donald Francis. *Thomas Morton.* New York: Twayne Publishers, 1969.

The Correspondence of Jeremias Van Rensselaer, 1651–1674. Edited by A. J. F. Van Laer. Albany: University of the State of New York, 1932.

The Correspondence of Maria Van Rensselaer, 1669–1689. Edited by A. J. F. Van Laer. Albany: University of the State of New York, 1935,

Coulter, Tony. *La Salle and the Explorers of the Mississippi,* New York: Chelsea House, 1991.

Crawford, Deborah. *Four Women in a Violent Time: Anne Hutchinson (1591–1643), Mary Dyer (1591?–1660), Lady Deborah Moody (1660–1659), Penelope Stout (1622–1732).* New York: Crown Publishers, 1970.

Cwiklik, Robert. *King Philip and the War with the Colonists.* Englewood Cliffs, N.J.: Silver Burdett Publishers, 1989.

Dalglish, Doris N. *People Called Quakers.* Freeport, N.Y.: Books for Libraries Press, 1969.

Davis, Natalie Zemon. *Women on the Margins: Three Seventeenth-Century Lives.* Cambridge, Mass.: Harvard University Press, 1995.

De Leeuw, Adéle. *Peter Stuyvesant.* Champaign, Ill.: Garrard Publishing Company, 1970.

Demos, John. *The Tried and the True: Native Amrican Women Confronting Colonization.* New York: Oxford University Press, 1995.

Dockstader, Frederick J. *Great North American Indians.* New York: Van Nostrand Reinhold, 1977.

Dolson, Hildegarde. *William Penn, Quaker Hero.* New York: Random House, 1961.

Dubowski, Cathy East. *The Story of Squanto: First Friend of the Pilgrims.* Milwaukee: Gareth Stevens Publishers, 1997.

Duncan, David Ewing. *Hernando de Soto: A Savage Quest in the Americas.* New York: Crown Publishers, 1995.

Dunham, Montrew. *Anne Bradstreet; Young Puritan Poet.* Indianapolis: Bobbs-Merrill, 1969.

Dunn, Richard S. *Puritans and Yankees: The Winthrop Dynasty of New England 1630–1717.* Princeton, N.J.: Princeton University Press, 1962.

Dupré, Céline. "Réne-Robert Cavelier de La Salle." In *Dictionary of Canadian Biography,* Vol. 1. Toronto: University of Toronto Press, 1967.

Earle, Alice Morse. *Child Life in Colonial Days.* New York: Macmillan, 1899; reprinted Stockbridge, Mass.: Berkshire House Publishers, 1993,

Eccles, W. J. *France in America.* Rev. ed. Markham, Ontario: Fitzhenry & Whiteside, 1990.

Eckert, Allan W. *The Conquerors.* Boston: Little, Brown and Company, 1970.

Eckert, Allan W. *The Frontiersmen.* Boston: Little, Brown and Company 1967.

Eckert, Allan W. *Wilderness Empire: A Narrative.* Boston: Little, Brown and Company, 1969.

Elgin, Kathleen. *The Quakers; The Religious Society of Friends.* New York: D. McKay Company, 1968.

Elliott, Emory, and others, ed. *American Literature: A Prentice Hall Anthology.* Englewood Cliffs, N.J.: Prentice Hall, 1991.

Ellis, Joseph S. *Passionate Sage: The Character and Legacy of John Adams.* New York: Norton, 1994.

Faber, Doris. *Anne Hutchinson.* Champaign, Ill.: Garrard Publishing Co., 1970.

Feest, Christian F. *The Powhatan Tribes.* New York: Chelsea House, 1989.

Ferling, John E. *John Adams: A Life.* New York: Henry Holt & Company, 1996.

Foster, Genevieve. *The World of Captain John Smith.* New York: Scribners, 1959.

Franklin, Benjamin. *Benjamin Franklin: A Biography in His Own Words.* Edited by Thomas Fleming. New York: Newsweek, distributed by Harper & Row, 1972.

Gates, Henry Louis Jr., ed. *The Classic Slave Narratives.* New York: New American Library, 1987.

Gaustad, Edwin S. *Liberty of Conscience: Roger Williams in America.* Grand Rapids, Mich.: Eerdmans, 1991.

Goodfriend, Joyce. *Before the Melting Pot: Society and Culture in Colonial New York City.* Princeton, N.J.: Princeton University Press, 1992.

Grabo, Norman S. *Edward Taylor.* New York: Twayne Publishers, 1962.

Guiterrez, Ramon A. *When Jesus Came, the Corn Mothers Went Away.* Stanford, Calif.: Stanford University Press, 1991.

Gunn, Giles, ed. *Early American Writing.* New York: Penguin Books, 1994,

Haile, Edward Wright, ed. *Jamestown Narratives: Eyewitness Accounts of the Virginia Colony: The First Decade: 1607–1617.* Champlain, Va.: Roundhouse, 1998.

Hamilton, Raphael N. *Father Marquette.* Detroit: William B. Eerdmans Publisher, 1970.

"Hannah Duston." In *The Young Oxford History of Women in the United States: Biographical Supplement and Index.* Edited by Nancy F. Cott. New York: Oxford University Press, 1995.

Harrah, Madge. *My Brother, My Enemy.* New York: Simon & Schuster Books for Young Readers, 1997. (Fiction)

Hays, Wilma Pitchford. *Rebel Pilgrim: A Biography of Governor William Bradford.* Philadelphia: Westminster Press, 1969.

Herbst, Josephine. *New Green World.* New York: Hastings House, 1954.

Innes, Stephen, ed. *Work and Labor in Early America.* Chapel Hill, N.C.: University of North Carolina Press, 1988.

Jacobs, William Jay. *Coronado: Dreamer in Golden Armor,* New York: Franklin Watts, 1994.

James, Edward T., and others, eds. *Notable American Women,* 3 Vols. Cambridge, Massachusets: Belknap Press of Harvard University Press, 1971.

Johnson, Allen, and others, eds. *Dictionary of American Biography.* New York: Scribners, 1946–58.

Johnson, Charles, Patricia Smith, and WGBH Research Team. *Africans in America: America's Journey through Slavery.* New York: Harcourt, Brace & Company, 1998.

Josephy, Alvin M. "The Betrayal of King Philip." In *The Patriot*

Chiefs: A Chronicle of Native American Resistance. New York: Viking, 1969.

Kamensky, Jane *The Colonial Mosaic: American Women, 1600–1760.* New York: Oxford University Press, 1995.

Kelso, William M., Nicholas M. Luccketti, and Beverly A. Straube. *Jamestown Rediscovery IV.* Richmond, Va.: The Association for the Preservation of Virginia Antiquities, 1998.

Kent, Zachary. *Jacques Marquette and Louis Jolliet.* Chicago: Children's Press, 1994.

Knaut, Andrew L. *The Pueblo Revolt of 1980: Conquest and Resistance in Seventeenth-Century New Mexico.* Norman, Okla.: University of Oklahoma Press, 1995.

Krensky, Stephen. *The Printer's Apprentice.* New York: Bantam Doubleday Dell Books for Young Readers, 1996.

Kupperman, Karen Ordahl, ed. *Major Problems in American Colonial History.* Lexington, Mass.: D. C. Heath, 1993.

Lambert, Frank. *Peddlar in Divinity": George Whitefield and the Transatlantic Revivals, 1737–1770.* Princeton, N.J.: Princeton University Press, 1994.

Lee, Susan. *Eliza Pinckney.* Chicago: Children's Press, 1977.

Levin, David. *Cotton Mather: The Young Life of the Lord's Remembrance, 1663–1703.* Cambridge, Mass.: Harvard University Press, 1978.

Lockridge, Kenneth A. *The Diary, and Life, of William Byrd II of Virginia, 1674–1744.* Chapel Hill, N.C.: University of North Carolina Press, 1987.

"Massasoit." In *Biographical Dictionary of Indians of the Americas.* Vol. 1. Newport Beach, Calif.: American Indian Publishers, 1991.

McCormick, Charles Howard. *Leisler's Rebellion.* New York: Garland Publishers, 1989.

McDaniel, Melissa. *The Powhatan Indians.* New York: Chelsea House, 1995.

McFarland, Philip James. *The Brave Bostonians: Hutchinson, Quincy, and The Coming of the American Revolution.* Boulder, Colo.: Westview Press, 1998.

Middleton, Richard. *Colonial America: A History, 1585–1776.* 2nd ed. Malden, Mass.: Blackwell Publishers, 1996.

Miller, Perry. *Roger Williams: His Contribution to the American Tradition.* New York: Atheneum, 1962.

Montgomery, Elizabeth Rider, *Hernando de Soto.* Champaign, Ill.: Garrard Publishing Company, 1964.

Morgan, Edmund S. *The Puritan Dilemma: The Story of John Winthrop.* Boston: Little, Brown and Company, 1958.

Morison, Samuel Eliot. *The Great Explorers: The European Discovery of America.* New York: Oxford University Press, 1986.

Morison, Samuel Eliot. *Samuel de Champlain, Father of New France.* Boston, Mass.: Little, Brown and Company, 1972.

Nagel, Paul C. *Descent from Glory: Four Generations of the John*

Adams Family. Cambridge, Mass.: Harvard University Press, 1999.

National Geographic Society. *The World of the American Indian*. Rev. ed. Washington, D.C.: National Geographic Society. 1993.

Osler, E. B. *La Salle*. Toronto: Longmans Canada, 1967.

Parish, Helen Rand. *Estebanico*. New York: Viking Press, 1974. (Fiction)

Pinckney, Eliza, ed. *The Letterbook of Eliza Lucas Pinckney*. Columbia, S.C.: University of South Carolina Press, 1997.

Pollock, John Charles. *George Whitefiled and the Great Awakening*. Garden City, N.Y.: Doubleday, 1972.

Putnam, William Lowell. *John Peter Zenger and the Fundamental Freedom*. Jefferson, N.C.: McFarland and Co., 1997.

Quinn, David Beers. *Set Fair for Roanoke: Voyages and Colonies, 1584–1606*. Chapel Hill, N.C.: University of North Carolina Press, 1985.

Rachlis, Eugene. *The Voyages of Henry Hudson*. New York: Random House, 1962.

Reich, Jerome R. *Leisler's Rebellion*. Chicago: University of Chicago Press, 1953.

Riforgiato, Leonard R. *Missionary of Moderation: Henry Melchior Mühlenberg and the Lutheran Church in English America*. Lewisburg, Pa.: Bucknell University Press, 1980.

Ritchie, Robert C. *Captain Kidd and the War against the Pirates*. Cambridge, Mass.: Harvard University Press, 1986.

Rountree, Helen C. *The Powhatan Indians of Virginia: Their Traditional Culture*. Norman: University of Oklahoma Press, 1989.

Rowlandson, Mary. *The Narrative of the Captivity and Restoration of Mrs. Mary Rowlandson*. Excerpted in *American Literature: A Prentice Hall Anthology*. Edited by Emory Elliott and others. Englewood Cliffs, N.J.: Prentice Hall, 1991.

Rudy, Lisa Jo, ed. *The Benjamin Franklin Book of Easy and Incredible Experiments*. New York: Wiley, 1995.

Sale, Kirkpatrick. *The Conquest of Paradise: Christopher Columbus and the Columbian Legacy*. New York: Knopf, 1990.

Salisbury, Neal, ed. *Sovereignty and Goodness of God*. Boston: Bedford Books, 1997.

Sando, Joe S. *Pueblo Profiles: Cultural Identity through Centuries of Change*. Santa Fe: Clear Light, 1995.

Saunders, Richard H. *John Smibert: Colonial America's First Portrait Painter*. New Haven, Conn.: Yale University Press, 1995.

Sewall, Marcia. *Thunder from the Sky*. New York: Antheneum Books for Young Readers, 1995.

Sherman, Josepha. *The First Americans: Spirit of the Land and People*. New York: Smithmark, 1996.

Sigerman, Harriet, ed. *Young Oxford History of Women in the United States: Biographical Supplement and Index*. New York: Oxford University Press, 1994.

Silverman, Kenneth, ed. *Colonial American Poetry*. New York: Hafner, 1968.

Smith, Carter, ed. *The Arts and Sciences: A Sourcebook on Colonial America*. Brookfield, Conn.: Millbrook Press, 1991.

Smith, Carter, ed. *Battles in a New Land: A Sourcebook on Colonial America*. Brookfield, Conn.: Millbrook Press, 1991

Smith, Carter, ed. *Daily Life: A Sourcebook on Colonial America*. Brookfield, Conn.: Millbrook Press, 1991.

Smith, Carter, ed. *The Explorers and Settlers: A Sourcebook on Colonial America*. Brookfield, Conn.: Millbrook Press, 1991.

Smith, Carter, ed. *Governing and Teaching: A Sourcebook on Colonial America*. Brookfield, Conn.: Millbrook Press, 1991.

Smith, Carter, ed. *The Puritan Family*. New York: Harper & Row, 1966.

Spaulding, Phinizy. *Oglethorpe in America*. Athens, Ga.: University of Georgia Press, 1984.

Stanford, Donald E. *Edward Taylor*. Minneapolis, Minn.: University of Minnesota Press, 1965.

Stephen, Leslie, and Sidney Lee, eds. *The Dictionary of National Biography*. London, England: Oxford University Press.

Stevenson, Augusta. *Squanto: Young Indian Hunter*. Indianapolis: Bobbs-Merrill. 1962.

Steven, William K. "Drought May Have Doomed the Lost Colony." In *The New York Times*. April 14, 1998, pp. A1, A14.

Stiles, T. J., ed. *In Their Own Words: The Colonizers*. New York: Berkeley Publishing, 1998.

Stout, Harry S. *The Divine Dramatist: George Whitefield and the Rise of Modern Evangelism*. Grand Rapids, Mich.: Eerdmans, 1991.

Syme, Ronald. *Francisco Coronado and the Seven Cities of Gold*. New York: Morrow, 1965.

Terrell, John Upton. *The Life and Times of an Explorer*. London, England: Weybright and Talley, 1968.

Tracy, Patricia J. *Jonathan Edwards, Pastor: Religion and Society in Eighteenth-Century* Northampton, N.Y.: Hill & Wang, 1979.

Trudel, Marcel. "Jacques Cartier." In *Dictionary of Canadian Biography*, Vol. 1. Toronto: University of Toronto Press, 1967.

Vachon, André. "Louis Jolliet." In *Dictionary of Canadian Biography*, Vol. 1. Toronto: University of Toronto, 1967.

Wainwright, Nicholas B. *George Croghan: Wilderness Diplomat*. Chapel Hill, N.C.: The University of North Carolina Press, 1959.

Waldman, Carl. *Who Was Who in Native American History*. New York: Facts on File, 1990.

Wallace, Paul A. W. *The Muhlenbergs of Pennsylvania*. Philadelphia: University of Pennsylvania Press, 1950.

Warfel, Harry R., and others, editors. *The American Mind*. 2nd ed. Vol. 1. New York: American Book Company, 1963.

Webb, Stephen Saunders. *1676: The End of American Independence*. New York: Knopf, 1984.

Wendell, Barrett. *Cotton Mather*. New York: Chelsea House, 1980.

White, Elizabeth Wade. *Anne Brad-street, "The Tenth Muse."* New York: Oxford University Press, 1971.

Whitman, Sylvia. *Hernando de Soto and the Explorers of the American South.* New York: Chelsea House, 1991.

Wildes, Harry Emerson. *William Penn.* New York: Macmillan, 1974.

Wilford, John Noble. *The Mysterious History of Columbus: An Exploration of the Man, the Myth, the Legacy.* New York: Knopf, distributed by Random House, 1991.

Williams, Selma R. *Divine Rebel: The Life of Anne Marbury Hutchinson.* New York: Holt, Rinehart, and Winston, 1981.

Winslow, Ola Elizabeth. *John Eliot: Apostle to the Indians.* Boston: Houghton Mifflin, 1968.

Winslow, Ola Elizabeth. *Jonathan Edwards: 1703–1758.* New York: Collier Books, 1961.

Winslow, Ola Elizabeth. *Master Roger Williams.* New York: Macmillan, 1957.

Winslow, Ola Elizabeth. *Samuel Sewall of Boston.* New York: Macmillan, 1964.

Wood, Peter H. *Strange New Land: African Americans, 1617–1776.* New York: Oxford University Press, 1995.

Wroth, Lawrence C. *The Voyages of Giovanni da Verranzzano, 1524–1528.* New Haven, Conn.: Yale University Press, 1970.

Yewell, John, and others, eds. *Confronting Columbus: An Anthology.* Jefferson, N.C.: McFarland and Co., 1992.

Ziff, Larzer. *The Career of John Cotton: Puritanism and the American Experience.* Princeton, N.J.: Princeton University Press, 1962.

Videocassettes

Benjamin Franklin Citizen of the World. A&E Home Video, 1994. Videocassette recording.

Benjamin Franklin Scientist and Inventor. Living History Productions, 1993. Videocassette recording.

Web sites

Africans in America. http://www.pbs.org/wgbh/aia old/part1/1i2992.html Available December 6, 1999.

"The American Colonies— New England" in *Documents Relevant to the United States Before 1700.* http:www.msstate.edu/ Archives/History/USA/ colonial/bef1700.html Available September 30, 1999.

"Anne Hutchinson." http://www.gale.com/gale/ cwh/hutchin.html Available December 6, 1999.

Bacon's Castle. http://www.sightsmag.com/ usa/va/surr/sights/bacon/ bacon.htm Available September 30, 1999.

"Bacon's Declaration in the Name of the People" (30 July 1676) in *Documents Relevant to the United States Before 1700.* http:www.msstate.edu/ Archives/History/USA/ colonial/bef1700.html Available September 30, 1999.

Bacon's Rebellion. http://www.infoplease.com/ce5/CE00404.5.html Available December 6, 1999.

Benjamin Franklin: An Enlightened American, http://library.advanced.org/22254.htm Available December 6, 1999.

"The Cabot Dilemma: John Cabot's 1497 Voyage & the Limits of Historiography" in *Documents Relevant to the United States Before 1700.* http:www.msstate.edu/Archives/History/USA/colonial/bef1700.html Available September 30, 1999.

"Charter of the Dutch West India Company (1621)" in *Documents Relevant to the United States Before 1700.* http:www.msstate.edu/Archives/History/USA/colonial/bef1700.html Available December 6, 1999.

"Charter to Sir Walter Raleigh (1584)" in *Documents Relevant to the United States Before 1700.* http:www.msstate.edu/Archives/History/USA/colonial/bef1700.html Available December 6, 1999.

"Charter of Massachusetts Bay (1629)" in *Documents Relevant to the United States Before 1700.* http:www.msstate.edu/Archives/History/USA/colonial/bef1700.html Available December 6, 1999.

Christopher Columbus and his Voyages. http://deil.lang.uiuc.edu/web.pages/holidays/Columbus.html Available December 6, 1999.

Columbus and the Age of Discovery. http://www.millersv.edu/~columbus/mainmenu.html Available December 6, 1999.

Columbus and the Native Americans. http://www.geocities.com/CapitolHill/8533/columbus.html Available September 30, 1999.

De Soto's Trail thru the Southeast. http://www.conquestchannel.com/inset9.html Available December 6, 1999.

Eliza Lucas Pinckney. http://wwwnetsrq.com/~dbois/pinckney.html Available December 6, 1999.

Estevanico the Moor. http://www.thehistorynet.com/AmericanHistory/articles/1997/0897_cover.html Available December 6, 1999.

The Estevanico Society. http://www.estevanico.org/ Available December 6, 1999.

Father Jacques Marquette National Memorial and Museum. http://www.uptravel.com/uptravel/attractions/3.htm Available September 30, 1999.

"The First Thanksgiving Proclamation (1676)" in *Documents Relevant to the United States Before 1700.* http:www.msstate.edu/Archives/History/USA/colonial/bef1700.html Available September 30, 1999.

Francisco López De Mendoza Grajales: "The Founding of St. Augustine, 1565" in Modern History Sourcebook. http://www.fordham.edu/halsall/mod/1565staugustine.html Available September 30, 1999.

Giovanni Verrazano.
    http://www.greencastle.k12.
    in.us/stark/verrazano/htm
    Available September 30,
    1999.

"Gottlieb Mittelberger, On the
    Misfortune [of?] indentured
    Servants" in Documents
    Relevant to the United States
    Before 1700.
    http:www.msstate.edu/
    Archives/History/USA/
    colonial/bef1700.html Avail-
    able December 6, 1999.

"Governor William Berkeley on
    Bacon's Rebellion" in Docu-
    ments Relevant to the United
    States Before 1700.
    http:www.msstate.edu/
    Archives/History/USA/
    colonial/bef1700.html Avail-
    able December 6, 1999.

Henry Melchior Mühlenberg: Patri-
    arch of American Lutherans.
    http://www.justus.anglican.
    org/resources/bio/261.html
    Available December 6, 1999.

Henry Hudson and the Half Moon.
    http://www.ulster.net/~hrmm
    /halfmoon/halfmoon.htm
    Available September 30,
    1999.

Historic Bartram's Garden.
    http://www.libertynet.org/
    bartram Available December
    6, 1999.

Images from the Salem
    Witchcraft Trails.
    http://www.law.umkc.edu/
    faculty/projects/ftrials/salem/
    salem.htm Available Decem-
    ber 6, 1999.

Indentured Servitude: A Culturally
    Historical Prospective of West
    African and African American.
    http://asu.alasu.edu/
    academic/advstudies/4b.html
    Available December 6, 1999.

Indian Pueblo Cultural Center.
    http://www.indianpueblo.org
    Available September 30, 1999.

The Indian Wars.
    http://www.geocities.com/
    Heartland/Hills/1094/indian.
    htm Available December 6,
    1999.

"Instructions for the Virginia
    Colony (1606)" in Documents
    Relevant to the United States
    Before 1700.
    http:www.msstate.edu/
    Archives/History/USA/
    colonial/bef1700.html Avail-
    able December 6, 1999.

Jacques Cartier.
    http://www.win.tue.nl/cs/fm/
    engels/discovery/cartier.html
    Available September 30, 1999.

Jamestown Rediscovery.
    http://www.apva.org/ Avail-
    able December 6, 1999.

John Adams.
    http://www.studyworld.com/
    John_Adams.htm Available
    September 30, 1999.

John Rolfe.
    http://www.esd.k12.ca.us/
    Cadwallader/Room%2020/
    Colonies Available December
    6, 1999.

"King Ferdinand's letter to the
    Taino/Arawak Indians" in
    Documents Relevant to the
    United States Before 1700.
    http:www.msstate.edu/
    Archives/History/USA/
    colonial/bef1700.html Avail-
    able December 6, 1999.

The Journals of Henry Melchior
    Mühlenberg.
    http://www.midcoast.com/~
    picton/public_html.BASK/
    catalog/books/1469.htm
    Available December 6, 1999.

La Salle Ship Sighted.
http://www.he.net/~archaeol
/9601/newsbriefs/lasalle.html
Available September 30, 1999.

The Life and Times of Henry Hudson, Explorer and Adventurer.
http://www.georgian.net/
rally/hudson/ Available
September 30, 1999.

Louis Jolliet: Professional Explorer.
http://www.mvnf.muse.
digital.ca/Explor/jolli_el.htm
Available December 6, 1999.

"The Massachusetts Body of Liberties, Numbers 1–49 (1641)";
"The Body of Liberties
50–98 (1641)" in *Documents
Relevant to the United States
Before 1700.*
http:www.msstate.edu/
Archives/History/USA/
colonial/bef1700.html Available December 6, 1999.

The Mayas.
http://www.indians.org/
welker/mayamenu.htm Available September 30, 1999.

"Mayflower Documents" in *Documents Relevant to the United
States Before 1700.*
http:www.msstate.edu/
Archives/History/USA/
colonial/bef1700.html Available December 6, 1999.

"Mayflower Genealogy and History" in *Documents Relevant to
the United States Before 1700.*
http:www.msstate.edu/
Archives/History/USA/
colonial/bef1700.html Available December 6, 1999.

*Motion: A Travel Journal—Time
Travelers: Sarah Kemble Knight
(1666–1727).* (Contains the
only known portrait of Sarah
Kemble Knight)
http://www.nearbycafe.com/
motion/motionmenu/

timetravel/knight.html Available September 30, 1999.

The New England Pirate Museum.
http://www.piratemuseum.
com/pirate.htm Available
December 6, 1999.

Olaudah Equiano.
http://www.atomicage.com/
equiano/life.html Available
December 6, 1999.

"Penn's Plan for a Union" in *Documents Relevant to the United
States Before 1700.*
http:www.msstate.edu/
Archives/History/USA/
colonial/bef1700.html Available September 30, 1999.

Pocahontas: Jamestown Rediscovery.
http://www.apva.org/history/
pocahont.html Available
December 6, 1999.

Pocahontas: Savior or Savage?
http://theweboftime.com/
Poca/POCAHO~1.html Available December 6, 1999.

Popé.
http://www.pbs.org/weta/
thewest/wpages/wpgs400/
w4pope.htm Available September 30, 1999.

*Quakers in Brief: An Overview of the
Quaker Movement From 1650
to 1990.*
http://www.cryst.bbk.ac.uk/
~ubcg09q/dmr/intro.htm
Available September 30,
1999.

*René-Robert Cavelier, sieur
de La Salle.*
http://www.knight.org/
advent/cathen/09009b.htm
Available September 30, 1999.

"Richard Haluyt, Discourse on
Western Planting (1584)" in
*Documents Relevant to the
United States Before 1700.*
http:www.msstate.edu/

Archives/History/USA/colonial/bef1700.html Available December 6, 1999.

"Robert Beverley On Bacon's Rebellion (1704)" in *Documents Relevant to the United States Before 1700.* http:www.msstate.edu/Archives/History/USA/colonial/bef1700.html Available December 6, 1999.

Roger Williams National Memorial. http://www.nps.gov/rowi/ Available December 6, 1999.

Salem witchcraft hysteria. http://www.nationalgeographic.com/features/97/salem/ Available September 30, 1999.

Samuel Champlain. http://www.blupete.com/Hist/BiosNS/1600-00/Champlain.htm Available December 6, 1999.

Samuel de Champlain's 1607 Map. http://lcweb.loc.gov/exhibits/treasures/trr009.html Available December 6, 1999.

Samuel de Champlain's Voyages. http://www.ccukans.edu/carrie/docs/texts/champlai.html Available December 6, 1999.

"Sarah Kemble Knight" in *The Puritans: American Literature Colonial Period (1608–1700).* http://falcon.jmu.edu/-ramseyil/amlitcol.htm Available December 6, 1999.

The South Carolina Business Hall of Fame. [Eliza Pinckney] http://theweb.badm.sc.edu/ja/jaelp.htm Available December 6, 1999.

"Spanish Conquest of Native Americans during the Sixteenth Century" in *Documents Relevant to the United States Before 1700.* http:www.msstate.edu/Archives/History/USA/colonial/bef1700.html Available December 6, 1999.

Spanish Exploration and Conquest of Native Americans. http://www.conquestchannel.com/ Available September 30, 1999.

Susanna North Martin. http:www.rootsweb.com/~nwg/sm.html Available September 30, 1999.

Tlingit Culture. http:www.geocities.com/Athens/Atlantis/4513/ Available September 30, 1999.

"William Bradford" in *The Puritans: American Literature Colonial Period (1608–1700).* http://falcon.jmu.edu/-ramseyil/amlitcol.htm Available December 6, 1999.

William Byrd II. http://marist.chi.il.us/~amlit/laurph2.html Available December 6, 1999.

Index

**Italic type indicates
volume numbers.**

**Illustrations are marked
by (ill.)**

Wesley, John *1:* 122; *2:* 360
West, Benjamin *2:* 347
Westminster Assembly *2:* 305
Weston, Thomas *1:* 94, 116
Westover plantation *2:* 372
Whales *1:* 196
Wheatley, Phillis *2:* 363
Wheelock, Eleazor *2:* 324, 324 (ill.)
Wheelwright, John *1:* 153–54
Whipple House *2:* 370
Whitaker, Alexander *2:* 323
Whitefield, George *1:* 122, 206;
    2: 304, 316–18, 318 (ill.)
Whitehall *2:* 373
White, John *1:* 81–82
Wigglesworth *2:* 360
Williamsburg, Virginia *2:* 211, 338
Williams, Eunice *2:* 283
Williams, Hannah *2:* 380
Williams, Roger *1:* 56, 97, 100,
    100 (ill.); *2:* 306
William III *1:* 98, 108, 114, 184;
    2: 293
Wilson, John *1:* 152; *2:* 358
Winnebagos *1:* 24, 68
Winthrop, John *1:* 94–98, 95 (ill.),
    100, 154; *2:* 215, 220, 358, 403
Winthrop Jr., John *2:* 385
Winthrop IV, John *2:* 385

Witch trials *1:* 148 (ill.), 150
Wolfe, James *1:* 78
Women, colonial *2:* 264 (ill.)
Women, Native American
    2: 262 (ill.)
Wonders of the Invisible World
    1: 149
Woolen Act of 1699 *1:* 198
Woolman, John *1:* 141,
    141 (ill.), 174
Wren, Christopher *2:* 373

Y

Yale College *2:* 339
Yale, Elihu *2:* 339
Yamasee War *1:* 17
Yeamans, John *1:* 118
Yumas *1:* 52

Z

Zenger, John Peter *1:* 175–76,
    176 (ill.)
Zinzendorf, Nikolaus von
    2: 309, 315
Zunis *1:* 46–47